How To Be The Best (In Business)

Insights from my 40-year career (as well as before and after).

Donald V. Almeida, PwC Global Vice Chairman (Retired) and Trusted Advisor

Special Thanks

Special thanks to Donna Rapaccioli, Mary Bly, Lerzan Aksoy, Martha Hirst, Tim Wilson, Gabriella Almeida, Sue Feeney, Dina Kali, and Mike Thiessen for your help and support along the way.

This book is dedicated to Gail, Gabriella, and Matthew.

A portion of proceeds from this book will be donated to Fordham University, Cardinal Hayes High School, The Wounded Warrior Project, Tunnel To Towers, and The Making Headway Foundation.

Thank you for supporting these incredible organizations.

Contents

PREFACE

Before we dive in, I want to take a moment to tell you exactly who I am:

Don is passionate (some say about everything he cares about), very honest and trustworthy, extremely hard working, very smart, very global thinking, and focused on diversity. He builds and sustains high-performing teams (and high performers), is very close to his family and his kids, loves a challenge, and always thinks BIG and out of the box. He doesn't run from confrontation—some even say that he thrives on confrontation. He is all about teamwork, is extremely loyal, is a great judge of people, and he has a great sense of humor. Don is great at making decisions quickly, communicates clear messages, is a great businessman, is great in the C-Suite, and knows everybody.

He also doesn't listen well, and he has a very short attention span (some say he has ADD (Attention Defecit Disorder)). Don hates administrative matters and people who always say "no" or make excuses for why something can't be done. He always tends to exaggerate, is known to use colorful language, makes decisions too quickly, can be curt or short at times, tends to interrupt you often, thinks he knows everything (some say he seems to know everything about everything), thinks he is always right, and always wants clarity and accountability (good and bad!).

Excerpt from Chapter 13, "Branding"

The above describes me in a nutshell and should give a little bit of context to those who don't already know me or my work.

Now that that's out of the way, you're probably wondering what this book is all about. It's a bit of my life story mixed with some straight-up advice on how to make it in the business world. It began with me jotting down some notes about my life, thinking it was just for my own reflection, to look back on the good and the bad. But then it hit me—some of the stuff I've learned the hard way might just help someone else skip a few bumps in the road.

I'm just a regular guy who's seen a bit of everything. I've sat in those high-stakes meeting rooms, made some bets on businesses, and put my time into giving back. I'm not about sugarcoating things or talking in fancy jargon—what you're going to get in these pages is straight talk, the kind you'd hear over a beer or coffee.

This book isn't just a rundown of my wins and losses: it's a map of the whole crazy journey that got me to where I am today. I'll share the lessons that have shaped my experience, from my first job to the big executive decisions, and how I kept my head in the game through it all.

I want to give you an insider's look at how a kid from Yonkers built a life he's proud of in the boardroom and beyond. It's about finding your groove in business and figuring out how to keep evolving, no matter what life throws at you. This isn't just my victory lap: it's a collection of the principles and the strategies that can help light up your path, too. Whether you're just starting on day one or you're thinking about what's next, I'm laying it all out for you.

Think of this book like a chat with an old friend—one who's seen a lot and is willing to share the playbook. After all, success isn't just about the finish line;

it's about the journey, the people you meet, and the person you become along the way.

Alright, let's get to it.

INTRODUCTION

I intended this book to be an in-depth look at what I learned in my fifty-five years of business experience: forty-one years with Price Waterhouse and then PricewaterhouseCoopers (hereafter referred to as PwC), and at least fourteen years before and after. The successes, the failures, and the lessons that I learned along the way.

I did not come from money. I did not grow up connected to the business world. I was a middle-class kid—maybe even lower-middle-class. What I did have was a great family and parents who believed that hard work and a good education would serve me well. Looking back, I believe that there were many things I learned from them that gave me the foundation to do things that I never imagined I could, and in some cases, things that had never been done before.

I went to Cardinal Hayes High School in the Bronx from 1965 to 1969—a Catholic school for about 2,500 first-generation boys. It has very famous alums, including Regis Philbin and Martin Scorsese. I also attended Fordham University from 1969 to 1973, a Jesuit university that aims to inspire high standards of success and personal development in students. Today, I sit on each school's board of trustees, and I am very active in both. I hope students at both schools read this book because I think it can show them what is possible. That each and every one of them has the potential to realize their dreams, and that with the right tools, anyone can rise to the top. These students are some of the smartest young adults in the world—I know many will go on to do great things.

Over the years, I've had great mentors who taught me much. Sometimes, I learned what I should do. Other times, I learned what I should not do. Both were very important. I used these experiences to form a kind of GPS that guided me. In a few, much rarer cases, I selectively used "what not to do" for very specific reasons—most often to make a point or an impact. I molded what I had been taught to fit my own style and personality, my strengths and weaknesses. This strategy of adaptation was key, and I will talk more about that in the chapters that follow.

Before I entered the full-time workforce as an adult, I had many jobs—either part-time during the school year or full-time in the summer. It was great to have them, and it was even better that they were across a broad spectrum of industries. The skills that have helped me most in my career were those I learned on these jobs. They also taught me what I liked and what I did not, knowledge that guided my career going forward.

There is a running joke in my family, especially with my kids, surrounding my "career" as a paperboy when I was ten. They believe my mom drove me around every day while I tossed papers at front doors from the passenger-side window. In reality, it was a tough job! Managing customers, the hours, and the physical labor were all things I'd never had to deal with before. By putting myself in new and uncomfortable situations, however, I learned a lot about myself and what it takes to succeed.

During this time, I started to learn things: finish what you start, meet your commitments, be nice to people, and last but not least, always act professionally. I began to understand what it means to be "good at what you do" or to be "wanted on a team." I also started to understand human nature—the differences in people's personalities, how people interacted, and what different people thought was important. All of this was fundamental to the success I had at the time and served as building blocks for the future, and all were taken to new levels as I gained experience.

The pages that follow take a close look at what I consider vital to my success and to the success of others I have worked with. Some of it may be intuitive or obvious, but hopefully, it is presented in a way that makes it more relevant or impactful. Some may not be so intuitive or obvious, but will hopefully grab your attention and make you think.

Some of what you read in this book may force you to expand your skills or raise your game. Other concepts I mention—like becoming the best in the world at what you do—may even sound impossible at first. I hope you will see through my life experiences that I share here that these things are not only possible but will become easy over time. Lastly, some points I make in this book may sound counterintuitive, or like they couldn't possibly work in real situations. In these instances, I will share examples and stories that show they do work if executed at the right time and in the right way. Almost every idea discussed can be applied to a broad range of circumstances and by different types of people with different skills. Others will not apply broadly, and some will be even more limited, requiring very precise execution to pull them off and make them effective. I will discuss these in detail in each case.

This book will give you all you need to be the best in business, and alongside that, the best version of yourself. It is for young and not-so-young executives, for business school students, and for all those who are in or want to be in business.

I hope this makes for an interesting read, and that you find great ideas to make your own. I consider this book to be the result of the extensive research that I undertook over the last fifty-five-plus years. Enjoy!

First Caveat

Those who know me know that I form opinions on many things, and that some of those opinions I hold strongly. In addition, I am not always right. I always have well-thought-out opinions that I believe are usually accurate. I am, however, always in search of new information and better ideas. You should keep this in mind while reading this book and, in particular, when interpreting the ideas and recommendations that I share here. You surely can make them better.

Second Caveat

I was a partner at PwC, and all my client interactions and dealings over forty-one years are confidential. For this reason, I may often give examples without naming a specific client or person. I will in some cases mention a person or company by name, and if I do this, it means it is publicly available information. It is also my firm's policy not to publicly mention client names or the names of client or PwC personnel. I have honored this policy in writing this book.

HOW IT ALL
STARTED

Chapter 1

A JOB IS NEVER JUST A JOB

E very job is a series of steps to achieve an objective or, more often, a group of objectives. These objectives are not just the things a role requires you to do, but things that you hope to gain from or achieve while working. Of these objectives, there will be a "primary objective"—the reason you took the job in the first place. In many cases, what we think is the primary objective really is not. A great example of this for me were jobs I had in high school and college which I had taken to make extra money and help pay for school. What I did not realize at the time was that I was putting in place building blocks that would add to my foundation for the next forty to fifty years, teaching me about people, work ethic, teamwork, finishing what you start, and so much more.

Paperboy Days

What a tough job rain or shine, but what a great learning experience! Having my paper route was my first foray into running my own business. I had customers, a product, sales techniques, and cash collections, as well as customer service and related customer complaints. If you ran the business correctly you made money, but if you did not, you either did not make as much or you lost money (though the latter was pretty hard to do). It was a cash-to-cash business with few timing differences. If you did it right, you collected all your cash each week.

The first lesson I learned was this: if you did not collect all your cash, you still had to pay for the papers. Ouch! I remember this teaching me very early on the power of cash, and how the basics of business were cash in and cash out. Later in my career, I remember often saying that "good business was about cash-to-cash and everything else was a timing difference." I also always reviewed companies' operations in terms of positive cash flow. If a company was not generating cash, there was a problem! Remember Enron?

Second lesson: there are all sorts of people in this world. In my encounters with customers on my route, some were fair and generous, while others were quite the opposite—even to a young businessman like me. The generous ones would always pay on time and give nice tips, sometimes even bigger tips around holidays. Others would try to stiff you and would use any excuse not to pay. I learned how to quickly tell the difference and remedy the situation. I coined the phrase "One strike and you're out."

I learned that certain things were "on" or "off" switches in a person—there was no middle ground for some qualities, and certain behaviors quickly sat you in one camp or the other. This was one of those. If you did not pay your paperboy on time—knowing it was his money, and that he was owed—you were a bad person! Period. I learned that the adage was true: if it looks like a duck, walks like a duck, and quacks like a duck, then it is probably a duck.

My time as a paperboy taught me to make quick decisions, cut my losses, and also to defend my decisions. When I cut off a customer and he complained to the company, I refused to take him back unless he paid his monthly fees upfront.

Construction Is Not Just Construction

After my tenure as a paperboy, I began working various construction jobs over the summer while I was off from school. I was a laborer and a mason, and I built in- and above-ground swimming pools and serviced them post-installation. Each of these jobs required long hours, often starting at dawn, and were physically demanding. On each project, I worked alongside an expert who would teach me the skills of the trade while using me as a helper. I spent hours on these projects and returned to work every summer in between visits to family and odd additional part-time positions.

Over time, I went from a helper to an assistant to an associate—a title given when you had learned the trade well enough to work with less oversight. I am not sure I was the best in the world at these jobs, but I tried my best to be really good. I remember always wanting to make an impact and be respected by others for the work I did. I also remember that while I was learning I was also teaching the men with whom I worked certain things in areas where I had more experience. Things like investing options, how to get a mortgage, how to finance a car, and how to use insurance, to mention a few.

It was during this time that I remember being given my first nickname: "the college kid." I was not sure at the time whether this was positive or negative. I learned later it was a surrogate for "the smart kid." It was also a sign of respect, shown by those with whom I worked who respected education but had been unable to get much of it themselves. I learned that they also respected my work ethic and were responding to *my* respect for what *they* did.

On the job, I learned each trade fairly well and certainly made a fair amount of money, but I was also learning what things I liked to do and why. I determined that I liked building in-ground swimming pools the best. Why? It was not the work itself that I liked, but rather the fact that you started at the beginning and saw the project through to the end. You started with digging the hole and ended with filling the pool and starting the filtration system.

You also worked on four- or five-man teams, so teamwork was really important. This was especially true when you were setting 300-pound forms which required the team to work together and for each team member to do his job. After a year or so I became a team leader, which I found very rewarding. This is when I first learned that leadership was not necessarily related to age. In all my previous experiences, I'd reported to someone many years my senior, so naturally I assumed that age and rank were directly connected. In this case, I was the leader—a college kid, by far the youngest on the job.

Another part I enjoyed was that I got to interact with the buyers of the pools. These were most often homeowners, local town officials, or other contractors. This was almost daily and marked the beginning of my learning both how to keep the customers happy and the importance of clear communication.

These eight years were foundational in many ways, even though they were jobs I would never do again.

One early lesson I learned was to finish what I committed to, no matter how difficult. At the time, I was a form setter's helper, and we were setting forms along a highway so that the concrete could be poured the next morning. The master form setter—a man in his late fifties—was an expert at what he did, and he was fast. I kind of came along for the ride; I got the forms and helped set them, basically responding to his direction.

I remember it was hot, and by three o'clock I was dog-tired. It was at this point that he told me we had committed to a certain distance, and that it would take us—he estimated—another four hours to finish. When I complained he said: "I agreed to do it, and I will finish with or without you." We finished together at about seven p.m. and I had my first (hot) beer to celebrate. He continued as one of my mentors for the next six years.

Driving A Taxi

During college I drove a cab, taking people from point A to point B whenever I had spare time. Pretty easy right? Wrong!

The first thing I learned was what a physically demanding job it was: really bad on your back from all the bumps in the road and on your legs and neck from not moving enough. The second thing I learned was how to read people: some were quiet, others talkative, some curious, some angry, some blue-collar, some white-collar, some locals, some tourists—you get the point.

I learned quickly that if I could carry on a conversation with my fares I could learn all sorts of things about them: where they were from, what brought them to New York, what they were planning to do while they were here. I also became a bit of a tour guide, making recommendations for what they should see, where they should eat, and so on. I found people interesting, and I discovered that I liked dealing with them; I was curious to find out all I could in a "simple" taxi ride.

Later in my career, I have reflected on this job as a foundation for why it was so easy for me to break the ice when meeting executives for the first time. It was natural for me to ask about their kids, their families, their hobbies, and the like. I also found it relatively easy to size them up. Were they serious types or did they have a sense of humor? Did they like sports, and if so, which ones and which teams? It's a cliché, but practice *does* make perfect—or at least makes you better—and talking to people is a skill like any other.

To this day, my wife and kids cannot stand that when I get into a cab or Uber I cannot help but talk to the driver. Where are you from, how long have you been in the U.S., how is business, and so on. This job was an early lesson that *everyone* has a complex personal life, and most of us like to talk about it.

I remember later in my career going to see a famous record producer who was essentially the CEO of a client we were trying to get. When I went to see him, I knew he would have formed a view of what it was going to be like to meet "a bookkeeper from PwC." His assistant showed me into his office, which was exactly what I envisioned: tons of platinum records, and pictures with famous artists. As we greeted each other, I said "Man, you have a lot of shit in this office!" He laughed, and *hard*. We spent the next half hour talking about which items were his favorites. As I left, he said: "You don't look or act like an accountant." I remember thinking "Maybe more like a taxi driver?"

Sears (Remember Them?) Customer Service

I have described this job often as standing at a counter in front of a line of people whom you have never met, most of whom are angry at the company and, by extension, at you. They were frustrated with some Sears product or service that did not work—every one different, with a different problem, posing a unique challenge. What made it even more difficult was the Sears motto: "The customer is always right."

Looking back, it is interesting to me the impact this Sears experience had on my life, my DNA, and how I approached problems. I only had this job for about a year or so, and only part-time, but did it serve me well! Looking back, this was one of the best business courses I ever took—and I got paid to do it!

Over time, I learned from coworkers and through trial and error how to defuse the anger and solve the problem. I also learned the art of listening and the art of understanding a problem from the customer's perspective. These were two great skills that I would refine throughout my career, but that I first became aware of at Sears. I didn't realize it at the time, but it was also at Sears that I started understanding the application of fairness and good business judgment.

I remember one day in particular when I dealt with two people in a row with similar but very different problems. The first was a man who'd brought in a seven-year-old toaster that did not work. It was under a three-year warranty. Though his coverage had lapsed, he demanded a new toaster; he was the "in-your-face-and-a-screamer" type. Long story short, I refused. Unsatisfied, he went over my head and up the chain, finally getting a new toaster from the store manager.

The second was an elderly woman with a brand-new toaster that did not work. She asked if she could have it fixed "if it wasn't too much of a bother." The store protocol at the time was to get it fixed; instead, I gave her a new one on the spot.

She was so low-key and nice that I wanted to give her two. You can imagine the effect that the difference between these two people had on me.

My time at Sears was one of those experiences that creates memorable story after story—most funny, though some not-so-funny. It taught me even more about the range of people out there, putting me face-to-face with everyone from the most abrasive and shameless to the meekest and mildest. The irony was that they both got new toasters. The abrasive customer because the store manager (the third or fourth line of defense) finally relented and said yes; the mild customer because I decided, in fairness, that she should get a new one.

It was in this job that I first learned the role of humor in defusing a tense situation. When I say humor, I mean saying something that makes the angry person laugh, or at a minimum stop their anger momentarily. I can think of countless examples from my time at Sears.

Some include repeating what the customer says. If they ask "Are you the dummy who sold me this product?" it's not a bad idea to reply in kind: "Yes, I am the dummy who sold you this product!" By just repeating what the customer says back to them, they hear themselves out loud and, in most cases, find it funny. By the way, the most common words used by customers to describe me did not include "dummy!"

Another is making fun of the problem but in a very sympathetic way. "The toaster just stopped working," a customer would say. Response: "Well, at least it didn't catch fire and blow up like the last customer's." You would be surprised at the laugh this causes!

And yet another is making it sound like theirs was the first problem you'd heard all week. When the customer is ranting—the product "just stopped working" and "you guys, better fix it"—the response is "Thank you so much, there's finally a problem I can fix. I was hoping there would be a problem soon, otherwise I thought I might lose my job!" I had to be a little more careful with this one and delivery timing was key; I couldn't come across as a smart ass.

I could go on, but you get the idea. Each of these situations was relatively low-stakes, but the skills I got from this experience were valuable all the same.

Running A Grocery Store

One summer I was asked to run a relative's grocery store for two months as a family favor. It was a small store that had a deli counter and a few aisles of typical grocery offerings. The team was similarly small: it was just me and two helpers for the whole summer. I had no prior experience in this kind of role, but by that time, I had pulled together a few years' worth of professional know-how from across my other jobs, and I was trained for two weeks before I started working. I had every confidence that I would rise to the occasion.

On my first day running the store, about ten construction representatives showed up and ordered sixty cups of coffee and every pastry we had. My crack staff and I nearly killed ourselves filling the orders while listening to complaints that we were taking too long. This happened again at lunchtime, with coffee being replaced by beer and pastry by sandwiches.

At three o'clock, we closed the store to stop the pain and tried to assess what had just happened. We came to find out that two new construction sites had opened nearby, producing extraordinary demand for our products, and that this increase in sales volume was something we'd likely have to contend with all summer. From there, we tried to figure out a way to address it, and *fast*—we were anticipating the same level of traffic tomorrow! The first part of the fix was trying to coordinate with the construction reps to determine ahead of time what they needed and when. The second was to apprise suppliers of our sudden surge in sales and to find cost-effective ways for them to help us meet demand. It took about a week to get everything working, and in the end there was still pain, but now it was manageable.

I learned very quickly the value of preparation, planning, and execution within controlled guidelines. The store was open from seven a.m. to six p.m., but we worked into the night to prepare for the next day. We scheduled certain deliveries to be made twice a day rather than twice a week to accommodate refrigeration space and other storage constraints. We limited deli offerings to specific items that were prepared the night before. We identified high-value customers and catered to them. General grocery shopping was discouraged between eight a.m. and ten a.m.—coffee time for the construction workers—and twelve p.m. to one-thirty p.m.—when they took their lunch. We asked for coffee and lunch orders the night before and gave incentives to get them done. These are just a few examples of responding to changing circumstances, and they taught me how to plan for most scenarios while remaining able to react to surprises.

This job also forced me to focus on how to motivate a team, albeit one of only two people. I would not call it a high-performing team (something I will discuss later), but it was certainly a team with clear objectives that we all understood, committed to, and tried to execute according to plan. My team members understood why we needed to do what we needed to do and agreed to the promised rewards should we succeed.

As an example, they agreed to work twice as many hours in exchange for three times the pay. Although this might sound overly generous, it was the result of my considering the upside versus the downside. The store stood to make twice the profit even after the added cost, and the employees and customers were happy. By the way, this is a good example of a job that can give you a great experience, but you would never want to do again! I would also be remiss if I didn't thank my twin brother Dave, who came to the store every day to help after working ten hours on construction.

Becoming An Eagle Scout

I need to mention my days in scouting and working my way up to Eagle Scout. I spent six years with the Boy Scouts of America, culminating in my achievement of Eagle in 1967. It is fair to say that many successful people, including business executives, were Eagle Scouts.

The journey to Eagle includes a very diverse and challenging set of experiences. For me, it meant camping out in all kinds of weather from the freezing cold to the sweltering heat, hikes of up to fifty miles over all sorts of terrain, and generally learning to adapt to whatever obstacle was put in front of me. I learned to finish what I started, which included individual tasks or projects, larger-scale events, and ultimately the road to Eagle itself.

I did not realize it at the time, but these were invaluable life lessons. I learned when the going gets tough, the tough get going. I learned "no pain, no gain" *before* that was a popular phrase. I learned that if something was easy, everyone would do it. I learned the value of a team. I learned the meaning of friendship. I learned about honor and honesty and to do what you say you will. I learned to be reliable and to trust that I could rely on others. Pretty foundational stuff when you think about it. Although I have not camped in years, I am still a supporter of the Boy Scout experience.

In college, I was involved in several activities and held some elected positions. I remember at the time doing it because I found it interesting and fun, but later I discovered it was because people, including people smarter than me, wanted to follow my lead.

Later, I will discuss leadership in more depth and give very concrete examples. I will tell stories from my experiences with leadership and explain why they happened. I will talk about high-performance teams, how they are created and sustained, and how they are led. I will talk about leadership versus management. These are all complex concepts. In some cases, they are easy to talk about but very difficult to execute. My only reason for raising the subject here is to say that my leadership experience started back at Fordham University, and I've been building on these early learnings ever since.

Enough about my pre-career days. Let's move on.

Chapter 2

MY CAREER AT PwC

About midway through my senior year at Fordham, I was offered an internship at PwC over the Christmas break.

My internship was on a major credit card client account, where I worked alongside a fabulous team and loved everything about it, including the long hours. I am not sure whether it was a high-performing team, but we certainly were working with a high-visibility client and led by a number of very senior and influential partners, whom I remember being very focused on "our intern" (me). The team also included managers and other team members, all of whom really knew their stuff. It was a life-changing experience for me in many ways, not least of all because it was the first time I'd seen a team where business and personal lives were so intertwined; the team and their families regularly spent time socializing together outside of the office. This was clearly *not* a nine-to-five job.

At the end of the internship, I received an offer for full-time employment. I remember this like it was yesterday—to a senior in college looking to land a role in business, it was naturally a really big deal. The offer was open-ended, meaning I could get back to them whenever I decided. I got several other offers, but all had end dates. This was a moment when I saw how a class organization operates. Should I choose to go to graduate school, I could take the offer after that. If I took a year off (yeah right), the job would be waiting for me when I returned. PwC was an organization looking to hire top talent. Timing was secondary.

With my open offer, my great internship experience, and PwC's outstanding review of my performance, the decision was easy. Interesting to me is that fifty years later, what I saw in those eight weeks was a perfect microcosm of what I would experience throughout my entire career.

So, looking back, what was it that got my attention? Beyond the prestige of working for one of the Big Eight, it was the experience of working with smart, talented, and highly motivated people. PwC was a meritocracy: if you worked hard and "did good," you progressed up the ladder. Further, even given this focus on individual achievement, the corporate culture was all about teamwork and collaboration—everyone wanted everyone else to succeed.

Suffice it to say that in August of 1973, I had a job: I was a new staff person at PwC. I made $10,500 a year plus overtime—a great salary—and I was one of the few new joiners who did not wear a hat! Today this sounds unbelievable, but back then businessmen wore hats. This lessened around the late 60s but still existed in 1973. Because I did not come from a "businessman" family, I did not own a hat. Looking back, I now know it did not matter—what mattered was how hard you worked and how quickly you learned.

I have described each year of this period as the equivalent of four years of college, where learning was exponential. This was my early training ground for determining what was and was not a high-performing team. It was dealing with clients, and in many cases, demanding clients. It was working on significant projects with deadlines and deliverables and pressure to execute. It was all about learning about business—process by process, and in different industries. Perhaps most importantly, I learned that I liked this kind of work, and moreover, that I was good at it. The more I worked, the more I learned, and the more I learned, the more I knew I needed to know. Also, this was learning "on the big stage," with the A-team and world-class clients—not bad for a kid from Yonkers!

It was during this time that I started to think in terms of being "really good at something." Later I thought in terms of being "one of the best," and eventually this evolved into being "*the* best." I will cover this later.

I wanted to be improving constantly; no matter how good I was, I could always be better. I will talk later about high-performing teams. For now, I'll just say that most teams think they are high-performing, but all true high-performing teams never think they are good enough. This is a crucial concept, to which I will devote a chapter.

People talk about "being lucky," or the role luck played in their careers. When it comes to luck, I believe in two concepts:

- First: luck is often defined as where opportunity meets ability, but opportunities don't come very often. This is to say that you shouldn't just wait around to "get lucky"—in many cases, you must make your own luck. I think this latter concept is the more important of the two, and the one that will sustain your career.

- Second: when you finally *do* get an opportunity, whether self-made or via dumb luck, you have to be ready to nail it.

In my early days, I got both—I got opportunities, and I nailed them. Opportunities came in a number of forms, often while working for some great people who mentored me and later looked out for me. I now know that these relationships were mutually beneficial; they helped me, and I tried my best to help them. This is also an area that crosses between the two concepts, meaning that when you get to work for some of the right people and begin getting a reputation for being a high performer, the best people want to work with you.

An Almeida Point: Seize Every Opportunity

Despite their rarity, many people don't take the opportunities they're presented with. There are many reasons for this, but one stands out above the others: **FEAR**. People are often afraid to jump on the opportunities they're given because they don't think they're ready to take on what the opportunity is asking of them. The only way to be successful is to risk failure, as the only **REAL** failure is not taking the opportunities when they come. Take every opportunity you're given, and always give your all—don't let fear hold you back!

I worked in several different roles with PwC across a number of industries. The industries included technology, entertainment and media, banking, forest products, oil and gas, and engineered products. My areas of focus included audit, performance improvement, risk management, acquisition due diligence, and some taxes. All of these areas and industries pertained to various business processes and the fundamentals of how the business—and in many cases, the global business—works.

My early days also had a dose of what we now call human capital. As a second-year associate, you had a degree of responsibility for the first-year staff; as a third-year, you managed a small sub-team of two or three; and as a manager, you managed the whole team. These teams ranged from four or five people up to larger groups. It was during this time that I saw what was being done right and what was not.

You could have two teams on similar projects working similar long hours. In one case they became friends forever, and in the other case, they could not stand each other. Why the difference? Later, I will talk about this alongside high-performance teams. I will also use examples which I hope will bring this to life. That said, the beginnings of my passion for the subject—my early learnings and "field research," as the professors call it—started here.

It was also during this time that I got to work with and study different types of managers and different management styles. PwC had every "flavor of ice cream," and in many cases, many different "flavors of vanilla ice cream"—teams were very diverse, even within bands. This diversity was instrumental to the firm's success, and I will talk about this in depth later as well.

I started understanding what type of businessperson I was. I was fairly independent, hardworking, unbothered by long hours, a people person, self-motivated, a global thinker, able to hold my own when challenged, and someone who always did what they said they would do. I started hearing words used to describe me such as "tough but fair," hardworking, honest, passionate, trustworthy, good with clients, a leader, and a team player. I also started to realize that some of these words were not used very often when describing others.

Looking back, it is clear that my early days at PwC were transformative for me. The skills I had gained in high school and college were a good foundation, but PwC was the big leagues, and now I was starting to learn the big league game.

The Impact of a Mentor

I'll discuss the topic of mentorship in more detail in a later chapter. For now, I'd like to share a story about an early mentor of mine.

When I was a first-year staff member, I was put on a medical equipment company. The PwC partner on the account was named Clem. At the time, I was twenty-two and Clem was in his late fifties. Every year, Clem would have a party at his house for the staff on each of his clients: four clients—four parties.

Clem was one of my early mentors, although he may not have known it. He would stop by whenever he was at the client and talk with the staff, of which I was the youngest. Clem was always supportive, always offering a one-liner like "Don, keep up the great work" or "Don, I know you're working hard, and I want you to know I appreciate it." He might follow up with "I used to do that, but my doctor won't let me do it anymore" and chuckle.

Clem was also the lead partner on a few other very large companies at the time, and everyone knew he was a very senior and important partner. The client thought very highly of our team, and very highly of Clem.

So, back to my first Clem party: I arrived at his house at exactly the stated time with my then-girlfriend (now wife) Gail. We were greeted at the door by Clem and his wife. I introduced both to Gail, and Clem told his wife how great I was and what a great addition to the team I had been: he saw a "great future" for me, and described me as a "future partner." The intro blew me away. The dinner party was for sixteen people, and it was the most personal, classy, friendly, and fun dinner I can remember. This was in 1974, and I still remember being surprised that someone had a dining room table that could seat sixteen people. I also still remember jokes between Clem at one end and his wife at the other about the rising cost of electricity.

I learned a lot from this party that has stayed with me—things like treat your people well, remember their names, and if you cannot have a first-class event do not have an event at all. I also saw a glimpse of how to motivate a team that you do not see very often and how to deal with colleagues of all levels at a client. Clem also instilled in me the concept that "all men put their pants on one leg at a time." He would joke with the CEO of our client one minute and with me the next.

An Almeida Point: It's The Little Things

WHILE GRAND GESTURES ARE CERTAINLY VALUABLE, DON'T UNDERESTIMATE THE EFFECT THAT THE LITTLE THINGS CAN HAVE ON A MENTORSHIP; SMALL GESTURES ADD UP OVER TIME AND OFTEN HAVE JUST AS MUCH (OR EVEN MORE) IMPACT. MY EXPERIENCES WITH CLEM SHOWED ME HOW YOU CAN MENTOR NATURALLY (IN OTHER WORDS, NOT AS PART OF SOME FORMAL PROGRAM) AND THAT A SERIES OF LITTLE THINGS (AND MAYBE A FEW NOT-SO-LITTLE THINGS IN SOME CASES) CAN IMPACT A MENTEE IN A VERY PROFOUND AND PERMANENT WAY. SOME OF WHAT CLEM DID FOR ME AND OTHERS IMPRESSED ME SO MUCH THAT I ADOPTED HIS TECHNIQUES AS MY OWN.

One last thing about Clem and his wife: they sent me holiday cards every year, each one handwritten with some little personal note. I got my first card from Clem in 1973, and then another every year for the next forty-some years until he passed.

I had the privilege of meeting and working with some of the greatest people and companies on the planet. I evolved from a kid from Yonkers into a truly global businessman with a network of thousands of friends and colleagues across over eighty countries.

Over the years, I had the honor of working with many esteemed companies. My dealings with these companies gave me opportunities to work with board members, CEOs, CFOs, business unit leaders, and others: people across the organization and the world. My dealings hopefully brought value to those I worked with, and every interaction—each of tens of thousands or more—certainly brought value to me. My goal almost always was to identify their problems and try to figure out how to solve them. I did this by myself sometimes, but most often with the help of my team or network. I did it then with PwC, and I do it now after PwC. If you are sticking with me, you will remember that job I had with Sears in customer service. That was a learning job. This was the big leagues!

I remember my first account where I was the lead partner. It was a company headquartered in New York. It was a major client of PwC and operated in the oil and gas, environmental, and technology sectors. Because of its importance, it had always been led by very senior and experienced partners, usually in their late fifties.

I had been the manager on the account for one year before making partner and knew the company's management and its board—although not for a long time at that point. I remember my first board meeting like it was yesterday. I was concerned that the client—and in particular, the board—might consider me too inexperienced to lead the account. I obviously took the meeting very seriously and prepared as well as I could. The meeting went very well, and it was very interactive between me and the board members. I was asked for my opinion on several matters and was also asked how I compared their company to others. At the end of the meeting, we had a private session—just the board and I—where we discussed my views on some strictly confidential matters. I remember, in particular, the head of the company being present and very engaged.

I learned something very important that day. After the meeting, the Chair—a man in his early seventies—took me aside to tell me how happy the board was to have such a young and energetic partner, especially one who knew their industries so well. He was focused on content over form, and so my age was irrelevant.

I have told many over the years, including some of my Fordham students, that having the knowledge and answers when it matters trumps most everything else—including age.

I remember like it was yesterday doing things that I had never done before—and in some cases, that had never been done by *anyone* before. This included, to mention just a few: the tech client's sale of their PC business; a leveraged ESOP (Employee Stock Option Plan) buyout; testifying in front of the U.S. Congress's Dingel Committee; meeting with the presidents and prime ministers of several countries; working on the first SAP R3 implementation in the U.S.; leading the technology practice during the "dot com" era and after, being one of the first to be reviewed by the PCAOB (Public Company Accounting Oversight Board); and working in seventy-four countries over the course of my career.

As an example, I remember being invited to an urgent meeting at a client—I was the lead engagement partner at the time. The topic was the sale of a business to the Chinese. PwC's role was to certify the financial statements related to the global business as well as to assist with deal issues in various locations, including Hong Kong. This required a global team to be mobilized to execute multiple workstreams. A fairly new partner—but one who was very familiar with the client's business—led the audit team.

This project was completed in roughly a year, which was the equivalent of lightning speed. It tested our global network, and the sale could not have happened without our involvement and help, although the majority of the effort was taken by the army of client and other collaborators all over the world who worked alongside us to make it happen. This was a great example of doing the impossible. I remember someone at the time saying, "If it takes 10,000 hours to finish, get 10,000 people and finish it in an hour." Obviously, this was a bit of a joke—but only a bit.

The project was massive and complex and had never been done before at this level and magnitude. It was also very strategic to the client and a topic of constant focus for over twelve months. When I look back, it is clear that the PwC network and my network were at their finest. Certainly, after this transaction, I was confident that there was almost nothing I could not do with my global team.

The chapters that follow will deal with topics that are important to me—topics that I believe are important for all those who want to be successful in business. They involve skills that I honed for over forty years and, in many cases, that I am known for within my former firm and worldwide. I have worked to live the values I will talk about and to refine the concepts through real-life execution. I have tried to do this in a high-performing way, knowing that it "was never good enough" and "could always be better"—I was always in search of a better way. I created very diverse teams of people smarter than me to constantly come up with better and better ideas and ways to do things.

When I reflect on my career, it is clear to me that I've lived a storied business life. I was given opportunities and challenges that I am frankly embarrassed to talk about. My superiors and mentors saw potential in me before I saw it in myself. They saw strengths in me that I did not realize I had, and were able to translate what I had done to what they knew I could do. I remember vividly the phrase "Give it to Don and he will figure it out." In the beginning, my reaction was "But I've never done it before" or "I don't know anything about that area." Over time, however, I learned to just get on with it without considering whether I could do it or not—it was a task or objective to figure out and get done.

For context, this role encompassed a range of critical functions. I was leading some of the firm's largest domestic and international accounts, managing the most challenging industry sectors (business units), and maintaining highly valuable and sensitive client relationships. The position was global, not to mention a role that had not really existed before, demanding the utmost in leadership skills—and frankly, every other skill I had. This included collaborating with a world-class global team. It also included helping merge two of the largest firms in the world and dealing effectively with high-level government officials (in some cases, those at the highest level) around the world, which was not a skill I initially thought I had.

One thing to get clear here is that I never had all the answers, and I did not always succeed. What I will tell you, however, is that my success percentage went up exponentially as time went on. What was impossible at first became possible but very difficult, then just difficult, and then almost easy. A quote I will never forget—from one of my global industry leaders from Sweden—is "Don does things which are not possible to do. We tell him it is not possible, and he says, 'I know it's not possible, but if it were possible how would we do it?' And then he just does it." This quote is directionally accurate, and it reflects my thought process. Most things that people say are impossible are actually possible, but require more analysis and, in some cases, thinking outside of the box.

One story that illustrates this comes to mind. I was sitting on a leadership team and a group from human capital came to get approval for a time-sensitive training program that needed to be rolled out across the firm. Their plan was to send everyone to locations across the country to receive training, and to do that over a two-to-three-month period at significant cost. Another member of the leadership team asked why we could not use a video with a short test to verify that the video's message had been received. The answer was that that would be impossible within the required timeframe: it would take too long to develop and produce. I always hated the word "impossible," so I jumped in, saying that I thought it was a great idea and asking how long it would take. The answer was between six and nine months from start to finish.

I continued: "How long would the video need to be?" Answer: "One hour." I said: "Is that all? We just did a twenty-five-minute video for a recently won proposal where our team was portrayed as a space shuttle team with significant moving parts and simulations included in the video. It was as high-quality as you could get." I was then asked by the HR leader in front of everyone: "How long did it take to develop and produce?" I intentionally hesitated for a second and said, "I think five days, but it could have been shorter." You could hear a pin drop! A nine-month project done in five days.

The difference here was a dramatic one in mindset. In one case, we had all the time we needed. In the other, a very short deadline with high stakes. The impossible becomes possible. HR would not normally think in terms of working 24/7 and putting a big team on it. To win a new client we did everything we could to get it done.

My years at PwC—which was and is a meritocracy—taught me many things about dealing with people and clients. I started by looking up the organization chart, so to speak, and I worked my way up to pretty near the top. I tried to use all the good things I had learned to make my teams and the organization better. I will discuss many of these things in this book. I will tell you, however, that great minds *do not* always think alike, and that good people can have dramatically different views on very important, foundational topics. I will try to point these out.

PwC is also a high-performance culture where we have over 75,000 people in the U.S. and 364,000 globally, with the average age in the late twenties. It is a culture that demands the highest ethics; fosters and creates diversity; drives constant learning, improvement, and advancement; and is quality- and client-focused. It hires the best and the brightest from the top schools around the world and, because it is a meritocracy, gives each new hire the chance to succeed no matter their background. One of my favorite things about PwC—and one of the things that kept me there for over forty years—was the opportunity to work with these really smart and motivated young people. I hope they learned a few things from me along the way, but I can tell you I learned a lot from them, and they always helped make me look good.

I have mentioned some of what is in this chapter to give you some context and color around what I will be talking about in later chapters. All large organizations are complex, most have strong corporate cultures, most reflect their demographics, some have cultures that are industry- or sector-related—for example, tech is fast-moving and fast-changing, governments not so much—and all need to change with the times. My biggest fear today is that if you are not a disrupter, you will be disrupted. Change is generally difficult for people and organizations. At PwC, I learned how to change, how to drive change, and how to understand the difficulties of organizational change. Hopefully, some of this will become clear in real-life examples that I share in this book.

Throughout this book, there are many stories that I use to prove a particular point. There are failures here and there, but not many. It is not that I never failed—I certainly did—however, failure for me was in most cases just a speed bump on the way to success. This is to say that when whatever I was trying to accomplish was not happening, I would change course, or work harder, or ask for help—whatever was necessary to achieve the objective and, in essence, not fail. This is most true when I didn't get admitted to PwC's partnership the year I thought I should have, and then I failed again the next year. Were these two failures? Objectively yes, but to me, they were just speed bumps that I had to get over and I did. I was finally admitted in my third year of candidacy, and I was a partner for more than twenty-six years with a great career. Also, in later chapters, I talk about setting ambitious goals and targets that may not be achieved, where your goal is twice the average goal. When these targets are not hit, some might call it failure. I view them as very lofty goals, where "success" could be considered 90% achievement—at 90% achievement you are still 40% above the average.

What I learned during my career is the basis for this book. It is decades of research and the application of that research. It puts together building blocks in a resume and in experience. It deals with how to meet people; how to build a network; how to deal effectively with executives or their equivalents (like college presidents or high-level government officials); how to build a high-performing team; how to build and manage trusted, complex relationships; how to manage big projects; how to manage global projects; how to manage and exceed expectations; how to run a business and make money; how to acclimate to different countries and cultures; how to handle adversity; how to win; how to lose; how to work a crowd; how to influence people; how to lead people; how to motivate people; how to reward people; how to tell stories; how to tell jokes; and when to just listen. I am sure I have missed some, but there you go.

It's now time to move on to the areas that are important to me and should be important to you.

HOW TO BE THE BEST: CORE VALUES AND CONCEPTS

Chapter 3

BE THE BEST IN THE WORLD

I know whenever I say "be the best in the world," most people smile or laugh or think I am exaggerating. You need to know, however, that this has been one of my core values for at least the last twenty-five years. It is a concept so important to me that I constantly apply it in almost everything I do: it is part of my DNA, part of my thought processes, part of my strategic thinking, and part of how I approach life.

The opposite of "being the best in the world" is "just getting by"—just doing enough to meet expectations, or even worse, not meeting expectations but being close enough that no one will call you on it. This opposite approach is an early topic in any college class I teach or lecture I give. I am an adjunct professor at Fordham University and I use this point to (sometimes) start to change the lives of highly intelligent young adults.

To "be the best in the world" is a concept that is demonstrated in life all the time, but it's rarely focused on as a core value to be incorporated into one's thinking. It is winning the Super Bowl in football, the Grand Slam in tennis, the World Series in baseball, and so on. It is doing these kinds of things so often that you start getting a reputation for being the best—like the New York Yankees in baseball, the New England Patriots in football, or the Los Angeles Lakers in basketball.

In business, it is marquee companies: organizations with long histories of quality that possess core competencies that make them the best in the world! I know some experts out there will think of times or areas where recognizable marquee companies have stumbled, but that is not the point I am trying to make; this is about sustained short-term and long-term performance.

Several important topics need to be considered before you can truly become the best in the world. The first—and arguably the most important—is how being the best is defined by those judging your performance. You can define the criteria, you can execute to the goals, and you can get to where you think you have to be to be the best. This is all important, but the only thing that counts is that the market considers you the best—that is, the market that a company operates in or customers that a company has or wants. For an individual, it is management and peers in your company or the clients and customers you deal with or want.

Too often we "talk to ourselves" and convince ourselves that we are the best. This is a major mistake, usually made by those who are slipping from first place or have never even gotten there, and often in a sophisticated way, with metrics and studies and the like. When determining whether or not you have become the best, do not ask yourself if you've beaten out the rest—listen to the marketplace. If the market is telling us that we are not number one, they are right and we are wrong. What we say or think is not what matters—the market's perception is the reality. Remember, it is all about changing perception.

The second major topic to be seriously considered is complacency. This happens very often: "We're the best in the world so they will come." What I do is unconsciously stop trying as hard—I relax! Almost always, those who are not the best try to copy or compete with you to become the best. The bar is always being raised. If you are not improving, you are losing ground. The result of this phenomenon is that if you are the best and you keep trying to be the best, you get better and better and better. The penultimate step is becoming the best in the world, and the final—and somewhat theoretical—step is becoming "the best there ever was." This last step sounds unattainable, though I am sure Muhammad Ali, Michael Jordan, Serena Williams, and Michael Phelps all thought so at one time.

To "be the best in the world" it helps if you know some of them, so you can use them as role models. I mentioned Clem in an earlier chapter; he was probably the first of "the best" I came to know. However, there were others who served as role models, mentors, and teachers. These individuals were partners and managers during my time as a staff person, then my peers when I became a partner, and they were certainly some of the best client executives and board members in the world.

Let me start with someone I'll call Jim. Jim was a manager when I met him, but he held various positions at PwC throughout his career. Jim was about five years older than me, and we met when I was a senior accountant at PwC and he was a senior manager. We had similar backgrounds—he from Brooklyn, I from Yonkers—and as I recall, we hit it off from the beginning. Jim was thought highly of and had a killer sense of humor. When I was admitted to the partnership—for reasons I do not know—I reported directly to Jim.

This was a challenging period for me with what my clients were doing, and Jim was someone I could reach out to for advice. I particularly remember being involved in a number of high-visibility transactions and projects, and in each case, I can remember Jim making sure that I was appropriately rewarded.

I will never forget moving to New York from New Jersey after two years of spending three hours a day commuting. It was not far enough to have the firm move me, but it was inconvenient enough for me to make the move myself. I never mentioned the move, but all of a sudden, I got a special bonus that just happened to equal my moving costs. When I thanked him for the moving bonus, I will never forget his reply: "What moving bonus? That was in recognition of your outstanding performance."

We worked together many times over the years, and we actually visited clients together. Jim gave me a great view of what leadership looked like at the highest level. He showed me how to make the younger partner (me) the main focus while with a client. At the start of a meeting, he would make it clear that I had requested that he come, "and when Don tells me to do something, you bet I do it," he'd say with a laugh. He showed me how to take control of a meeting or a room: he did it in the way he walked in—like he owned the place, and he was dressed like he did. He showed me a number of ways to use humor to your advantage. He always had a few one-liners at the beginning, in the middle, and at the end of a meeting. This made people tend to like him. He even showed me how to use what you normally should not do "to get people's attention." For example, walking into a meeting in progress and disrupting it by telling a joke to get their attention.

Another "best in the world" is someone I will call Sam. I visited many clients with Sam over the years and I reported directly to him while I was a Vice Chairman. Sam is a nice person who happens to be a great salesman and a true global leader. Sam, like Jim, also has a great sense of humor. Sam can turn on the charm and is great around people, whether it's one-on-one or in large groups. He came across as a very savvy businessman who was steeped in global experience. I modeled all these traits in my endeavors, although I probably applied them using my own personality.

One trait I remember about Sam—which was one I had myself and have always felt strongly about—was how Sam took care of his people and his teams. While I was reporting to him, this was true for me and my team.

I had the opportunity to work with a number of PwC partners and client executives who, like Jim and Sam, were some of the best in the world. I have agreed not to name them here, but they should all get credit for what they gave to me and what I learned from each of them.

Let's now turn to the "best in the world" teams. Whenever I would strategize with new teams, I would always strive to target being the best in the world. This often resulted in cocktail conversation on the subject, with some team members thinking we could, some convinced we could not, and some unsure and in the middle. Believe me when I tell you that if you prove able to do it once, others will tend to believe you in the future and always.

One example of this was when I was asked to lead our technology practice, which was both a humbling honor and an awesome responsibility. The first thing I did—which I highly recommend—was identify my leadership team and together define what success looked like. In this case, success was being number one in all major markets (out of about five or six in the U.S.), as well as in a number of skill areas like IPOs (Initial Public Offerings), venture-backed companies, and in certain sub-industries like software, internet, and the like. It also included the critical objective of being number one in Silicon Valley. This last one I recognized as key to being the best in the world; the mantra I used was "to be number one in technology we must OWN Silicon Valley."

I will never forget the first team meeting in San Jose where the new guy (me) outlined our strategy. It was a group of 200-ish and I was experiencing a whole host of emotions. The first question—and I knew it was coming—was: "Do you really think we can OWN Silicon Valley?" My answer: "Yes!" I then went on to discuss the targets we needed to hit in order to get there, the help we could expect to receive (the money and the resources that I had to deliver to the San Jose team), and what the leadership team's responsibilities were going to be.

I was asked: "What does it mean to OWN Silicon Valley?" We had a list of metrics and I outlined what they were, but I told them the key was: "Being number one by such a margin that number two is convinced they could never become number one." You should have seen the debate this caused! It went on—and I let it—for more than an hour. As an aside, I later became marginally famous for using the word "own" and for the adage of "being number one by such a margin that number two stopped trying because they knew they could never get there."

As part of this debate, I told them a story. Early on in a CEO's tenure, he concluded that the number one company in his industry was ahead by such a large margin that it was not possible for him to surpass them. When the competitor launched a huge ad campaign around them being number one, the CEO's answer was to create a counter-marketing campaign maintaining that his company was number two, but they were better than number one because they would try harder. In doing so, he created a situation where number two was considered better than number one. This example clearly showed how a company could own the market as number two, knowing it could not be number one, but this is the only time in my career I ever saw this.

There are many advantages to being the best in the world. It's easier to sell yourself, it's easier to sell your product or service, pricing becomes less sensitive since you are viewed as the leader, talent wants to work for you, and you tend to be more profitable. I have competed in business in all sorts of circumstances, and over time you learn how to compete, even if at a disadvantage. For example, suppose you are competing for an automotive client and you do not have any automotive clients. In that case, you argue that the firm that owns the auto industry will dilute their best resources over many clients, whereas you will put forth *only* your best people, and the firm in question will be your number one client in the industry: they will get 100% of your effort and focus. That said, it is always easier to win when you dominate.

Another dynamic of dominating occurs inside your prospective customers or clients: they view you as a lower-risk option. When a potential customer makes a selection decision, they know there is a risk of being wrong. If you are small or not dominant, you are a bigger risk—if I pick you and the venture fails, *I* made a bad decision. The bigger the project and the more money spent, the bigger the risk. If I pick a small company or a company that is not dominant, I may be wrong, and if I am wrong, I may lose my position or even my job. If I pick the best in the world and it fails, then it becomes *their* fault, not mine. How can I be criticized for picking the wrong company when I picked the best in the world?

This mindset of "becoming the best in the world" occurs in many industries—in some cases, one company stands out as the top dog, and in other cases, a small group of companies have (nearly) equal claim to the title. It also applies to specific business units or specialties within companies.

In the industry I worked in, there are what is known today as "the Big Four." They are four global giants with very extensive worldwide networks. I believe PwC is the best of the best (meaning the best of the Big Four and more broadly the best in certain areas), and I can tell you why in an elevator speech, a one-hour presentation, or over a day or week, depending how much time you have. PwC is one of the most widely recognized brands and is known and respected in virtually every country in the world. Opting for PwC is a great example of a foolproof choice—selecting them will almost never be wrong and will rarely be subject to criticism.

That said, there are components of PwC where they are clearly the best in the world and not just the best among the Big Four. These include specific industries (technology and banking), skill sets (audit and consulting), technical areas (due diligence and accounting), geographies (many), and other focus areas. In these cases, they lead the debate, identify the issues, and predict the future. They are an integral part of the ecosystem, and they are very well-networked (they know everybody, and everybody knows them); above all else, they are a "player."[1] I think you get the picture of what I think and what the endgame looks like.

Let me give you a few more examples of what striving to be the best in the world looks like in practice:

---

1. "Players" are those that are at the top of their game, boasting a potent mix of skill and influence. They perform at a high-level and are generally regarded as being some of the best there are at what they do.

Back in 2014, I met with a high school freshman I was beginning to mentor to discuss his grades and plans for college. He was just finishing his first semester when we met and had an overall average of 72. He played basketball on the school's team, and—being that his focus was on his extracurriculars—72 was a "good" average by his standards. I told him that it was good to be a really skilled basketball player, but it was much better to be a really smart *and* really skilled basketball player. This is what all the college coaches are looking for: not just a talented athlete or a gifted student, but both—the next "best in the world." After some long talks with him and his mom, he finally got the message. By his senior year, his average had soared to around 90%, and he was being recruited for basketball by highly-ranked colleges—even some in the nation's top twenty.

Another example is related to my normal counseling of staff on my teams. I remember meeting with a young staff person on one of my teams. She was really smart and doing extremely well. In our discussion, I asked her what she wanted to do over her thirty-to-forty-year career and what she wanted to be known as the best in. These two topics surprised her, and she clearly had never focused on either. Ultimately, she landed on wanting to manage a large global client. This objective had clear experiences she had to have, expertise she had to accrue, and specific things she had to do. This also set her focus on the thing(s) she had to be the best in. She chose deals and transactions as her area of focus, and large multinational clients as the target clientele. This enabled her to move up the ranks and ultimately be admitted to the partnership. Although she may not yet be the best in the world, she is certainly moving in the right direction.

The last example is from when I worked on a deal team early in my career. It was a very diverse group—brought together from all over the U.S. and at least two foreign countries—that supported deals for a leveraged buyout firm. We worked on a number of deals which I will never forget, but the acquisition of one company in particular was a very special and unique one. This project required the team to work 24/7 in a high-stakes and high-pressure environment, but they rose to the occasion. Everyone committed to doing whatever it took to get the deal done, and they did: it was long hours under significant pressure, in areas never explored before or since, reporting to an extremely demanding client. Throughout it all, it was the team's focus on being the best in the world that kept us motivated and consistent, producing quality work even when the going got tough. By the end, the team members, the client, and I concluded that our team was one of the best in the world, and you can bet that we were proud of it.

An Almeida Point: The Best Mindset In The World

BEING THE BEST IN THE WORLD IS NOT JUST ABOUT WHAT YOU'VE DONE OR WHO YOU ARE. IT IS A MINDSET—A CONSTANT PURSUIT OF BEING BETTER AND BETTER, REGARDLESS OF WHAT YOU'VE ALREADY ACCOMPLISHED. THE BEST IN THE WORLD SET NEW GOALS FOR THEMSELVES AS THEY ACHIEVE THEM, ALWAYS LOOKING AHEAD TO WHAT THEY CAN DO NEXT. SO, BEING THE BEST IN THE WORLD NEEDS TO BE A CONSTANT AREA OF FOCUS. NO MATTER HOW GOOD YOU ARE, YOU ARE NEVER GOOD ENOUGH—DON'T EVER STOP IMPROVING.

Chapter 4

WHAT IS A "PLAYER"?

I n the world of professional sports, a "player" is someone who performs at a high level. Michael Jordan was a player. Mickey Mantle was a player. Pelé was a player. Serena Williams is a player. Tom Brady was a player. If you're not a well-known or famous athlete and I call you a player, it means I think of you in the same way I think of these guys. Conversely, backups, journeymen, rookies, and practice squad guys are NOT "players."

In business, players are normally high-performers, and thus they tend to occupy high-level or executive roles. Chairpersons are players. CEOs are players. Board members are players. Senior VPs tend to be players. Lower-level executives do not tend to be viewed as players.

As defined above, a "player" is someone who is widely thought of as extremely qualified with a significant sphere of influence within their area of focus or more broadly. The context for determining whether someone is a player certainly changes based on the circumstances, but is also beholden to the discretion of the one making the determination. Being a player in baseball is different than in business, and so the criteria for how "players" are defined is different from the point of view of a baseball fan as compared to the CEO of a company. Most baseball fans would view Mantle as a real "player." They may not even know who the chairman of the largest bank is, but to myself and many others, he is definitely a player!

I want to focus on the term "player" as it pertains to the business world, and by extension, the areas that influence or drive business. High-level executives and board members are usually players, but so are those in politics: people like the president of the U.S. and members of Congress are clearly players in the world of business, as they can have a major influence on how business is done. For the same reason, other senior people in roles that influence the outcome of business can also be players. High-level regulators, for example, are normally players as well.

When I was in charge of PwC's Technology practice, players included CEOs and CFOs of large or fast-growing tech companies, senior executives at relevant banks, partners at venture capital and private equity firms, partners at law firms, and other significant influencers. PwC partners were often on the list of players for those firms, and in some cases, they may have been high on the list.

If you are still wondering who the players are, pick a topic or area (you can pick technology, motion pictures, banking, universities, healthcare, whatever—any industry will do), then research your chosen area using a search engine. You will quickly get lists of players in the given category. I would always do this when we were proposing to a potential client, especially if their area of operation was in a country outside of the U.S. My purpose was to identify as many influencers (players) as I could. Often, my next step was to identify which ones I knew, and which ones I could get to through my networks.

The Importance of Being a Player

When you live in the world of serious business, players want to deal with other players. In my own work, I understood that it was important that client executives and the like viewed you as a player. If they did, you could become a trusted advisor; if they didn't, they went somewhere else for advice and counsel.

In this book, I deal with many topics that I think are important to being the best, many of which also help make you a player. Areas such as being an expert at something, being the best in the world, having an opinion, being a leader, building your network, making a decision, dealing with CEOs, and being global are all critical for any player-in-the-making.

Becoming a Player and Understanding the Game

So, how can you become a player, and what is the "game" that the players are playing?

The game is life first and business second. As the title of this book implies, its tenets (if followed) will give you the opportunity to be a player in business. All it really takes is being viewed as an expert, albeit usually one with multiple skills and connections to a large group of relevant people. Being known as the best or one of the best in the world at something will certainly help. Obviously, doing what is necessary to become a player takes time, hard work, and refined interpersonal and leadership skills.

I have always found it interesting that real players do not really compete with each other: they only have to if they go head-to-head in a deal. They are always world-class professionals who have real, tangible skills and networks. As I said before, players tend to want to deal with other players, and so many players actually go out of their way to mentor others and create new players. To the extent that I was a player, I certainly had this kind of help. Also, in my experience in building and sustaining high-performance teams, I certainly loaded up on as many players as I could. My last role at PwC saw my collaboration with the partners on our 150 largest clients from around the globe. Many of these partners were certainly players, and most were players on an international scale. Some were even major players in their respective countries, with the clout and success to match. This group was high-performing and worked extremely well together. This included everything from sharing information and technical expertise to sharing contacts from their respective networks.

Within this group some were not players—most knew the difference. One of my charges was to build a high-performing culture that "raised all ships," as the saying goes. Every one of the 150 partners knew their roles and responsibilities, and we worked together as a global team. This group included partners from thirty countries, including India, China, South Korea, Russia, and Brazil.

So, as you are gaining experience and growing your networks, there will come a time when you are recognized as a player, most likely within a certain geography or industry. In my case, it happened before I was a partner, when I first became an expert in something important. It happened when I worked with a group that was trying to "save New York City."[1] I was twenty-six years old, and an expert in accounting and financial reporting. I was representing PwC in the trenches day-to-day, to the mayor, the governor, the lawyers, and the bankers. No one else was doing what I did: I was one of one—the go-to guy. I was a player, and I got it done.

At the time, I didn't even use terms like "player," let alone think of myself as one. What I *did* think was that I was capable of handling the task at hand and working almost literally 24/7 to get it done (though I'll admit to being a little anxious at times). Importantly, those I reported to and our client had no doubt I could do the job, and all knew the stakes we were facing. Everyone got to know me, including major players from all relevant organizations. I even remember, on subsequent deals with new players joining, being one of the players who introduced new players to older players. This is when I first learned that being a player was not connected to age: I was twenty-six and introducing players in their sixties.

You will notice when you are becoming a player and in what areas your influence is growing as a result of what and who you know. You will start forming relationships with (important) people who other players know, and maybe even

---

1. See "On knowing what nobody else knows based on experience," Chapter 7.

some that they don't know. The terms "name-dropping" and "name-dropper" tend to have a negative connotation. Not to me. If you're talking to a player and know (*really* know) many of the same players as them, then they will understand that you too are a player. Be careful though: when I say that you "know" them, it means you know them somewhat well, and that they would recommend you.

Much of being a player is related to substance, as in what you know and who you know. Some of it, however, is about presence—one's ability to act like a player. You can be a genius and have a huge rolodex, but if you are quiet and don't let anyone see what you have to offer, then you can never be a player.

I strongly suggest that you always be truthful. That said, how you react, what you say, and how you say it can send a big message and determine whether or not you're viewed as a player yourself. Let me give you one example:

I was meeting with the CEO of one of PwC's famous marquee clients. I didn't know him very well at the time, and we were meeting one-on-one in his office. He had just returned from Washington D.C., where he had met in the White House with a number of high-level officials, including the then-president. He was recounting the experience and blurted out "Do you have to deal with this guy (the president) very often?" I said, "No, not really. Our chairman gets that privilege!" He said, "Thank God!"

I'm sure that this gave him the impression that I dealt with the president in some capacity. In reality, I had only shaken the president's hand once at an event, and that was before he was president. The point here is that the CEO of my client viewed me as someone who would possibly meet with the president in the same way he did, and my (factually correct) comment did not change his view. He already viewed me as a potential player when he asked that question, and I reinforced that. A non-player might have responded with something along the lines of "Are you kidding me? Why would I ever meet with the president?" Though that said, if you weren't viewed as a player you wouldn't have even been in the meeting, and you wouldn't have been asked the question.

The CEO and I would go on to cultivate a close relationship over the next ten years. This was a guy who if we met at events (business or otherwise) would always introduce me this way: "This is Don Almeida. He is my senior partner from PwC. Don knows everybody" (which was flattering, but obviously not true). You can see how he viewed me; even though he was an industry luminary with no shortage of his own connections, I was able to introduce him to people he didn't know but wanted to meet. Had I not worked to identify myself as a player during our first few meetings, I doubt the relationship would have flourished the same way.

Chapter 5

HONESTY AND INTEGRITY

H onesty and integrity are mutually inclusive: to be honest means having integrity, and to have integrity means being honest. I talk about the importance of these two attributes throughout this book; they are key to almost everything we do in life and business. People are either honest or they are dishonest—there's no such thing as "partially honest." I firmly believe that one must always be honest, and further, constantly exhibit and reinforce their integrity in their behavior.

Dealing honestly with people 100% of the time is critical to success. Your word must be your bond. To gain trust is difficult; to lose it takes a nanosecond, and once lost, it can never truly be regained. Honesty and integrity are the foundation of business, and they become even more important as the scale of one's business becomes more significant—the bigger the deal, the more vital one's integrity. It is very often a tiebreaker in differentiating you from others: "I'll do business with Don because I know he will be honest with me."

It has always amazed me that I am sometimes called "too direct" (which is usually meant as a negative) simply because I have honestly answered a question. If you ask me a question, I will always give you an honest answer. Most people don't! They don't for many reasons: some answers are not politically correct, some may potentially offend the other person, some are what used to be called "white lies," and some are just plain lies!

When you do what I do, the positive side is that you are known as a "straight shooter," a "bottom-line guy," or a "no BS guy": someone who will tell you the truth, and who can be trusted. Conversely, pulling punches or telling white lies can give rise to a reputation that you are not honest.

Indisputable Honesty

I had a client once who paid us millions of dollars for years without any competitive proposals. Why? They trusted that our fee would be fair, that our team would be the best in the industry, and that we would deliver what we promised when we promised it, anytime they needed us and anywhere in the world.

In business, one's personal brand tends to become widely known. It ought to always include honesty and integrity. Everyone hears everything!

Great Ideas

Sometimes people hear an idea from someone and introduce it to other groups as their own. This happens very often in business, especially with what I call "empty suits." An empty suit is someone who has never had an original idea. They typically take someone else's idea and start to socialize it. Once they get positive feedback ("What a great idea!"), they act as if it's their own. An honest person would give credit to the person whose idea it was and join up with them to help take it forward. The irony here is that sooner or later, the facts always become known, and when this happens, the empty suit who stole the idea is outed and branded with a bad reputation.

Performance Counseling

Performance counseling is rife with dishonest feedback. Usually, this relates to bad performance or prospective advancement in rank or compensation. Telling someone that they are not doing well is not easy, and is a management skill that needs to be acquired. Also included here are candid conversations on how to improve and what needs to be changed. Helping the person understand the issues, explaining how to resolve them, and even assisting in the resolution personally are all opportunities to reinforce your honesty and build trust.

Very often these conversations are watered down, not specific, and in many cases misleading. The person receiving the feedback may actually leave the conversation thinking they are doing fine when in reality they are not. Then, when more direct action is taken as a consequence, those reviewed are liable to feel blindsided, making comments like "I was never told" or "I didn't know." Invariably, these situations result in a lack of trust and a conclusion that the person giving the feedback is dishonest.

Discussions about advancement and compensation often give rise to similar issues. The person giving the feedback may try to motivate the other person by implying that a promotion is imminent, or that a significant raise is near. While these rewards may be possibilities, it is rare that they are as likely as they are made out to be. Later, when these positive things do not happen, the person who "promised" them will blame a higher-up executive, in many cases maintaining that they are "not even at the decision-making table" and therefore "didn't even get a vote." These situations can be devastating to a coworker's morale and can result in a complete lack of trust between the individuals and potentially within the entire organization.

When put in these types of situations, you must do your best to be honest with the person, even if it results in more conflict in the moment. Conflict now usually results in a better outcome later.

Long-Term Potential Counseling

"What are my prospects?"; "Do I have what it takes?"; "Do I have the right personality?"; and "Do I have the right background?"

These are questions I am asked very often by college students, but also by relatives, employees, partners, and others. For as long as I can remember I have always tried to give my best, honest advice—good or bad.

In most cases, the answer is not black and white. That said, people are either cut out for something or they are not. It is usually a probability analysis based on the facts, which is to say that the 80/20 rule applies: there is an 80% chance you either are or are not right for a job or career. If you're an outside guy (like a salesperson), you're probably not suited for an inside job like tax accounting. If you don't like blood, you probably shouldn't be a doctor.

Promises Kept

Promising something and then not following through is a great way to get a reputation as being dishonest, and unreliable to boot. This is something that many people do (sometimes even on a routine basis), and it's essentially the same thing as lying. In some cases it is minor, but more often it's not. Politicians are notorious for this type of dishonesty. There are people who are known to always make empty promises, and everyone knows they have no intention of keeping their word—some are called BS artists. I think this is one of the highest levels of dishonesty because it impacts your reliability. If you are dishonest and not reliable, then no one will want to work with you.

Lack of Honesty

If one is dishonest, they fall into a large category of people. There could be any number of reasons for a person's dishonesty. Sometimes it's how they were raised. Sometimes it's genetics. Sometimes it's greed or financial hardship. Whatever the reason, my only advice is to stay away from those that you cannot trust.

Chapter 6

THE ART OF LISTENING (AND UNDERSTANDING)

S omeone once said, "You have one mouth and two ears for a reason." This is one of these sayings that for whatever reason I can't forget; it has come into my consciousness over and over again for many years. I think this happens because it is one of those truths that is almost always relevant.

Now, let me start by saying that there are two things very often thought and said about me. The first is that I do not listen well, and the second is that I have a propensity to interrupt people who are speaking.

The fact is that listening is a priority for me, and I listen well. Having said that, I do often encounter people who just want to go on and on and on. You have heard the adage "A picture is worth a thousand words." Well, I coined a phrase to describe these people: "Why use a picture when 10,000 words will do?" So, I do listen intently, but there comes a time when we've *got it* and ought to be moving on.

The second criticism of interrupting people is true, but only on occasion. It usually comes as the result of me disagreeing with what is being said, or asking for clarification of some general statement that's being made: platitudes like "everybody knows," "this was agreed," "this was already approved," "you know we don't do this," and the like. Who is "everybody"? Who agreed? When was it approved and by whom? And how do I know that? I do interrupt, but it is usually directly related to the lack of clarity and specificity of the speaker. Said differently, if you thought I interrupted you a lot, it was probably because you were not being specific or clear enough.

Good. I'm glad I got that off my chest, and for you reading this who know me, now you understand. Also, you may want to read the chapter on leadership (Chapter 18), particularly the part about "restlessness." There is no doubt I was and am restless. I consider it a big strength.

Now, back to the art of listening.

I used to tell my teams: "Never say no unless you can't say yes, and never say 'it can't be done' unless you *know* it can't be done." In my experience, the vast majority of people think they know the answer even before they hear the question. This tends to be truer the more of an expert in something they are, and gets even more true the less of an expert the other person is. Also, it always seemed to be even more true when a left-brained person was talking to a right-brained person: it was like left-brainers thought they were smarter.

Here is an example: I came from the world of accountants and financial people—classic left-brain people, most being experts in one or more areas. In many cases they were high performers, and as a consequence would normally go into meetings well-prepared. That said, what often happens is this: they walk into the meeting, and as the CFO, CEO, or whomever is talking, they conclude that they already know the answer to what is being proposed. In some cases, the answer is "no" or "it cannot be done." WRONG!

Before you can start forming any conclusions, you must first fully understand the objective that the CFO or the CEO is trying to achieve, including nuances. This requires very careful listening, and further, listening with an open mind. You can have no predetermined answers—none! Very often, a clear understanding of the situation and objective(s) requires the speaker to expand on what he/she is saying, diving into any specifics that may be important to the answer.

More often than not, the other party has already had numerous discussions about an issue or objective and has formed views around what can and can't be done before they've even met you. In some cases, these views may be incorrect. Also, people from different backgrounds may not be familiar with the language or specific words normally used to describe something—even when both parties think they're speaking plain English. Individual manners of speech might mean that "maybe" is taken as "no," or that spirited debate is perceived as pointed confrontation. I often remember kidding CEOs of my clients about "what the president *really* meant to say."

All this is to say that there are any number of factors that can complicate productive conversation (as well as productive listening), and so the process of understanding the objective is key. Getting that clarity requires a sort of Q&A interchange as well as a discussion of "what-if" scenarios to better understand potential options and how they compare to one another. This is critical to getting a correct answer—if these conversations have not taken place, you are not finished yet. It was always interesting to me that you might start with a "no" answer and end up with a number of "yes" options (in other words, more than one "yes" answer). In some cases, the CEO was happy with any of them, but one was ultimately considered preferable.

This good listening and understanding can be a huge value-add to the other party. This is particularly true when the left-brain experts I referred to before put their brainpower to work creating a solution rather than explaining why "no" is the right answer. I have seen many cases where in just one meeting, listening, followed by understanding, followed by Q&A, followed by "what-if scenarios," followed by discussion produced great solutions, or even changed the objective with a slightly different focus or timeline.

These types of interactions drive significant value as I mentioned, but can also illustrate your working or partnership method to the other party: "They not only listen to me, but they go out of their way to understand my problem and help me solve it. They understand my objective and help me achieve it." If you are good—and I know you are or can be—then it is also a chance for you to demonstrate qualities like intelligence, expertise, good bedside manner, and pragmatism, as well as your knowledge of the subject matter, industry, and the rule and its application.

Being a good listener and understanding the issue or objective can turn "these guys don't understand my problem or issue, get me someone who does" into "wow, these guys are smart, know their stuff, and are really good—make sure we bring them in the future." This is true even if at the end of the discourse the answer is "no," which will occasionally be the case. That said, even in those cases it will be clear that you listened and tried to find a way. The quote then will be "If they can't find a way, no one can."

One last thing: in 1975, I took a half-day communications seminar. The only thing I remember from it is a slide with two stick figures and a speech bubble above each. One said "This is what I said," and the other said, "This is what I heard." I have never forgotten that slide, and think of it often. As we all know, much of what is said in a meeting or at a seminar—or even in one-on-one interactions—is not clear or is not understood. This happens all the time.

There is some rule of thumb, some average percentage of how much of what's spoken is actually heard. It's really low. I have been at meetings where a question was asked and answered. One-third thought the answer was "yes," one-third thought it was "no," and one-third was not sure. This is why you should always confirm the answers to important questions.

One of my pet peeves—and this connects to honesty—is the term "They lied to me." I always ask "Are you sure you understood?" If they say yes, I ask "Are you sure they understood *you*?" All too often, what was really a misunderstanding or miscommunication is interpreted as a lie. This is often true when an implied commitment is made that one party takes as agreed while the other considers it as a possibility. This often happens around timing. An example is "I'll get back to you on that"—one party is waiting for a call, and the other will never call because what they were hoping would happen did not.

I remember one case and on a big deal where our answer was "I'll get back to you shortly." The client interpreted this to mean in an hour and my partner meant next week.

An Almeida Point: Always Confirm Your Understanding

IT IS CRITICALLY IMPORTANT THAT YOU CONFIRM YOUR UNDERSTANDING OF WHAT WAS SAID AND AGREED UPON. IF YOU ARE THE SPEAKER, THEN SUMMARIZING WHAT YOU THINK YOU COMMUNICATED IS A GOOD HABIT. IF YOU ARE THE LISTENER, THEN CONFIRMING WHAT YOU HEARD WITH THE SPEAKER IS ALSO A GOOD HABIT. I ALSO OFTEN RECOMMEND SENDING A NOTE CONFIRMING EITHER WHAT YOU SAID OR WHAT YOU HEARD. IF IMPORTANT IT WOULD INCLUDE SPECIFICS, SUCH AS "WE AGREED TO MOVE

FORWARD WITH THE PROJECT, AND ALSO THAT I WILL TAKE THE LEAD."
THE OLD ADAGE STILL HOLDS TRUE TODAY: "YOU CAN'T COMMUNICATE
TOO MUCH."

Chapter 7

BECOME AN EXPERT

As I have reflected on my career, it is clear to me that to be relevant in business you must have some expertise in something. Said differently, to be invited to join the party, you must be viewed as bringing something to the table. In the beginning, this is a specific skill set or area of perceived expertise. As your relationships move forward, the other parties will hopefully perceive broader areas of expertise.

When I started in business, I was once asked "What is an expert?" My answer, somewhat jokingly, was "Someone who knows more about something than the other people in the room, and who has slides." In the consulting business, the answer could be "When the other person has never done something, the expert is the person who has done it once."

I graduated from the Fordham University Gabelli School of Business in 1973 with a degree in Accounting. I joined PwC shortly thereafter, and for some six years learned more and more about the accounting and auditing profession. This was cumulatively ten years of experience in accounting and auditing, which I would understand over time as a foundational element in business and finance. By 1979, I had gained significant experience with various companies and industries, as well as a solid grasp on how businesses worked from the inside out and from the outside in. I dealt with regulatory agencies, Initial Public Offerings (IPOs), highly technical accounting and tax issues, and many experts in fields different from mine (attorneys, investment bankers, bankers, etc.). I also started to acquire the skills for solving complex problems. In my view, I was entering the early stages of being a well-rounded businessman. This, as I would understand later, was expertise that most did not have. I also came to realize that my skill as a businessman was built on the experience I acquired when I was young and that it would continue to improve over time.

So, being a business-focused thinker is clearly a skill, but I view it as a core competency. It separates you from all those who don't think that way and aligns you with all those who do, like business owners and CEOs.

ON BECOMING AN EXPERT ON SOMETHING...

Remember the credit card company from my internship? Well, I worked on that account for two more years after I'd been hired. As part of my responsibilities, I had to review their credit card processing system. I knew the system from start (when you charge at a restaurant) to finish (when your bill is paid each month), and all fifty steps in between. What this meant was that I knew the credit card business—period. There were all sorts of "what if" scenarios, and I would be consulted by my superiors, fellow staff, and even the client because everyone knew I knew the company's processes inside and out. Interestingly enough, fifty years later, the processes have not changed much; some may now be computerized, but the steps are the same.

When you think about being an expert, it is important to understand that your expertise is generally valued by others as a function of their own level of competence in the area taken together with how important said area is to them. In other words, both expertise and its value are *relative*. An easy example would be filing a tax return when your tax rate is 50%, your income is high, and you know nothing about taxes. The expertise you need is someone who knows personal income tax rules, so you hire a professional to help you file. Because you know little about taxes yourself and it's important to you that your taxes are filed optimally, you would view your hire as an expert even if they are not the best tax professional in the world.

This concept of relativity is extremely important in understanding the definition of "expertise" in business terms. In my career, I was often referenced by clients and colleagues as being an expert. In most cases, I was not an expert, and I would say as much all the time. That said, I often found myself in situations where I was extremely knowledgeable on the given topic (or maybe only somewhat knowledgeable) while the other party had zero relevant knowledge or experience.

A *true* expert is typically one who has an extreme depth of knowledge and experience in a relatively narrow area or on a particularly niche topic. Many of these experts spend their entire careers gaining more and more expertise. A true expert could be a brain surgeon, a historian specializing in Roman history, or a New Jersey real estate tax accountant. The flip side of this coin is someone who is "a mile wide and an inch deep"—someone who knows a little about a lot, but is not really an expert in anything.

In my view, in my career I was neither—and candidly, I never wanted to be. What I *was* was someone who knew a lot about many things. I had a level of expertise beyond merely superficial knowledge in many areas, but was not really a true expert as defined above. These areas included a number of hard skills but also included soft skills and people skills. I had a high level of knowledge on topics like global business, solving complex problems, how business is done within various countries, strategic planning, and building and sustaining high-performance teams. In addition to these was the deep knowledge of accounting and tax matters and how they impacted sophisticated global companies that I'd learned early in my career.

ON KNOWING WHAT NOBODY ELSE KNOWS BASED ON EXPERIENCE...

In my fourth year with PwC, I was asked to work with a group of entities that was going to try to help save New York City. This large group worked for a number of years together with most major political and other figures with interests in NYC's survival. I can not go into detail for client confidentiality reasons, although most of what was done is in the public domain. I mention it here as a great example of how I, at the age of twenty-six, became an expert in what needed to be done for each transaction. After the first one, a small group of advisors including me were in fact the world's experts in what had been done and what needed to be done.

This was also a time when I learned the art of meeting famous people. In many cases, this was the result of them wanting to meet me.

An Almeida Point: Own Your Experience

OFTENTIMES, PEOPLE ARE AFRAID OF CLAIMING EXPERTISE FOR FEAR OF SOUNDING CONCEITED OR OPENING THEMSELVES UP TO CHALLENGE. IN REALITY, THAT'S NOT HOW IT WORKS. YOUR EXPERIENCE—THE PROBLEMS YOU'VE DEALT WITH, THE SKILLS YOU'VE GAINED, THE KNOWLEDGE YOU'VE BUILT—ARE WHAT MAKE YOU VALUABLE TO A TEAM, PARTICULARLY IF IT'S IN AN AREA THAT THE REST OF THE TEAM IS UNFAMILIAR WITH. IF YOU HAVE REAL EXPERIENCE, THEN YOU HAVE REAL EXPERTISE; DON'T BE AFRAID TO LET IT SHOW!

An important point to focus on is that there are different levels of expertise. To (over)simplify, I will put them in three main categories, plus one honorable mention: Deep Expertise, Significant Knowledge, and Broad Understanding, and the "plus one" is Soft Skills.

Deep Knowledge represents your areas of true expertise. They are areas in which your understanding deepens and expands over time. In my case, this was mostly in financial areas, but over time expanded to other subjects like doing business in certain countries.

Significant Knowledge refers to things that you know a lot about, but that you are not an expert in. These are areas where you can carry on significant conversations on the topic, but where your knowledge is not deep enough to solve complex problems. To those with little to no knowledge of the subject in question, significant knowledge looks a lot like deep knowledge, to the point where the former is often confused for the latter. I was often introduced at social gatherings as an "expert" in something that I knew I was not, and I would always respond "I know a lot about it, but I am certainly not an expert."

Broad Understanding means that you might be able to carry on a conversation about a given topic, but not much more. You have read up on the subject or had a number of relevant experiences, so you understand the area, but your detailed knowledge is limited. A good example for me came from doing business in various countries. I never had deep knowledge and was not an expert, but I did have significant knowledge of Italy and a few other countries where I'd lived and worked for three years. I also had broad knowledge of more than fifty countries where I had done business.

"Soft Skills" is a term often used in business to refer to a suite of interpersonal skills—though I would always say they are not so soft. Some soft skills like communication skills, people skills, the art of negotiation, presence, humor, and projecting honesty are critical to success and are learned and refined over time.

So why is this important? Becoming a real expert and being viewed as one requires all of the above types of knowledge. Also, effectively dealing with different types of people is helped by all these areas of expertise, but each is considerably less effective without a number of soft skills. Being the world's expert on something may be worthless if no one knows who you are and you are unable to communicate your expertise in a way that engages people.

Having all three levels of knowledge is truly what makes you interesting, engaging, and someone that people seek out for advice. Also, shoring up your broad understanding of a wide range of subjects allows you to react to a conversation or discussion no matter where it leads. This goes beyond the business sphere, and includes conversational topics like sports, or maybe golf, basketball, or baseball specifically; it includes music, or maybe rock or classical specifically; it includes the best restaurants in NYC, London, or Paris. You get the point.

Most experts have a dominant pattern in their thinking, reflecting a preeminence of one of the four quadrants of the brain. These quadrants could be described simply as follows: upper left, analytical; lower left, organizational; upper right, conceptual; and lower right, humanistic/artistic. I call these dominant pattern experts "singletons." Singletons can be beholden to any of the four quadrants, but one is usually more influential in guiding their thinking. Possessing the range of expertise I described above is typically seen in people who are "quads"—those who reflect all four quadrants of the brain. You see this very often with CEOs who have broad knowledge across a spectrum of areas. Curiously, most are also musical, playing instruments or singing.

So why is this important? In business and life, it always helps to try to understand how the people around you think. This kind of knowledge helps you navigate conversations and deal with issues. Remember the two stick figures: one says, "This is what I said," and the other says "This is what I heard," and they are not the same. This happens very often, and in many cases is caused by what I refer to above. A predominantly left-brain person will likely misunderstand a predominantly right-brain person. I see this often when academics deal with people from the business world. Academics can be very literal and businesspeople tend to have hundreds of phrases that are used but are not meant to be literal. Things like "shoot the guy" means fire him, or "she's a black belt" means she's an expert and has nothing to do with karate, or "blow it up" means stop doing it and has nothing to do with explosives.

In working with someone, once you understand how the other person thinks, you can be more effective in dealing with them. I always found this brain analysis helpful. This was an area where I at best had a broad understanding, and maybe not even that. That said, it was an interesting perspective, and it did help me take a conversation to the next level. I might say to a CEO, "You're obviously a quad—and so am I." This could, if done correctly, cause an instant bond. It also reinforced the myth that "Don is someone I need to know."

I need to be very clear here. A CEO, president, or someone of a similar rank must be a broad thinker with broad experience, but they also can and do have deep expertise in one or many areas. All CEOs ascend to their rank via an area of focus or expertise—marketing, sales, finance, or HR, to name a few—and likely accumulate broad expertise in other areas along the way.

Over the course of my career, I gained experience in accounting, technical accounting, tax, and business. That said, I was certainly not PwC's expert in any of these areas. This was for several reasons, but it was principally because our true experts spent all their time in that area, and in most cases, a specific segment of that area. They were not only experts in accounting but specialists in areas like revenue recognition and even the subsegments thereof like software revenue recognition.

My expertise in these areas was drawn from thirty years of experience in the technology sector and with IPOs and deals. Clients understood that if they were doing something important, I needed to be there to advise them—sometimes alone, sometimes with one of my real experts. Most deals crossed various areas, and thus my ability to add value required both broad knowledge as well as specific expertise. Both were critical to success, but I found that broad knowledge was often the more valuable of the two. Knowing what you needed to know and knowing what was important to the deal were valuable skill sets; getting the exact right technical answer was usually step two.

Securities and Exchange Commission

Doing business as a public company requires knowledge of SEC rules. Many of these are legal rules, but many are also related to accounting and disclosure. Knowing the rules—which I did—was definitely a valuable skill set, but knowing current SEC practice and interpretation was even more valuable. Having a core group of expert advisors who were experienced with SEC matters was key when dealing with any public company, and this was especially true with IPOs. If you were one of those experts, you were invaluable. If you *also* had other business and technical skills, you became a trusted advisor.

I knew I had become a trusted advisor when the client (CEO/CFO) asked my opinion on matters that I was not known to be an expert in. In these instances, I understood that they wanted an opinion from a business advisor whose judgment they trusted, and that person was me.

International Authority

This is an area of expertise I could write chapters on. At the highest level, it is experience in doing business outside of your home country. There are a plethora of complexities to be understood in just doing business in other countries and assessing their impact on a U.S. company. There are also high-level understandings of things like geography, history, risks, geopolitics, skills, technology, and so much more knowledge that is useful, if not requisite, to succeeding in foreign dealings. Having broad experience across the world is a very valuable and relatively unique expertise.

As an example, I worked in seventy-four countries in my career, spent significant time in more than fifteen of them, lived in Europe for three years in the early 80s, and completed major projects or ran businesses all over the world. I have multiple global networks: one within PwC, one comprising our current and former clients, and one of friends and associates that I have built over more than fifty years. I have helped domestic clients expand outside the U.S. for the first time, international clients expand to more countries, and global companies that operated almost everywhere in the world set up new structures like distribution hubs, outsourcing operations, or manufacturing operations. I have also assisted in strategy and risk assessment across the world.

When you have broad global experience—and I say you must in this day and age—you become a valuable expert: your other areas of expertise are weighed in the context of your global experience, thus elevating the value of both. They (whoever they are) will require your insights and input almost always, whatever the matter or issue.

Having specific country expertise is also a great and valuable skill. Sooner or later, issues in a specific country will have to be dealt with. My country experience together with my global network made my expertise and ability to help solve issues very unique. Countries where these two capabilities worked in tandem included Russia, Kazakhstan, India, China, UAE, Japan, Brazil, Argentina, South Africa, Italy, France, Germany, the UK, Ireland, Mexico, Canada, and Singapore.

Leadership Experience

Having leadership skills and being a leader is clearly a high-value and rare skill. At the very least, good leaders are quickly recognized by clients and colleagues. At the highest level, it facilitates the creation and leadership of high-performance teams. Whenever I promoted someone to a leadership position, I would always say "I can give you the job, but you will only keep it if your team thinks you are the right person" (i.e., a leader).

Many of my examples of becoming an expert tend to not come from my early career. That said, I did gain some expertise "ahead of the curve": working with a group trying to save New York City, becoming very knowledgeable on doing business in Ireland, and my tour to Italy were all experiences I had in my twenties. These are great examples of what I'm talking about, but they likely won't apply to most. My mindset, however, was always to become an expert in (or at least really good at) whatever I was doing. If I was the most junior person on a deal team, I would try to learn all there was to know about all areas of the deal, not just my areas of responsibility. This allowed me to be (or at least look like) an expert when the next deal came around. On my credit card client, for example, I not only became an expert in the area I was responsible for but in the credit card business and industry as a whole.

I am going to end here. My message is to gain a skill—or even better, multiple skills—so that you are clearly able to differentiate yourself as an expert and often get invited to the party. Amass as much knowledge as you can, across all three levels of expertise. Learning new things is always worthwhile, and no knowledge is ever truly useless.

Chapter 8

HAVE AN OPINION – BE BOLD!

I have a reputation for having an opinion—some would say a strong opinion on everything! When I think back, there were several factors that came together over the years to cause this to be at least partially true. I wanted to be an expert in certain things. I wanted to always be the most prepared. Over time, I gained a lot of experience—and *global* experience at that. I knew people (CEOs, executives, high-level government officials, etc.) who asked for my opinion. And lastly, I found that my opinions over time were becoming increasingly well-informed, and in many cases, with very unique perspectives.

I've found that extreme value comes from having an opinion that's different from the person doing the asking, and then being so compelling in your defense of your own opinion that that person changes their mind. This becomes even more valuable when the discussion surrounds the other person's business or business model. An opinion can become an expert opinion, and then an opinion they need to have as input before making a final decision.

All chief executives have an opinion, be they CEOs, university presidents, or heads of state. Most of these opinions are strongly held and forcefully stated. If you are a "player," you need to have one. Being asked for your opinion and not having one is sending a signal that you do not think the topic is important enough to have thought of it, or that you are not in the "in-crowd" that talks about such things, and in either case, that you are not a player.

The "be bold" piece refers to the forcefulness of your view and your ability to defend your position. Is he or she convinced they're right? Have they thought it through? Do they know the facts? Do they have the details? Even if I disagree, do they have a point?

An Almeida Point: Be *Bold*, Not Close-Minded

HAVING AN OPINION AND BEING BOLD IN YOUR DEFENSE OF IT DOES NOT MEAN YOU CAN'T CHANGE YOUR STANCE IF SOMEONE MAKES A CONVINCING CASE FOR ANOTHER POSITION. IN FACT, THE BEST (MOST OF WHOM HOLD STRONG OPINIONS THEMSELVES) ALWAYS SEEK ALL POSSIBLE VIEWS BEFORE MAKING AN IMPORTANT DECISION, AND DISCUSS AND DEBATE THOSE VIEWS BEFORE SETTLING ON A FINAL OPINION. IN TODAY'S ENVIRONMENT, THERE ARE TOO MANY WHO ARE UNABLE TO DISCUSS AND UNDERSTAND THE VIEWS OF OTHERS, PARTICULARLY IF THOSE VIEWS ARE DIFFERENT FROM THEIR OWN. HIGH-PERFORMANCE CULTURES REQUIRE OPEN DISCUSSION AND DEBATE TO GET TO THE BEST ANSWER. HAVING AN OPINION AND BEING BOLD SHOULD NOT CHANGE THIS, AND IN FACT, IT SHOULD LEAD TO MORE ROBUST DEBATE AND BETTER ANSWERS.

The irony in business is that most people do not have opinions, or have them but are unwilling for some reason to share them. This is so common that just having an opinion sets you apart from the rest. Most people who have opinions but do not share them neglect to do so for many reasons: they may be afraid to offend someone; they may think their opinion will be unpopular; they may not want to go against the boss; they may just be meek or scared to do so. The list goes on.

To get a reputation for knowing certain subjects and having a valued opinion is a trait of those who are the best in the world. Most players will see you as a peer—or at least as an advisor if not a peer—if they believe you have knowledge, opinions, and contacts that can bring value to them. If you do not have knowledge, opinions, or contacts, you are not a player. It sounds funny, but my opinion is that having "an opinion on everything" is much better than having "an opinion on nothing."

To form valuable opinions, I believe you need to first identify the areas you know and those that you need to get to know in order to bring value. This obviously needs to be focused on the elements of the environment you work in: the relevant industries, geographies, and skills (e.g., business, the arts, music).

I remember in my early days, for example, going to Ireland three times a year for work. I started becoming very knowledgeable about Ireland and forming opinions: the best restaurants or hotels in Dublin; where you should visit in Ireland; how taxes work; the best way to ship products back to the U.S.; and so on.

This started a career where global travel was key, and what started with Ireland multiplied and expanded to encompass dozens of other countries. I am generally known for having traveled to many places and for knowing something (or a lot) about what goes on there. I also freely share my opinions, and am known for that as well. As a consequence, people reach out often for my views—even now.

When I dealt with clients, I would always try to identify three to five areas most important to them and their leadership (to the CEO, for example). I would then do whatever I needed to do to expand my knowledge of the subject matter and understand how it impacted my client.

I remember a client to whom India was becoming critical in their business. My team and I spent significant time in India understanding Indian issues, and in particular, the client's current and future business there. This included the local regulations, customs, and laws, and how each of these could impact our client. We also analyzed the risks that faced the client at the time and in the future.

I gave my opinions to my client on their Indian business many times throughout our work together. On numerous occasions—particularly early on in the relationship—my views were not shared broadly by the client. As time went on, however, I grew to be viewed as an expert who needed to be listened to and whose opinions needed to be seriously considered. This outcome was brought about by multiple situations where my opinion and the opinion of my firm proved to be correct, particularly when we advised on future risks the business might face. Our advice gave way to strategic adjustments that helped to limit vulnerability, which in turn resulted in us having a seat at the table. This was a great example of opinions being of high value.

To be an expert and not share your views is like having a Ferrari but no gas. Conversely, to be an expert who brings extreme value by giving their opinion at the exact time it is needed makes you a player. This is truly when maximum value can be delivered.

There is also an area I want to mention which I call "soft opinions." As a consultant, you are constantly asked "How do we compare," as in "How good are our financial controls compared to the average or the best" or "How good is our executive management compared to such-and-such other company's?" For whatever reason I would always have a view—one that I considered an educated view based on my experience—and I gave my opinion. Most would be reluctant to do this, but what I found was that this approach was truly high-value. It was taken for what it was—my opinion—not as though it had been based on a scientific review with statistically valid samples and the like.

Another area of opinions is the extremes, like "I never saw anyone doing it like this" or "I never saw this done with this complexity, which means it must be really expensive and inefficient." These opinions were obviously not based on me knowing what *everyone* else did, but rather on a high-value directional view. These were normally well-received.

One other thing that is important here is that opinions are personal. They are yours. They do not always have to be correct, and in many cases, there is no one correct answer. This is important to remember when considering how to bring value and whether to give your opinion or not. Remember, I always tended to have one, offer it, and defend it.

So, without belaboring the point, suffice it to say that having an opinion and being bold are traits I think are important. They are also things that clients pay for, and which help identify and solve problems.

Chapter 9

MAKE A DECISION

To some, this may sound like an odd chapter for this book, but in reality, it is one of the most critical skills in business and life. Your ability to make a decision is critical to your success!

In my experience, there are two kinds of decision-makers in this world.

Indecisive: People with 95% of the information who are continuously in search of the remaining 5% before they can make a decision. Some with 99% are in search of the last 1% before they can finally decide. However, they will likely never find the remaining information, and therefore *never* make a decision.

Decisive: People with at least 51% of the information who weigh the pros, cons, and risks, and make a decision there and then. They know that in some cases they may have to make a course correction and change their original decision. This is okay because they believe that the risk of waiting is worse than the chance of a course correction.

I am someone who makes decisions very quickly. If it's an area I know very well, an area where I am getting a recommendation from someone whose opinion I value, or an area that is not that important to me and comes with a recommendation, I will make a decision with little or no research—some have even said "without facts." The indecisive types think I am crazy. They say loudly: "How can he make a decision when he has no facts?!" They are wrong: about me, and maybe even about all decision-makers.

In business, you are very often paid to make decisions. Highly paid executives—no matter who they are—make numerous decisions every day. If you are in certain professions—surgeons, air traffic controllers, pilots, battlefield commanders, to name a few—you make decisions minute-by-minute or even second-by-second. They all fit the profile of decisive decision-makers and act more or less as I described myself.

Here is a very important point: in many areas of work and life, making a decision means taking on some risk. In many of those areas, not making a decision avoids taking that risk. In my experience, the majority of people prefer not taking risks, and therefore prefer not to make decisions. In some cases, that predisposition goes unnoticed. In others, however, it's a really big deal.

In high-performance cultures or when dealing with high performers (especially in business), it is expected that teams, consultants, and the various people around them will make decisions and make them quickly. Also, the ability to make decisions quickly can bring extreme value. The old adage "time is money" is very often true. Also, quick decision-making can in turn make things happen quickly.

In the business I was in, it was important to establish relationships with key executives at our clients. One common theme with these executives was that they moved quickly, made decisions quickly, and wanted advisors around them who could do the same. Naturally, one of the primary requirements to do this was being an expert on the subject matter in question. Close behind, however, was the ability and authority to make quick decisions. I remember once as a senior with four years' experience asking, "When is this answer needed?" The response: "Instantaneously, if not sooner!"

As I mentioned before, I dealt with people who could NEVER make a decision more often than I would've liked. As we all have seen, there are two kinds of people (here he goes again) in this world: those who want to say no and those who are looking for yes.

Those who want to say no ask endless questions. After each answer, there is yet another question, and another, and another, and another. In many cases, the bar for what it would take to get a "yes" answer gets raised again and again, and we rarely get an answer before we run out of time. If we do get to an answer, it's a "NO," but we are not sure why.

Those who want to get to a "yes" answer either get there quickly if parties are aligned or—if a no seems likely—start looking for alternative ways to get to a yes. In my career, I advised all who would listen that when dealing with a colleague or client, NEVER say no unless you have concluded that yes was completely impossible. A no was only ever given after we obtained a clear understanding of the objectives that the other party was trying to achieve and concluded they were not achievable. This usually required a small group of really smart people getting together and doing "what-if" scenario planning. Only after all scenarios had been vetted could a "no" answer be given. Sharing our scenarios with the other party also showed our reluctance to end on a no.

Later in my career, I was often put in the position of trying to fix a bad relationship with a client. A client's unhappy senior executive was usually the result of many things, often including our inability to give a timely answer on an important matter. In some cases, my team and I were able to get the client an answer that worked for them, but in other cases, we could not. In almost every case it was too late to cure the problem, and thus, too late to preserve the relationship between the client and my partner—the best I could do was to salvage the relationship between the client and our firm.

In the art of quick decision-making, there is a skill that drives decision and client management. This takes a number of forms, each with its own process or series of steps. It is by the use of these skills that even more categories of decision-makers emerge (it's never just two!).

The first I will call the "Expert Decision-Maker." I was called this by several clients. This was because whenever I was expecting a meeting (e.g., with a client) on a complex topic, I would study and be briefed on the areas that I anticipated would be covered during the meeting. I would not only become well-versed in the subject matter but also project how it would impact my client. I also would educate myself on the firm's positions on various topics, including recent guidance on the matters. This allowed me to look like an expert not only on the technical subject matter but also on its practical implementations and what contemporary organizations were doing. This may sound logical and normal, but I was surprised how many prepared *after* such meetings—fewer people prepared before. I would often say that I was always the most prepared at the meeting no matter who else was there.

The second I will call the "Decisive Decision-Maker." This was where a question was raised and I answered it there and then. I mentioned this before, but it bears repeating, as the impact of this in a meeting can be game-changing. Its effect can be further elevated by others in the room (attorneys, investment bankers, and the like) having to get back with an answer. I will confess that this happened to me infrequently in my early career, but more and more as I became more experienced. It can also be the result of preparation as in example one.

The third I will call the "Complex Decision-Maker." This is where you answer the question but introduce one or more complexities to the answer. An example would be "Yes, but have you considered A, B, and C?" This could be when A, B, C, or some combination thereof could change the question, and therefore change the answer. I was party to many discussions that revolved around a question that was either too simple or overly complex or whatever! I often said, "All questions are simple, but all answers are complex."

The fourth I will call "Mr. No." You know this one. No matter the question, the answer is "No." We all know these people. In dealing with these types, we all go somewhere else for an answer unless we have no other choice. If you want to destroy a good relationship, just introduce Mr. No.

The fifth and final I call the "Pragmatic Decision-Maker." This is someone who works with the client to get to either a yes or a no answer. They usually have a really solid rationale for the answer and will have the client fully briefed along the way, believing all avenues were pursued and exhausted and agreeing with the answer by the end of the meeting or conversation. The pragmatic decision-maker very often gets the client a different answer than they wanted, but one that helps them meet their original objective(s). Managing this process requires a multitude of hard and soft skills.

An Almeida Point: If You Can, Be A Decision-Maker

IN MY EXPERIENCE, YOU WANT TO BE KNOWN AS SOMEONE WHO MAKES DECISIONS. THIS CAN AND WILL COME FROM ONE OF THE TYPES OF DECISION-MAKERS I REFERRED TO ABOVE, BUT YOU DO NOT WANT TO BE MR. NO. YOU DON'T WANT TO MAKE DECISIONS TOO QUICKLY, BUT EVEN WORSE IS NOT MAKING THEM AT ALL OR MAKING THEM TOO LATE.

Chapter 10

DEFUSING ANGER

There are several strategies that I used, and that you can use yourself, to defuse anger and manage major conflict situations. For better or worse, some of the businesses that I ran required me to put myself in these types of situations fairly often. If a client felt they had been treated badly and wanted a partner change, wanted to fire us, or wanted to sue us, it was my job to try to fix it. In many cases, this meant dealing with clients I did not know, and who didn't know me except maybe by reputation.

Some things must be said so that the points are clearly understood, and the learnings can be assessed and implemented (or not). In order to do that, I must quote actual dialogues in this chapter, which in many cases have "colorful language" associated with them. Naturally, it should be understood that when people are angry, they do and say things they normally would not. In some cases, they regret what they have said. In other cases, they do not.

In all these situations, I followed these three process points:

1. You must (and I did in all cases) **get a detailed assessment of the facts and circumstances** from the people and teams involved. When you do this, you must speak with those whom you trust will tell you the truth, the whole truth, and nothing but the truth. You need to know, however, that even if you source your information from only trusted parties, their accounts will be the truth as seen from their eyes. In other words, it's impossible to completely separate the objective truth from

someone's subjective account of it—"there are always two sides to every story," and there could be even more. This process also requires an understanding of the history of the relationship. This knowledge is critical in pinpointing exactly when the relationship turned bad, and determining what triggered the decline. Contacting people who have worked with the individual and know them well can also be key to this end. I always assumed that the client had some valid reason to be angry with us, but that said, in many cases, the issue was ultimately one of communication or lack thereof. Further, many cases involved some degree of what I call "guilt by association," which is to say that something had gone wrong, and although we may not have caused it, we were viewed as letting it happen.

2. You then need to perform a **risk assessment**. By this I mean you need to assess the probability that the issue can be resolved. If you are fairly sure the problem can be fixed, then a "normal approach" might be appropriate. A "normal approach" entails a clear, direct discussion that's intended to arrive at a mutually agreeable resolution and then execute it. In cases where the client is threatening to fire or sue you, a normal approach will rarely get the job done. In these cases, a fairly unorthodox approach might be required. This includes approaches like agreeing with the client and being angrier than they are about it. It could be "in your face" action, where from the moment the meeting begins you are already informing the client of actions you have already taken to address the problem before even being asked. In rare cases, it could be telling the client that *they* messed up, not you or your firm. It could be "raising the temperature" in the room to communicate you are not backing down. Or lastly, you might have to resort to the old "you can't fire me, I quit." These are only examples, but I have used each in one situation or another.

3. Be ready to "**go with the flow.**" One thing I can tell you from experience is that these meetings never go as planned—for better

or worse. From the minute you walk in, you need to be assessing in real time all comments, words, and body language, identifying any deviations from the norm—particularly as they pertain to interpersonal niceties or lack thereof. These sound like insignificant things, but "Do you want coffee?" or "Please sit on the couch" or "How was your trip?" and the like are always great signs, and usually indicate that a "normal approach" might work. In these situations, the client may have already concluded that you are part of the solution, not part of the problem, and will be willing to work with you to figure out a solution. Conversely, comments like "What do you want?", "I'm really busy, so can we do this quick?", or "Are you here so I don't sue you?" would normally indicate a tough meeting, and likely mean you'll have to adjust your approach. Even in seemingly agreeable situations, the temperature may change in a moment with little or no notice. When this happens, you need to "go with the flow": assess the other person's energy and adapt accordingly. This might mean changing your tone, pulling back on certain points, or sticking to your guns. Above all else, communicate that you are there to help, and understand that even a perfect response might still fail in some situations.

I now want to give some real-life examples. These events actually happened, and I will try to describe them in the most factual way possible. Remember, however, I'm describing these situations through the lens of my own experience, and as I saw them at the time.

Case 1 — It can be worse than you think!

This first instance occurred while I was running the Technology practice of PwC. On the day in question, I received two phone calls: one from the engagement partner on the account, and another one from our senior partner (my direct boss). Both calls were about the same issue—we had a long-standing client who wanted us fired. The presumed issue was an accounting error which required a restatement of their financials. The CEO was angry, blamed our engagement partner and PwC, and wanted us gone.

The engagement partner was one of our young superstars, who was devastated that the error occurred and that we were being fired on his watch. He knew the CEO well, but from a purely business perspective. He, the CEO, and the CFO had discussed the competencies and weaknesses of their accounting staff on a number of occasions, but no changes had been made. The error appeared to be the company's fault, with no involvement by PwC. In fact, the error had been *found* by PwC, though unfortunately too late.

My first step was to speak to the CFO. He was clear that he disagreed with the CEO, and that he did not believe PwC was at fault. He believed the CEO was overreacting given the implications from the Board and Audit Committee, and he was concerned that he would get blamed for the error and its negative impact on the company. I needed to meet the CEO face-to-face.

I called to schedule a meeting with the CEO, but his office would not take the call, and the president's office similarly refused to schedule a meeting. I knew we had to meet in person to make any progress, so I found out what day the CEO would be in the office, and told the CFO to tell him I was coming and that I needed at least five minutes. The CFO emphasized that the CEO *would not see me*. Regardless, I traveled to his office.

Since I was coming anyway, the CFO set up a number of high-level meetings as a courtesy, but the CEO still would not meet me. I finished around noon, at which time I asked the CFO to tell the CEO that I was waiting in the lobby, and that I just needed five minutes. I was told every half-hour for the next five hours that the CEO would not see me, and each time I responded with "I've come all this way to see him. It's really important, and I'm not leaving until I see him. I only need five minutes."

It was about five p.m. by the time I'd finally made some headway. The CEO's secretary approached me, and apologetically told me that the CEO would see me—but only for five minutes or less. She indicated without saying that he was in a very bad mood, and very annoyed that I was forcing the meeting. We walked to his office, and here is what happened.

I walked into a very large office. The CEO was working at his desk with his head down. He pointed to the couch, which was a football field away, with a hand gesture indicating that I should sit down. No greeting. I said nothing and he said nothing. My strategy was to let him speak first. After what seemed like a very long time (but was probably only two minutes), he said without looking up: "What the fuck do you want, and why are you wasting my time?!"

I waited and waited and waited, and did what I recommend you consider doing in this situation. I repeated "What the fuck do I want?!" five times in a row! I then paused and said: "Easy! I want you to tell me how great PwC is, how great my partner is, and that you would never consider using any other firm. My problem is I know you're not going to say that, so I'm here to see if you and I can agree on the issue, and see what I can do to fix it." I also told him that I had decided without consulting him that if we kept the account, the partner would be changed—"already done."

At this moment he looked up and was laughing uncontrollably. He had concluded (1) he didn't scare me; (2) I was as stubborn as he was; and most importantly, (3) I had come to help him!

He then buzzed his secretary, got us each a coffee, and we talked for almost two hours. He was very angry at what happened, but quickly agreed it was not our fault, although he wished we had caught it. We agreed on some changes to his process, and maybe a personnel change or two—changes he knew he should have already made. He also made me promise not to change the partner, who, as it turned out, he respected highly and thought brought a lot of value.

My partner (who now joined the meeting) and I convinced the CEO that the issue wasn't as big a deal as he had thought. We also agreed to (and later did) participate in the discussion with the board.

Case 2 — Sometimes it can't be fixed.

A public company client of ours had acquired another client of ours. Without getting too technical (and the rules have since changed), the financials of the two companies had been combined to form the new company. About a year after the merger, it was determined that the acquired company's financials were wrong. That meant that the acquirer's financials were wrong and needed to be restated—a big deal.

At the time, I was running a practice that included these two clients. An urgent meeting was set up with the client, and I flew that day to attend. The meeting was held in a huge conference room filled with about thirty client people and attorneys. I attended with our engagement partner and another partner—only three of us. The partner present was the partner on the acquirer and therefore had not been involved with the company that had the issue.

Leading the meeting from the client side was the CEO, and leading from our side was me. The CEO was outraged, and rightfully so. In his view—and I agreed—his company had done everything right. He prided himself on leading a company with very competent management who tried to make sure all rules were followed, including financial. He had been blindsided, as the error was not caused by him or his company but rather by the company he had acquired—the company that PwC had audited.

I discussed with him the fact that in the last twenty-four hours, I had brought in our top experts to explore any and all possible alternatives to restatement, and they had maintained that there were none. As you can imagine, he was impressed and completely unimpressed at the same time.

For the rest of the thirty-minute discussion, the CEO was on his feet and yelling at me—and frankly, "yelling" doesn't adequately cover it. The rest of the room was absolutely silent. At one point, I thought he might dive across the table at me. That said, he knew that I was not the enemy. He knew I had flown in to try to help, he knew I had not caused the problem, and he knew his PwC team and partner had not caused the problem. Despite his frustration, I was pretty sure he understood that the management of the acquired company had caused the problem. They now worked for him—at least for a short time. He knew all of this, but he was livid, and he wanted someone—*anyone*—to say "It's my fault."

He—still standing and still yelling—said the same thing over and over and over again: "Will someone please tell me it's their fault? Please will someone tell me it's their fault? Please, please, please!" At that point, I looked him straight in the eye and said, "Jim, I don't know what to tell you." He looked at me stunned for five seconds, then burst out laughing.

The CEO ended the meeting and asked for a private one-on-one with me. During that meeting, we discussed my view as to what had happened. I tried to communicate that I hated that it had happened, but that PwC was not at fault. I also gave him some input as to how to minimize any negative market reaction. He clearly appreciated my input. That said, as we continued the discussion it became clear that he would be forced to change firms. I didn't like the answer, but I clearly understood his position. He and I still keep in touch twenty years later.

Case 3 — Sometimes you need to trust your gut.

We were having a significant issue in a certain foreign country. The issue was not related to anything we did or didn't do, but rather had arisen from a misunderstanding of sorts. I am unable to describe in detail the facts surrounding the issue, the country, the official, or almost anything else, though I wish I could because you would find it very interesting. So, with that as background context (or lack thereof), I will tell you what happened.

I was put in a situation of having to meet a very high-level government official at his equivalent of the U.S. White House. I had never met him before and had never been to his office. My objective was simple, to make him aware of our firm, to give him insight into how we were helping other countries, and to apprise him of our global network and how it could benefit him and his country. I flew in the day before the meeting and was briefed for several hours on what would happen, who would be there, what his agenda would be, and very importantly, the dos and don'ts of the meeting. There were two main takeaways from this:

- First, some details regarding the meeting: the meeting would not be in his office, there would be ten to fifteen of his people there, our team would be four people (including me), and the meeting would be in the local language, with each of us having an interpreter. In addition, the meeting would be about fifteen minutes long, it would be very formal, and, since it was our first meeting with this official, it would primarily function as a meet-and-greet with very little substance discussed.

- Second, regarding me: I was to be very serious (there was to be none of my normal joking around), and I was to call him "Mr. Vice President"—*never* by his first name. I was not to sell our firm, but only talk about how we could help. I was told he didn't speak English, and that he probably didn't care much for Americans. I also found out early on that none of our people had ever met him or been to his office.

That night, as I always did, I searched the internet for information on the official I was going to meet the next day. After about ten minutes, I found something very important. The VP had an MBA from Duke. This told me the following: (1) he definitely spoke English; (2) he was very familiar with America's lack of formality (e.g., using first names); (3) he probably was a basketball fan, as Duke had recently won the national championship; and (4) we may know someone in common, as I knew the dean of the business school fairly well.

The next day, my team and I were led on a ten-minute walk to the VP's office, and thus I recognized what would be the first of many Incorrect Briefing Facts (IBFs). When we entered the room, he was alone (IBF). He immediately rose from his desk and came to greet us. In English (IBF), he said "Don! (IBF) Nice to meet you. How was your trip?" Taking my cues from him, I responded as I always would, calling him by his first name in my reply. He smiled. I introduced him to my team, and as we were getting ready to sit down at the conference table, I decided to revert to my normal self and we had the following exchange in English (I'll call him "Bill," which is not his real name):

Don: "Bill, I read somewhere that you got an MBA from Duke. Is that correct?"

Bill: "That's correct—great school—and I spent two years in North Carolina."

Don: "Did you know my good friend Jim, who I think was the dean at the time?"

Bill: "Yes, I knew him well and we still keep in touch."

MY SHOT — Don: "I can't remember, but didn't Duke start a basketball team back then?"

Bill (standing and yelling): "Start a basketball team? Hell, we won the national championship! Come with me!"

Bill then took me to the corner of his office where he had two basketballs: one signed by the championship team and one signed by Coach Krzyzewski. He then asked if I had seen last night's game. When I said no, he joked that I should get international cable at the hotel.

Both in the meeting and afterward, my colleagues were stunned by what happened, and frankly, at how I'd acted. I told them I was bulletproof—"Everyone knows Americans don't know how to act!" On a serious note, we made a key contact that day, and it was a good start to achieving our objective.

Case 4 — Sometimes NO is NO

The next case involved a public company client that had materially misstated their financial information. Unfortunately for them, this occurred at the beginning of a stock issuance. As soon as we found the problem, we communicated our position to the client, which was that they needed to immediately report the matter to the regulators and stop the stock issuance process. I got a call back shortly thereafter and went with the partner on the account and our attorney to see the client the next morning.

Unbeknownst to me, the CEO had put together a senior group of top executives and outside advisors and attorneys with the intent of making the problem go away. For those reading this, this chapter is titled "Defusing Anger," but in some cases, the facts are the facts and the outcome is the outcome—anger or no anger.

I walked into the meeting with my team of three. The room was standing room only. The CEO, who I quickly concluded was a dominant force, had decided that the problem was not a problem and that either I would fix it or he would get someone who could. I took him through the company's issue at a high level and explained why it needed to be corrected immediately and the regulator notified. I told him he had the right to consult with counsel, but that the stock offering gets stopped *now*—no further discussion. Either he called the regulator or I would.

This was one of those situations where no is no, and anger—real or theatrical—doesn't change the answer or its severity. He finally got it. He reluctantly did the right thing. We never spoke again, and PwC resigned from the client.

Defusing anger is a very complex area that requires multiple skills to execute successfully. It is also one where practice leads to improvement. I also found personally that humor and self-deprecation helped (e.g., "I'm not that smart, but...").

Chapter 11

NEVER BE THE SMARTEST GUY IN THE ROOM

When I say "never be the smartest guy in the room," I mean it in a very derogatory fashion. In my experience, the "smartest guys in the room" are not actually the smartest, but instead are those who have the audacity to *think* they are the smartest. You know who they are almost immediately because they will usually tell you upfront—they go out of their way to make sure everyone knows who they are.

It usually goes something like this: "Hi, my name is Dr. So-and-So. I teach at Harvard, and I have multiple Ph.Ds. I am a sought-after lecturer by all the big investment banks, and I really didn't have time to attend this meeting. I did so as a favor and can't stay for the whole thing. My assistant will stay after I leave and report back to me. We'll have to make all the key decisions before I leave. Thanks."

I mean no disrespect to Harvard, of course.

It could also go like this: "My name is So-and-So. I am the world's foremost expert in mortgage-backed securities. These are very complex and very hard to value. I have created the such-and-such model, which has been named after me, to value them. If we need to discuss how it works, we will have to take it offline since it will be hard for you to understand, unless you have a Ph.D in quantum physics like me. If we take it offline, I will speak slowly so you can understand. Ha ha ha (no one else laughs)."

I tell my students that it does not matter if they are the smartest guy or gal in the room if no one wants to work with them. In my experience, these "smartest guy" types are the most insecure people in the world. They may be smart, but they are usually no smarter than the many other smart people in the room. What's more, they usually have little business experience and even less business acumen. They, as I say, "have read the book but never actually done it." For the really bad ones, I add "and they haven't even read the book."

The *Real* Smartest Guys

In my experience—and this is important—the real smartest guys in the room are those with the most hands-on experience, the highest level of expertise in the area being discussed, and those who have actually read the contract and/or know the deal. It becomes clear very quickly who the real smartest people are and what they can contribute, and when it does, the "smartest guys in the room" types are quickly ignored and marginalized. They are usually not invited back unless they have a required seat for some reason.

Also, the real smartest guys (male or female) always listen before they speak, speak only when they can add something, have a clear basis for their comments, and have the experience to draw conclusions, offer solutions, and make decisions. These real smartest guys usually make an impact with their first comment, and from then on their opinions and input are requested.

In my experience in trying to always add value to meetings, I tried to be well prepared and, as often as possible, the most prepared. If there was a contract or deal involved, I had read the contract thoroughly or knew the terms of the deal cold. If there were specific technical areas that were relevant, I did my homework and became an expert, which often included meetings with our technical experts who would not be at the meeting. I remember often pointing out that "that's not what the contract says" or "that is not what the terms of the deal are" when discrepancies arose, and it amazed me that many people at the meeting had not read the contract or the deal terms. Once you do what I just mentioned, the group quickly recognizes that you know the contract and the deal terms well, assumes you have a certain degree of expertise, and begins to make a point of asking you for your thoughts.

I would also prepare a few questions—and in some cases, a lot more than just a few—about things that I thought needed to be looked at or changed. In many cases, this gave rise to a debate as to why it had been done the way it was in the first place and whether there was a better way. This is where real value is created.

For those of you who think age matters, or years of experience matters, it really does not. What matters is what you know, how you prepare, and whether you will come across as one of the real smartest guys in the room. Also, for those of you who constantly look for an excuse—a reason why you didn't succeed, or why the meeting didn't go well, or why they picked someone else for a role you wanted—stop now! It does not matter where you came from, what your ethnic background is, what school you went to, who you know, what your gender is, or anything else. What matters is that you know what you need to know at the time you need to know it—only that makes you the *real* smartest guy in the room.

Chapter 12

INSIDE GUY VERSUS OUTSIDE GUY (AND A FEW OTHERS...)

I have been using this example for my entire career. It is the first good example of extremes in personalities that I use to start the discussion of differences in people that are important to understand in life and certainly in business. These differences will also be very important to understand for ourselves. Let's get started.

An "inside guy" is someone who prefers their own company, and is most effective when they don't have to manage others. They opt for one-on-one interaction, or maybe even no interaction at all. They generally like working alone or in groups of two or three. They don't like crowds and likely avoid situations that see them speaking in front of groups—their best work is often done behind the scenes. They tend to excel in careers like technical engineering, tax accounting, research, and the like.

An "outside guy" is someone who loves being with people, and works best in collaborative settings. They thrive in a crowd, and they love to be the center of attention. They love to talk, and may even become restless without debates and discussions about their ideas and proposed executions. They gravitate toward careers in communications, sales, marketing, entertainment, and media.

If you put an inside guy in an outside job, they will hate it: they will be uncomfortable at the outset and become more so as time goes on, which will likely result in failure. Conversely, if you put an outside guy in an inside job, they will also hate it and likely fail: they will feel trapped and grow progressively more unhappy.

My leadership style was to pick team members to work on projects. Once a project was completed and it was ready to be presented to a group (e.g., leadership or a client), I would always ask the team leader who led the work to make the presentation. I would then do what I called "color commentary." I found this to be a good motivator for the team and I still do it. That said, I remember a time early in my career doing this and seeing the person selected go into a state of extreme discomfort. They did not really say anything that indicated as much, but I noticed very unusual behavior. They had about two days to prepare—a lifetime, especially given the fact that they knew the information cold. They had practiced incessantly, but despite this preparedness, I could see that they were extremely apprehensive about giving the presentation. They asked if they could present to me first, and I agreed. In this private presentation, they were nervous, sweaty, and reading from a printed script. Afterward, I had a one-on-one meeting to discuss whether they should be the one to give the presentation, and we agreed that I would do it instead. I could see the weight of the world lifted off their shoulders right before my eyes, and I understood what had happened: this was an inside person asked to do an outside person's job.

I would use this example with my students to start a discussion about what major they might want to select, what kind of career path they might want to take, or which industry they might want to go into. I often found that this very simple factor had not been considered. It often triggered a lengthy discussion on how someone's personality can impact their success, which I think helped them frame the topic.

Now, not all people fit neatly into these two categories, and even those who do will not all be the same. Some may have attributes of both or, with training, go from one to the other. Although this is true, all people will broadly align with one or the other. As an exercise, you can go down the list of your friends and see which fit where.

I am clearly an outside guy, but I have an accounting degree. At first look, that might seem kind of like an outside guy in an inside job. Not exactly. If you track my career, you can see I dealt with clients from day one and was pretty good at it. You can also see that it became more and more of an outside job as I went along. Also, I often heard the words "You don't act like an accountant." Many of those I encountered were expecting one type of person (probably a stereotypical accountant) and got another. The fact was that PwC was a place where both outside guys and inside guys could thrive and excel.

This was only one of the personality differences in life and in business that I thought important to understand. Let me cover a few more.

Decision-Making

As discussed in *Make A Decision* (Chapter 9), there are generally two types of decision-makers. The first is cautious (indecisive): they only move forward if they have all the information that might influence their choice. For these folks, even having 95% of the available information might not be enough, and they fervently search for the remaining 5%. Those in this category theoretically can't make a decision until they get 100%. I say "theoretically" because very often they take so long that the decision is made for them or the need for a decision passes.

The second extreme—the bold (decisive)—are those who make their decisions once they get 51% of the information. They believe they have enough information to make a good decision and that if they are wrong they can change it later.

The cautious group usually thinks the bold group is crazy, and maybe even negligent. They can't believe that anyone could make these decisions without all of the information. The bold group thinks the cautious group is scared to make *any* decision, and can't believe they would rather jeopardize a project by way of inaction than risk making a mistake. The bold group will often chastise the first—"Just make a decision, will you!"—and believe that their refusal to make a decision means that the real decision was to keep things the same all along. The cautious group finds this laughable.

Understanding these extremes and how they interact is important when you are dealing with a counterparty who is on the opposite side of this paradigm. It is even more difficult when the other person is your boss or reporting to you.

In my experience, you will almost always find both extremes in every meeting, which is why most meetings don't result in a decision—someone is always asking for more information. Unless you have a strong leader and an environment that accepts conflict, you will most often NOT make a decision. By the same token, however, an effective leader can leverage these opposing stances to make informed decisions, as debate between members of these groups can give way to a prudent approach. This, in turn, speaks to the natural balance that comes from splitting the difference between extremes, and why input from both groups is useful: without cautious input, the bold group might make decisions too rashly and without enough information; without bold input, the cautious group would be too indecisive to actually accomplish anything.

Leader *vs.* Follower

You can read Chapter 18 on leadership—and should—but for now, let's just say people can typically be described as either "leaders" or "followers."

If you put a follower in a leader's role, they will not lead well and they will not be successful. Also, the group that you have asked them to lead will know fairly quickly that it's not working.

If you put a leader in a follower's role, you will not maximize their potential. While it may work better than the inverse—particularly if you have a very strong leader in place who can manage other leaders effectively—more often than not, the leader in a follower role will over time start challenging their leader, stepping into the role and leading the team or a subset thereof themselves.

Again, these are extremes, and all people are not necessarily exclusively one or the other. That said, they do tend to fit into one category or the other. This extreme is a little different than "inside guys versus outside guys" in that the latter seems to be a 50/50 split across the population, but a clear majority of people in my experience are followers, not leaders.

High-Level *vs.* Detail-Oriented

This category not only has extremes but also levels of difference that drive management styles. These management styles are critical to understand in order to succeed in business, yes, but also even just to survive it. It's interesting that at the highest levels, people are known to fall into one of these extremes. For example, U.S. presidents Ronald Reagan and George W. Bush were notorious for being high-level (not detail-oriented) guys, and Jimmy Carter was known for diving into the details.

Leaders who manage at a high level feel comfortable doing so. They generally believe in the "80/20 rule," which in this context means that 20% of the facts drive 80% of the outcome. They usually lead by picking the right experts for the right positions and letting them do their jobs. They monitor progress through high-level metrics and reports. They also use their gut feelings and experience to guide them.

Leaders who manage using detailed information only feel comfortable if they have all the information they think they need. They typically use the details to assess the high-level result. They tend to rely more on data as opposed to people. In many cases, they try to become experts in areas outside their natural expertise.

An example of this was a CEO with a sales background trying to become an accounting expert.

Personally, I was a high-level leader who would only concern myself with the details when it was really important, and moreover, when things were not going well. If something was "going sideways," as I used to say, I would dive into the details with laser focus and try to help the team get it fixed. The key here was knowing when to make the move: if you did it too early, you were usurping the authority you had given to your team, and if you did it too late... Well, it was too late.

I worked with and for many great leaders. Some were high-level leaders, and some were the detailed type. What was important for me was knowing who was who so I could best adapt to their management style. It was not hard to tell.

An Almeida Point: There Are Always Two, But Never Only Two

AS A PROFESSOR (AND IN LIFE), I ALWAYS USE "TWO" AS THE SURROGATE—AN OVERSIMPLIFICATION FOR THE SAKE OF CLARITY. THERE ARE ALWAYS MORE THAN TWO OF ANYTHING, BUT I USE TWO EXAMPLES TO MAKE THE POINT I AM TRYING TO GET ACROSS SO THAT ANALYSIS OR DISCUSSION CAN BE MORE PRODUCTIVE, AS COMPARING AND CONTRASTING TWO VERY DIFFERENT THINGS IS EXPONENTIALLY EASIER THAN EVALUATING A DOZEN MORE COMPLEX THINGS.

AS I HAVE STATED OFTEN, MY EXPERIENCE AND MY GOAL OF COMMUNICATING WELL HAVE TAUGHT ME TO TRY TO OVERSIMPLIFY WHERE POSSIBLE TO MAKE A POINT. THIS IS A HABIT OF MINE THAT HAS SERVED ME WELL, HELPS ME COMMUNICATE MORE CLEARLY, AND AIDS IN CONDUCTING BUSINESS MORE EFFICIENTLY. I THEREFORE OFTEN

USE THE PHRASE "THERE ARE TWO TYPES OF PEOPLE." I DO THIS EVEN THOUGH THERE ARE ALWAYS MANY MANY MORE THAN TWO. IN THIS CASE, THERE BEING TWO TYPES—AN OUTSIDE PERSON AND AN INSIDE PERSON—IS DIRECTIONALLY TRUE. PEOPLE REALLY DO GRAVITATE TO ONE OR THE OTHER. I USE IT OFTEN WITH YOUNG PROFESSIONALS WHO ARE CONSIDERING CAREER CHOICES, BUT THIS IS ONLY ONE AREA WHERE IT APPLIES

I LOVE IT WHEN A STUDENT OR FACULTY MEMBER SAYS: "PROFESSOR, THERE ARE ACTUALLY MORE THAN JUST TWO." IN BUSINESS, I WOULD ASK THEM TO LEAVE THE MEETING. IN ACADEMIA, I TELL THEM IT IS JUST A SIMPLE EXAMPLE TO ILLUSTRATE A POINT.

Chapter 13

BRANDING

"If you have to think anyway, why not think big?"

—A U.S. President

B randing is a very important topic to me. It is somewhat linked to the themes discussed in *Building Your Experience and Profile (and Resume)*, but also many other chapters in this book. I lecture at a graduate school on the topic of branding, and I always start the same way: I speak first about personal brand.

Personal Brand

I start by asking: "What is a personal brand? Do you need one? And can you describe yours?"

Very often the conversation starts with students talking about what they think their brand is from their perspective. In many cases, their view is more aspirational than actual: it often describes what they want it to be. In other cases, they have never even thought about their brand before, and seem to have no idea as to what it is. They might even say they don't have one.

The conversation continues with me saying "I am 100% certain each of you have a personal brand, and if you don't know what it is you need to know."

A personal brand, like most commercial brands, is how you are viewed by the outside world. The view is never 100% the same across all audiences, but its key elements are generally the same. Your personal brand first develops from people who know you, then spreads to people who do not know you at all. It has always amazed me that a person's brand is widely talked about by people who do not know them well, and even those who have never met them. We see the following phenomenon all the time. "He's a really good guy." "How do you know?" "Everyone says it." "He's really smart," "He's hardworking," "She's very tech savvy," and so on. How do they know? Everyone knows.

Another thing about personal brands is that they tend to be multifaceted. An example is "She is smart, very professional, hardworking, a team player, a great leader, and not a whiner." In some cases, the personal brand in circulation is largely correct; in other cases, it is only partially correct; and in the remaining few, it is not correct at all. In my life, and certainly in my career, I often asked people who knew me (and some not that well), "How am I viewed by you and by others?" The answers were very rarely the same. I remember asking it once and the answer was, "People who know you love you, and all want to be on your team and work with and for you. Those that don't know you are generally scared shitless."

A personal brand evolves over time, and in my view is influenced by actions that you take, intentionally or otherwise. In some cases, a brand can be "spun." In other cases, it cannot because it reflects fact. For example, honesty, integrity, and trustworthiness; you are either honest 100% of the time, or you are not.

My recommendation here is that you decide what you want the elements of your personal brand to be and you work hard to live them and in some cases refine them and accentuate them.

My personal brand after all these years goes something like this:

Don is passionate (some say about everything he cares about), very honest and trustworthy, extremely hard working, very smart, very global thinking, and focused on diversity. He builds and sustains high-performing teams (and high performers), is very close to his family and his kids, loves a challenge, and always thinks BIG and out of the box. He doesn't run from confrontation—some even say that he thrives on confrontation. He is all about teamwork, is extremely loyal, is a great judge of people, and he has a great sense of humor. Don is great at making decisions quickly, communicates clear messages, is a great businessman, is great in the C-Suite, and knows everybody.

He also doesn't listen well, and he has a very short attention span (some say he has ADD (Attention Defecit Disorder)). Don hates administrative matters and people who always say "no" or make excuses for why something can't be done. He always tends to exaggerate, is known to use colorful language, makes decisions too quickly, can be curt or short at times, tends to interrupt you often, thinks he knows everything (some say he seems to know everything about everything), thinks he is always right, and always wants clarity and accountability (good and bad!).

Regarding my personal brand as stated above, the positives and negatives tend to be overstated, particularly by those who focus on select elements. All in all, I believe it is a fair depiction of my traits. That said, upwards of 90% of those who view me this way have never really met me. Despite this, many of them hold the view strongly. When I speak in front of groups (of all kinds and ages), I often tell stories that intentionally or unintentionally reinforce parts of my brand.

There is a word I want to introduce here: "intimidating," as in "he can be intimidating." At times, this word has been used to describe me. My view is that I can be intimidating when I want to be, but also that I am sometimes intimidating without meaning to be. An example of the former case is if my team were proposing against a competitor, I would certainly try to intimidate the competitor in order to win. This was usually done by comparing our expertise and experience to theirs and demonstrating that we were clearly much better. The latter case was most often an unfortunate result of my personal presence (which is hard to change), and sometimes my title (i.e., Global Vice Chairman). That said, after spending fifteen minutes with me, most people are no longer intimidated.

Let me end this segment by recommending that you determine your personal brand—good and bad—and work on refining it through your actions. Some elements are easily refined, and some are not, but if you remain focused on your behavior, you can impact your brand. I would start with the three to five elements that are most important to you, and I would strongly suggest that honesty, integrity, and being trustworthy lead that list.

Developing A Brand

Your brand is how you are known. If you are an organization (like a company or a business), it is what you are known for or even famous for. Brands can relate to the overall organization or only parts of the organization (e.g., PwC audit), or parts of the organization which have different names (e.g., Bud Light/Budweiser). It can pertain to different products or services or even different people (e.g., LeBron James, Michael Jordan).

When I think about brand architecture strategies, I think about the following:

- What do we want to be famous for?

- How are we distinctive?

- How can we differentiate ourselves?

I generally start from one of two perspectives: either what we ARE really good at that differentiates us, or what we WILL be good at that can differentiate us. Both of these can be best understood if the organization does a review of its core competencies and builds from there. Deciding what you want to be famous for is the key starting point. Once this is decided, determining the best ways of publicizing it comes next.

Core Competency

I mentioned the term "core competency." I have my own definition of what this is, and you won't see it very often. To me, a core competency is something you do better than anyone else, which differentiates you—something that makes you one of one (or one of a very small group).

When I think of core competencies and how to identify them, I think of a bull's eye: the center is a core competency, the next circle is a competency, and the outer circle are things you are really good at.

One of my relationship steps with new clients was to offer to do a review of their competencies at no cost. All I needed was one hour with each of their top ten executives. I would interview each executive together with one or two associates, asking:

1. Did they think they had any core competencies?

2. What were other competencies they thought the company had?

3. What other things did they think the company was good (and bad) at?

These were wide-open discussions. After our interviews (whereby we got to meet all ten top executives in a very friendly environment), we put together two summaries—one with attribution, and one without.

The first summary was what the executives had said, and the second was what we thought. 100% of the time, the executives thought the company had core competencies that were NOT close to being core competencies, proven by our identification of companies that did those things at least as well but often better. Also, the listed competencies (the second circle) were very often not differentiators at all, either because the company was not that good at them or many (*many*) companies did them well, so it didn't make the company different or better! A favorite phrase of mine that I use to make this point is "It didn't sell any tickets."

In each case, we sat down with the executives as a group and went through our findings and conclusions. This was usually a two- to three-hour meeting where emotions ran high ("my baby is cuter than your baby" syndrome). In the end, however, the executives understood and agreed with our conclusions. This gave them a starting point in determining "what they wanted to be famous for," and how it might be branded.

A really good example of where this process is extremely helpful is with conglomerates. A conglomerate is a company that has amassed a portfolio of different companies. Good examples are companies like General Electric, United Technologies, and even Exxon. Their respective taglines (or brands) are "We bring good things to life," "This is momentum," and "Energy lives here." I'll leave it to you to decide what you think of these.

In the pages that follow, I've included some examples of effective branding. In some cases, the objective(s) can be obvious, but in others they're really creative.

The Avis Story

For a little history, Avis was started in 1946 by a former Air Force pilot Warren Avis. His first rent-a-car location was at the Willow Run Airport in Detroit. I met Warren in the early 90s. He told me that pilots at the time had to carry their own bicycles or motor scooters to get from the airport to town. This gave him the idea of renting cars at airports—a first at the time.

Back in 1962, new Avis CEO Joe Vittorio together with his ad agency created the original Avis tagline, which exists today as "We Try Harder." The original line, however—which most don't remember—was "We're #2, but we try harder."

The story here was that Joe had come from Hertz, which at the time was more than twice the size of Avis. Both companies did basically the same thing—rented cars—and they did it in basically the same way—in cities and at airports. Also, their products were essentially the same: fairly new, clean, and low-mileage cars. Joe, knowing that Avis could never grow to Hertz's size, decided to make number two better than number one. They did that by concluding that because they were number two they would have to try harder to satisfy customers. This meant friendlier, quicker, and on-the-whole better service. Was this true? You decide.

True or not, this related branding strategy gave rise to the tagline. Back then, every Avis TV commercial, advertisement, Avis sign, Avis pin, Avis bus, Avis courtesy car, and Avis uniform included the tagline "We're #2, but we try harder."

Global Network, PwC

In my PwC career, I was fortunate to have had the opportunity to lead several major clients and major business units both domestic and global. Early on in my career, I got to understand the extent, value, and core competency of the PwC global network. It is very large, very extensive, very high-value, and very connected. As an example, a global relationship partner with the right experience on a large global client can execute across the globe with great speed using the PwC Global Network. The network comprises people (experts) based throughout 150 countries, with strong relationships in each country and more broadly, using world-class technology. The PwC Global Network is clearly a core competency—in other words, it's one of one!

In my view, from a branding perspective, the PwC global network is synonymous with the PwC brand.

The PwC Technology Practice

For the period from 1994 to 2002, I led the PwC Technology practice and (later) the Technology, InfoCom, and Entertainment and Media practice (TICE) of PwC. When asked to lead a business unit, I followed a series of loosely defined steps. This included deciding on my core team of leaders; together with my team putting together a strategic plan covering three to five years; deciding on our structure, in this case, industries (software, semiconductors, etc.) and geographies; and most importantly, defining what "being number one" meant and the strategy needed to get there. Naturally, this process included assembling the total team across the relevant industries and geographies—hundreds of partners, managers, and staff. A key point here was that our proposed strategy—including our strategies for implementation and (of course) for branding—had to be clearly defined, clearly understood, and embraced by the team (more on strategy in Chapter 23).

One of the key elements in our strategic plan was branding our practice as the "PwC Technology" practice, and later, the "PwC TICE" practice. The branding effort aimed to establish PwC as the number one firm in the technology sector, particularly within our key geographies and industries, but also across the U.S. more broadly. At a macro level, that meant penetrating the ecosystem in each industry and geography—easy to say, but hard to do. We would have to impact every bank, law firm, venture firm, industry organization, and eventually, all clients in our chosen areas. We did this in a number of ways, with each team trying to achieve the same objective in their own areas, but also coordinating across the country.

One of the ways was through the PwC Venture Capital Survey (later the PwC Money Tree Survey). We decided to start a quarterly survey of venture firms across the U.S. to obtain data on where their technology investments were being made by industry and geography. This created a very unique set of data that no one else had and everyone wanted, including the members of the venture firm community themselves. Our reputation for confidentiality put us in a unique position to do this.

So, what did we do with the data? We issued quarterly reports to all participants, clients, and prospective clients, along with a few other members of the ecosystem. We also hit the major cable channels quarterly in every geography (CNN, CNBC, etc.) with FLASH hot off-the-press highlights. Oftentimes, our data was put on loops, so the two-minute segment played every hour or two for two to three days. This also gave our partners high visibility by way of local programming—there were different PwC partners in each major geography presenting the report on TV.

We also put together high-tech videos highlighting each quarter's cable reporting. Imagine a three-minute video with partner after partner and cable logo after cable logo flashing across the screen with the words "PwC presents its Venture Capital Survey" over and over, again and again. I called that "branding on steroids."

Fordham University

Fordham University is the Jesuit University of New York, and often cites the tagline "New York is our campus—Fordham is our school." These are two fairly well-known brands (NYC and Jesuit) of Fordham University. That said, the university has for years been improving everything Fordham. It has been very successful in doing this, but maybe not as successful in communicating it to the world at large.

There are several strategic initiatives underway to try to fix this and to help raise the profile of the university in the U.S. and globally.

One of these key initiatives is men's basketball. This means using men's basketball to help raise the university's profile. How is this done? First, several decisions were made by the Board of Trustees and the president to improve the quality of the staff and team. The objective was to improve our quality in order to move to the top of the A10 (the league Fordham is in) and to periodically go to the NCAA Tournament.

By having a much more competitive and winning team, the university would be more visible on TV, in newspapers, and around New York, which in turn boosts visibility across the U.S. and globally. Basketball is the vehicle, but the university's quality and qualities are the content and selling point—the *brand*.

IBM

What follows is a list of IBM's publicly available taglines over its many years of operations:

- THINK (famous and in many languages)

- WE MAKE IT HAPPEN

- SOLUTIONS FOR A SMALL PLANET

- IBM COMPUTERS HELP PEOPLE HELP PEOPLE

- THINK 3.0 and LET'S CREATE (2022)

In closing, branding is always connected to what you want to be famous for, and what you want to be famous for is always a strategic decision and connected to your core competencies or the competencies you are building.

Chapter 14

BUILDING YOUR EXPERIENCE AND PROFILE (AND RESUME)

B uilding one's experiences, solidifying one's profile, and representing oneself through an effective resume are all keys to success in business, and I have focused on these three topics for most of my career. I have done this with my kids, high school students, college students, employees and partners in my firm, clients, and executives at companies and not-for-profits that I've worked with.

Building Your Experience

Let me begin with experience. Your experience is the sum total of everything you have done. It is the result of the hundreds of thousands of decisions you make. It is influenced by choices you make for yourself, choices others make for you, and plain old luck. It can open doors, but it can also close them. In most cases, it adds to your value, but in some cases, it can detract, and for better or worse, you add to it every day.

Your experience is put together over years, assembled from the building blocks of all the various skills and learnings that you pick up along the way. It makes you more broadly valuable in some cases—with more and more experience across a wide range of areas; it makes you more uniquely valuable in others—a lot of experience in one or a few certain areas that make you a real expert. In most cases, you determine what your areas of focus are, and by extension, what kind of experience you accrue. Let there be no doubt about it, however, that over time no one is exactly like you—the shape of your experience evolves and differentiates you from even your contemporaries in similar roles and industries. I have many examples of times when I was not your average accountant.

When I look back on my career, it is clear to me what some of the key choices that I made were, which key choices were made for me, and what developments were the result of luck (I always said that luck was where opportunity met ability).

Some of the key choices I made included going to Fordham University, deciding to be an accounting major, joining PwC, going to Europe (Italy) on a three-year tour, coming back to the New York office, and staying to make partner.

Some of the key choices made for me were being offered/put on some of the great clients I had the opportunity to work with, working for some of the partners and managers I worked with (especially in my early career, and then again later), being given the opportunity to travel and become global (before it was mandatory), and being offered positions to run businesses.

Some luck I had was having the parents and family I have, getting into Fordham University, getting an internship while in college at PwC, and having some phenomenal mentors throughout my career, particularly in my early years.

Set A Direction

When I go into "career counseling mode," which can be related to almost anyone at any age or point in their career, I always ask the same question: "When you're retired and looking back on your career, what would you want to have done?" Interestingly, in most cases, this question has not gotten any focus. For those in college or early in their careers, two things are usually true: (1) they haven't given it much thought, despite its criticality at this time in their journey; and (2) when they finally *do* focus on it, they tend to keep the bar low. This is to say they grossly underestimate what they can achieve, and thereby limit their potential.

I talk very often with high school and college students about their futures. What I always emphasize is that they should do something they like or (ideally) love to do. If they did this, they would tend to work harder, and if they worked harder, they would tend to do better. If they *really* worked hard, they might even end up being one of the best—if not *the* best—in their chosen field.

Discussions about "setting the bar" usually happened with staff or young partners at PwC, or occasionally with clients. Almost always, their view was usually the low end of where I saw their potential could take them.

In both cases, the question led to a long discussion about what was possible (or even likely) and my views of their potential. This discussion also focused on things that would be critical to their success. A common example was the need to live and work overseas to gain global experience. I would always emphasize that this was optional in my day, and even a differentiator, but today it is mandatory if you want to achieve any standard of success. In all cases, no matter what the advice, I could see course corrections being made right in front of me.

I remember one high-performing partner in our transactions group who was around thirty-five years old and asked for me to be his mentor. When we met for the first time, I asked him, when he retired and looked back, what would be his last job? He said he would ultimately like to run the transaction group in New York. Now, do not get me wrong, that position was held by very senior and highly-compensated partners and was highly sought after. That said, I asked whether that was it—was that the highest he would set his sights? He was surprised and asked me what I thought. I told him that I thought he could be the lead partner on one of our largest clients, lead the transactions group in the U.S. and globally, and should think about being on our U.S. and global boards. I will never forget his stunned look, "Do you think that could be possible?" he asked. Yes, yes, and yes was my answer. We then spent almost two hours brainstorming what he would have to do and what experience he would have to have to get there.

So why is this topic so important? The basic tenets of knowing what you like, doing it, and then excelling at it are key to being able to build your experience to support your ultimate goals. I always thought of it as a puzzle that was filled in over time, albeit a very aggressive puzzle that will never be fully filled in, but committing to specific foci means that your experience will grow to support what you want to be "when you grow up." The puzzle will also change and expand over time as you fill in your experience.

When you have a vision of what you want to accomplish, you can then define the building blocks necessary to get there and start assembling them piece by piece. As an example, if you want to be the lead partner on a major client at PwC, there are pretty specific experiences you have to have to even be considered. They include international experience, experience in the industry the client is in, a proven track record in managing large accounts, people skills that show you will be able to lead a large team, and so on.

Identify What *Not* To Do

As you manage your career and gain needed experience, you also need to try to identify what *not* to do. This is extremely important to gaining the experience you need while not wasting time in areas that will not benefit you. This may sound pretty fundamental, but I have seen the opposite happen often, usually when a promotion and a significant salary increase or overseas assignment are offered.

In the first case, the opportunity for early promotion entices someone to take a position that they do not really want, will probably not like, and, most importantly, will slow down their experience building or take their career in the wrong direction. I have seen this happen time and time again, and it almost never works out. We called these "accelerated promotions," and they were offered to get people to take positions that nobody really wanted.

The second case—the offer of an overseas assignment—is equally common, however, the foreign experience is usually a good thing and has long-term benefits. That said, similar to the first case, if it is not work experience relevant to where you ultimately want to go, it will take you off track and maybe in the wrong direction. Also, these tours are usually multi-year, which is good in terms of learning what it's like to work abroad, but can put a speed bump in your career path. The bottom line is that a foreign tour can be phenomenal if it consists of work experience you need in addition to overseas experience.

The potential irony in these two cases is if you do well you will be asked to stay and proceed up this new path. I have often seen this when a high-performer chooses either of the aforementioned cases and they improve core elements of the company's business—in other words, where the money is made. When you perform well, and the odds are that you will, then you may get stuck there. This is especially true when you are high-performing but many others in your group are not. I used to call this "In the land of the blind, the one-eyed man is king!" I remember many cases where team members or mentees would leave the firm—in my view, for all the wrong reasons. One case I remember was a high-performing partner who left the firm to be the CFO of a joint venture between two large companies. The primary reason for his decision was money. I was as supportive as I normally was, but cautioned that he was leaving a highly compensated position that he both loved and was great at. He understood, but believed it was a once-in-a-lifetime opportunity. After a year and a half, the venture folded and he was back in the job market. Where did he ultimately end up? Back with us, with me as his sponsor. This was in the days when re-admitting a partner was very unusual. He retired with PwC.

The "Must-Haves"

As you guide your career and navigate towards your ultimate (or interim) goal, you need to identify your "must-haves." These are a very select group of experiences that you must have to achieve your career objectives. Mentors, advisors, or other trusted parties can help you explore the possibilities, but only you can truly decide what your goals are and what you need to do in order to get there.

That said, there are chapters in this book that discuss areas and concepts that you should consider. You already know that I think international experience is high on the list: the experience of working and living in one or (preferably) more than one country. Only if you do this will you develop a true appreciation for global business, which is critical to your success no matter what you do.

Also key are people skills, like how to create and lead a team and how to influence others. These skills are discussed in other chapters and are gained through different job experiences and trial and error.

To give a concrete example, my must-haves were (1) graduating with an accounting degree; (2) getting a job with a Big Eight firm (I picked PwC, which clearly was a great choice); (3) getting my CPA; (4) going on tour to Milan for three years and working all over Europe when I was twenty-eight years old; (5) working on bigger and bigger clients over the years; (6) working in various areas such as transaction support, IT systems implementations, restructurings, and derivatives; and (7) running different businesses.

These experiences gave me subject matter expertise as well as broad business aptitude. They also included competence in running a business, which helped me better connect with the CEOs of our clients who ran their own businesses.

My must-haves developed over time as I was better able to see what would be needed to succeed to get where I wanted to go. Because your aspirations will change over time, your must-haves will change as well. In my case (and hopefully yours), my ambitions were constantly expanding. In college, I knew I needed to graduate, I knew I wanted to work at one of the preeminent firms, and I knew I needed a CPA as a minimum credential. After a few years of working, I got a better view of my future professional objectives, and thus, my necessary career choices: becoming a global businessman, becoming an expert in certain areas, and becoming proficient in running businesses were high on my list. As I accrued these skills, I was offered new opportunities, and so my must-haves evolved again. Ultimately, I decided that being a partner, leading major client teams, and running global businesses were what I wanted to do.

Your Profile

Let me take the next step. Experience and personality taken together make up your "profile." Your experience evolves over time, and your personality can change over time as you age and grow, but in my view, changes less significantly. If you tend to be quiet, you tend to stay quiet. If you are an introvert, you tend to stay an introvert. In my case, I was extroverted and became more so over time. On the other hand, I did not like public speaking until I was about twenty-five years old—then I grew to love it and became really good at it.

What is most important here is that you go in the direction of things you like to do. If you like to do something, then you will tend to work hard to be good at it (remember *Be The Best In The World*). Your style and personality will definitely influence the direction you go in. They also will determine how you do things, and that in turn will impact your profile, and certainly how you are viewed.

If you put an inside guy (a person who does not gravitate toward dealing with people, like a researcher, for example) in an outside job (like a salesman), they will usually not succeed, and in fact, will get extremely frustrated. The same is true if you put an outside guy in an inside job.

As your career progresses, you should look to expand your experience in the broad areas that fit your personality and core long-term skills. This is how you can maximize the building of your experience and your profile. I use "inside guys and outside guys" here because it was always one of the key filters I used in trying to guide my career. For me, the outside guy definition included leading teams, running businesses, dealing with clients, and generating revenue. It also expanded over time to doing all of this globally. I was trying to refrain from doing things that did not align with this definition while doing all the things that would enhance it. I have many examples in my career where I, as an outside guy and a type-A personality, was offered inside jobs. In my case, these were all people-facing jobs, but they did not necessarily deal with clients and were not profit centers. No, not for me. I coined the phrase "highest and best use." If you put someone in a job that utilizes their skills, that is the highest and best use. I followed this theory throughout my career for not just myself, but also for those who worked for me and those I mentored. It served me well.

I caution here that the route I took was very specific to me. In all these decisions there are pros and cons which must be considered.

My Profile

I am a global businessman with experience in seventy-four countries. I have core technical skills in accounting, finance, sales and marketing, human capital, and client management, alongside other broad business skills. I have started businesses, turned businesses around, grown businesses, and shut businesses down. I have dealt with boards, all levels in the C-Suite with particular focus on CEOs, and all levels in governments including presidents, prime ministers, and a prince or two and all over the world. I also have experience with companies of all sizes, from startups to Fortune 50.

I am an honest, direct, clear, and blunt (at times) New Yorker who does not sweat the small stuff unless it is important (rarely), who makes informed decisions quickly, and whose word is his bond. I am all about the team and delivering what was promised. I am also all about creating and keeping trusted relationships. I usually don't start conflict, but I never run away from it—I believe spirited discussion and healthy debate always result in better answers. I love to have a good time, and I use humor to solve problems, cut tension, break the ice, or make a point. I am known as a ballbuster because I come at you all the time with one-line jabs...but only if I like you. I am also loyal to a fault. Oh, and I also use colorful language at times.

This is my shot at my profile—I believe it is factually correct. It reflects my personality, my physical attributes, my timing, my age, where I came from, my DNA and genetic makeup, and so on. As you can see, it only describes me and no one else.

Throughout my career, I cautioned younger partners and staff to "be careful not to do what I do or say what I say." It worked for me (though sometimes it did not), but it may not fit their style or personality. This is a really important point. Occasionally I would see someone say something or do something that was not consistent with their style or personality. It was usually obvious, and I would always say: "Obviously they read the book, but never really did it." You see this very often with team members who are taking on the style of the team leader or boss. What may work for the boss may not—and in many cases, *will* not—work for you.

A profile is something you plan for and create over time. It is who you are, reflecting your experience, your skills, your personality, and how you are viewed by others. I have often spoken to my classes (and my kids) about building experience and building a profile—two different things, but both are important. They both evolve over time.

Resume Building

Let me switch to a briefer topic which is converting experience and profile into a resume. I mentioned before that a resume is very often the first thing people will look at to determine whether they want to meet you (and maybe actually offer you a job). Therefore, it has to sell them on you, and it needs to effectively reference your experience to do that.

90% of all the resumes I have read over forty years sound the same. They look the same, have the same content, and are written in the same way. The key is to include experiences that are different than most and send a signal. The irony here is that many people have these experiences, but for whatever reason do not include them.

Here are examples of what I look for: (1) leadership experiences—president of the school or your class, or president of your fraternity, or captain of your team, or you started something like your school newspaper, or ran a holiday trip to Mexico; (2) a unique skill—languages, music, sports, medicine, writing, community service; (3) a special experience—participating in the Olympics, professional sports, climbing Mount Everest, the Tour de France; and (4) team experiences—working with a group like Habitat for Humanity, or the Catholic Relief Services, or tutoring at an inner city school (not one-offs, but working with people together over a period of time). As a rule of thumb, highlight anything that makes you unique: speaking a foreign language, playing an instrument, being in the military, or winning an award are all key parts of your story.

When you think about your resume, you also need to focus on what it will be used for: it should always have a career objective that is focused on the job you are seeking. This is to say it must change over time as your experience grows, but also as you focus on a new job. It must scream out "I want this job!" Most resumes don't.

Also, you must constantly consider not only what experience you need, but how it will impact your resume. Let me give you a clear example of this. I have tried to connect Fordham University students to students at Cardinal Hayes. The Fordham students volunteer to be tutors and mentors at Hayes, helping Hayes students who need additional assistance. The Fordham students are giving back to the community, and this is the reason they do it, but it also looks great on a resume.

On a resume, this might be written as "volunteered at a local high school to help students with their schoolwork"—an accurate description of some quality work, and something that could stand out on a resume. That said, what I tell Fordham students is that in addition to giving back, "they were a core group who created and executed a learning program at Cardinal Hayes High School in the South Bronx that grew from ten students to fifty students over three years and helped raise the students' average SAT scores by 100 points." From the perspective of someone who assesses applicants' resumes, the first version was just fine, but the second would get their attention.

Your resume is a document that sells you. It sounds a little superficial, but as I tell my classes, it will in many cases be the first thing someone sees. It needs to reflect experience, but it also needs to be crisp and impactful and differentiate you—to make you look different and more interesting than others.

When I think about experience and resumes, I think about what I call "hooks." A hook is a reference to an experience that grabs the reader and makes them want to meet the person. It also very often makes hirers conclude (at least initially) that this is an applicant they want to hire. Hooks are very specific experiences that are typically very rare or unusual, or that indicate disproportionate value.

Examples that I have seen on business resumes have included working in the White House, speaking Mandarin, winning an Olympic medal, playing on a pro sports team, and being a Rhodes Scholar, to mention a few. I once saw one that said the applicant helped perform brain surgery. This ended up being someone who interned in a hospital and actually got to be an assistant in the operating room, before later concluding that being a doctor was not in the cards.

Whatever is on your resume needs to be factually correct. This does not mean you should not embellish a little—you should. However, I cannot tell you how many resumes I have seen that had items that were simply not true. It only takes one and you are done. You also need to be able to discuss every item on your resume to "bring it to life." Believe me when I tell you that enthusiasm and passion around what you have done and to some extent why you did it are huge sellers.

Going back to the candidate with the brain surgery experience: I took a quick review of her resume and noticed a reference to "having assisted a team in performing brain surgery." It certainly got my attention, and I could not wait to see and talk to her about what this was. When we met, she explained that she had been a hospital volunteer and at the time was considering going to medical school. She worked with a surgical group that, among other things, performed brain surgery. The doctor leading the team would select certain volunteers to assist in the operating room, and she was the one selected. She explained that she was clearly the most junior member of the team, but did actually assist in the procedure. She explained in detail the operating process and her role. She also explained how she got selected, which was also impressive. She got an offer!

On the negative side, I remember interviewing someone who was not Chinese whose resume said he was fluent in Mandarin. After a long discussion where he tried to explain, unsuccessfully, how he became fluent, it was clear that he was not, and had only taken lessons for six months. Surprise, he did not get an offer.

Another resume said the person had managed an SAP R3 systems implementation. I found this odd on a college resume, especially from someone who had not had a prior career. When we talked about it, it became clear that he, at best, had been an administrative assistant or intern working on the project. Surprise, he did not get an offer.

My resume has some very unique experiences. Two of the many questions my resume raises are: (1) "How did you get on the Foreign Investor Council of Kazakhstan and get to know the Prime Minister?" and (2) "How did you get on the Financial Center Advisory Board of Russia?"

I have given a few examples of what kinds of things might differentiate you. Your experience and whether it differentiates you for a position are most important. That said, do not underestimate the value of a well-targeted resume.

Chapter 15

BUILDING YOUR NETWORK – CONNECTING THE DOTS

B y the time I retired from PwC, my network had become my most valuable asset. A number of CEOs and others would say "Don knows everyone." Although I liked to hear that, it was obviously not true. What *was* true was that I knew many people all over the world through various networks. If I wanted to get to someone almost anywhere in the world and I didn't already know them, I almost always knew someone who did. This made my reach incredibly broad. Also, because of the length of my career and the trusted relationships I had built over time, I had trusted friends all over the world, many if not most of whom were happy to help me in any way they could. This did not happen by accident!

From early on in my life and career, I liked meeting people, and my personality was such that if I could help them, I would. In many cases, I helped someone by making an introduction that benefited the parties on both sides and in turn benefited me. If I introduce two people who would like to meet, both parties appreciate it and I bring value to both sides; it's a three-way benefit.

How to Build a Network

Building a network effectively requires **thought**, **skill**, and **execution**.

"Thought" in this context means you have to decide that networking is important—a priority—and commit to actually *doing* it. Over time, this becomes intuitive, and you'll find yourself employing your networking skills all the time and over and over again.

"Skill" means you know how to approach people with the intention of meeting them. This requires a certain caliber of confidence, and certainly requires you to be comfortable meeting people you do not know. Refer to *How To Meet (Famous) People* (Chapter 28) for some tips in this area.

"Execution" refers to the actual building of the network person-by-person, but at the same time leaving what I call "fingerprints" on each—little touches that make sure you will be remembered. This can be done in many ways, but the best way (surprise, surprise) is to bring value to the other person, be it in your first interaction or shortly thereafter. Even a brief conversation in a casual setting reveals facts that may lead to possible opportunities to bring value. For me, this was very often at broad business meetings—Davos, the Saint Petersburg Economic Forum, and the like—where groups of people from different countries gathered. This is a perfect setting to introduce "friends" to one another. After each such event, I always followed up with email notes—though I'd still hand out business cards. Each note was personal and, in many cases, either offered my assistance in some way or asked how I could help. Often the other person's note came first, thanking me for an introduction I'd made or some help I had given.

Areas of Expertise

Later in my career, I found it much easier to network because of my experience, and frankly, because of the expansive network I'd already established. In international settings—or domestic settings with international people—I was often one of the more experienced with local customs, business culture, etc., and was a good source of knowledge. Also, being a senior partner at PwC, I was able to offer connections to experts that could help, be it in the country where we were or (almost) anywhere else in the world. My PwC "toolkit" together with my contacts and experience made me pretty impactful.

At the beginning of my career, however, I used all the tools I had to make connections—though I didn't have many. I used my firm, PwC. I used firms I worked with like law firms, banks, investment banks, technology industry connections, client connections, etc. The key here was always trying to find a connection to create an "in," and then trying to find how you could bring value.

When I say "bring value," I mean personal value to the other person. This takes many forms, and may not be obvious immediately. As a conversation progresses, there will always be relevant questions that either party will ask. A question can lead to an answer, and an answer can lead to value:

"How long have you worked at PwC?"
"Four years. I work on clients A, B, and C."
"Do you know Paul?
"I do. Do you know him?"
"No, but I would love to meet him."
"Done, let's have lunch"

This is a very simple example, but it represents thousands of interactions I have had in my career.

Many people find the thought of building a network as I describe here very difficult, and some may even think it's impossible. When I speak to younger people on this subject, I immediately point out that they all already have networks, and most often many different ones. They have their grammar school network, their high school network, potentially their college network, their sports network, their religious network, and so on. In sports, there are sports camps; in music, there are music schools and performances; in college, there are fraternities; etc. These are all methods most people use to connect to specific groups or ecosystems—maybe they have created these networks naturally, or maybe they've built them intentionally. In any event, these early connections are the start of building networks, and everyone does it, albeit some do it better than others. When you connect with these different groups, you are most often connecting to people with similar interests to you, and you are showing them that you have similar interests to them.

In business or life, expanding your network requires some of the skills you already have, further refining those skills, focusing and targeting those skills, and expanding them. This means, as I have already mentioned, that your ability to expand your network gets easier all the time as the tools you have evolve. You get to know more people, and you have more experience and skills. In some cases, you yourself may be the person many other people are looking to network with or connect to.

Enhancing the Dot and Better Connecting It

Making a new contact by meeting a person and sharing an interaction represents what I call a "dot." Over time as you build more dots, you start connecting them to each other. This in turn creates a network of interconnected relationships that naturally puts you at its center, as you're the "common connection" between those you've introduced. These days I get three to five calls a week from friends who are calling to say that they were somewhere and met someone who said they knew me and to pass on their regards.

With the help of my Executive Assistant, I created a system where all of the contacts I'd made over the years were loaded into a database alongside their contact information. I would periodically review this list to see who I might send a note to. To this day, I send holiday cards electronically to hundreds of my friends. I generally get a 95% response rate. Many of these responses result in a follow-up note from me or a phone call.

It is extremely important to try to keep your network as functional as possible. I also use LinkedIn and, although it may sound odd, I do try to wish everyone a happy birthday. I learned the value of this in a number of countries where birthdays are a big event, but it's a worthwhile practice anywhere in the world.

Life After PwC

For the last ten years of my post-PwC life, I have been involved with several corporate and nonprofit boards. As a result, my network has grown significantly during this time, both in its size and its value. I still do the same things now that I did while I was at PwC, and I draw on my network often. Now, in my nonprofit world, I am constantly using the value of my network and my contacts to bring value to the new organizations I am involved with.

Chapter 16

MENTORSHIP – GIVING AND RECEIVING

A ll successful people have had great mentors. All really successful people have also *been* great mentors.

So, what is a mentor? Simply put, a mentor is someone who looks out for you. They are someone who spends time "teaching you the ropes," so to speak. This happens in a wide variety of ways: some are intentional and obvious, while others are very subtle and often go unnoticed. Mentors are usually (but not always) senior to you in life or in an organization. They could be your boss, a senior executive at your company, a client, a fellow board or clergy member, or someone you succeed in a role; almost anyone who has experience you have not yet acquired can be a mentor.

Some have asked me: "Do I need a mentor?" My answer: "No—unless you want to be successful."

In all likelihood, you've already experienced the positive effect of mentorship. Early in your life, particularly in school, you have teachers who help you learn necessary skills. Many teachers are in essence mentors, and they can have a dramatic impact on your life. During this time, you also have your parents, relatives, older friends, and hopefully others who are mentors. These mentors help you decide what you want to do in life, and some may even help you do it. This set of relationships continues in life and business. There are plenty of ways to learn skills and information by yourself, but it is mentorship that helps you bridge the gap between knowing something and fully understanding it.

Most successful people have numerous mentors, each of whom may mentor in different ways and different areas. For example, I had many mentors throughout my career. Though some of these mentors are no longer with us, those who remain are very dear friends of mine. They know who they are, and I owe them each a significant debt of gratitude. I could not have done what I did without them.

Mentorship is unique to every situation; there is no standard list of things that make someone a good mentor or a good mentee. Every person in almost every situation acts differently, and "mentorship" interactions could occur as infrequently as once a year or as often as twice a day, depending on the mentor, the mentee, and the circumstances. As life and business situations change, so do these interactions.

When I think back on my life to date, I have had many mentors and many mentees—it's hard to pick out just one or two. My mentors have all been different: some have given me broad guidance, others have given me very specific advice; some have helped me get promoted when I was doing well, some have helped save my business life in times of struggle; some have been twenty or thirty years older, and others have been my age; some were my mentors on purpose, and others didn't realize they were. They came in all shapes and sizes, in all religions and colors. I am grateful to all of those who helped me—in my career and otherwise—and there are a few I want to acknowledge specifically.

In your career, you meet people you can never forget. One that comes to mind for me is someone I will call "Bob." Bob recently passed. When I first met him in 1982, he was one of the most senior partners at PwC. He had just been asked to lead one of the firm's largest accounts (the same account I would be asked to lead twenty years later), and I was returning from my three-year tour in Italy. He picked me to be his senior manager on a major client, reporting to him. I worked extensively with Bob for two years and traveled internationally with him. Before

I knew him personally, I had been told that he was "tough to deal with," along with a bunch of other negative stuff. Instead, what I found as I began working for and with him was a consummate professional and a fount of knowledge, with a great personality and sense of humor to boot. He was a great mentor to me, and I owe him a ton of gratitude. It was an honor to have known him.

Another career find for me was the aforementioned Jim. I referred to Jim in *Be The Best In The World* (Chapter 3), and he certainly was, in addition to being a great mentor to me. When I made partner in 1987, I reported directly to Jim. I'd met Jim early in my career, and although he was only four or five years older, he quickly became a longtime mentor and friend. For some reason, Jim had always looked out for me, and when I was admitted to the partnership, that continued. He gave me great counseling and great advice. I also saw his "fingerprints" at times when the firm recognized I hadn't been treated fairly—which is my way of saying that wrong decisions were made and later changed—and though I never knew for sure who influenced the change, I noticed some small details that indicated Jim had been involved.

I was playing golf with a gentleman I'll call "Paul" the other day, and I'd be remiss if I didn't mention him here. I first met Paul in 1973: I was working with my first client and Paul was my point of contact. I was twenty-three and he was maybe ten years older. We hit it off almost immediately. When I was on location, I would often stop by his office at the end of the day and we'd sit together and talk for a while. We would talk about everything, personal and professional. Whether he knew it or not, he was giving me great advice on both business and non-business matters. Years later, he is still giving me great advice, and at times on really important stuff. I would never call him a mentee, but some years ago I started also giving him input on various things. It is a trusted, privileged relationship.

I would also mention someone I'll call "Dennis." I met Dennis just before he was admitted as a PwC partner. He had been called to New York to review two audits, both of which were mine. The partners I worked for at the time on these clients were two of the most senior partners at PwC, and they had been tasked with assessing Dennis' qualifications to be a partner. He obviously passed their test. Dennis later went on to do great things at PwC. Dennis counseled me often, and I actually counseled him on occasion. He was a mentor to me, and someone who connected me to a number of significant career opportunities. We also worked together on some of the most complex situations in my career. He always helped when I needed it, and I am forever grateful.

In this chapter and throughout this book, there are countless examples of situations wherein I was mentored or where I mentored someone myself—it's part of my DNA. I've also found that it is a phenomenon that particularly permeates high-performance teams, wherein all team members are invested in the success of their peers.

I once thought the inclination to mentor someone was just human nature—and I still think that to some extent it is—but I have learned over the years that there are dramatic differences in how people view the topic. Some view it as a "light touch": they may step in and help a mentee once or twice in specific circumstances. Others (like myself) view it as a long-term commitment. To me, someone I consider to be a mentee is someone I help, nurture, and support for most of their lives—including a healthy dose of "tough love" when needed. Real mentors give life- and career-changing advice. They may open doors that would otherwise not be open. They may accelerate the accumulation of experience.

When it came time to become a mentor myself, I found that mentoring was something I was naturally drawn to, but also a way of repaying the kindness I'd been shown over the years: I couldn't adequately repay my mentors, so I pay it forward, doing for others what they have done for me.

So how would I pick my mentees? The true answer was in a lot of different ways. I always respected and gravitated toward people who were hard-working and who wanted to excel at what they did—those who wanted to be the best they could be. When I saw someone like this, I tended to try to help them. I would meet these people in all sorts of ways and all different kinds of circumstances:

some were young staff, others more seasoned partners in my firm; some were new members of one of my teams, others not on my team at all; some thought they knew exactly what to do, others were concerned that they didn't; some looking for help, and yes, some not looking for any help at all.

To me, mentoring is a 24/7 undertaking. Yes, you can set up meetings, lunches, or formal calls, but the magic comes when the mentor and mentee trust each other and reach out when needed. As I mentioned earlier, "when needed" could be as infrequently as once a year or as regularly as twice a day depending on the circumstances. Also, mentors need to know their mentees well enough to give input even when not asked for it—sort of like preemptive advice. I do it all the time with those I mentor, including my children.

By the way, "mentoring" is not just a business term: it's a *life* term. As an example, I am very involved with Fordham University and Cardinal Hayes High School in the South Bronx, and I mentor many students and alumni from both schools. Again, my criteria are usually (but not always) students who are hard-working and want to excel at what they do. At Hayes, some of these students are outstanding basketball players on our nationally-ranked team.

So, what exactly do I do? Let me give a few real examples. I will refer to them as my "guys." I often say when asked about someone I mentor that he or she is "one of my guys."

Guy Number 1

He is connected to Cardinal Hayes but did not attend the school. He graduated from college and became a New York City grammar school teacher, though he was a basketball player through college and had always wanted to be a trainer. Guy Number 1 came from a challenged background, with not a lot of experience in business or finance. This notwithstanding, he wanted to start a training business. He and I talk about everything—life *and* business—and

I have helped in several ways. The highest impact however has been around financial matters and starting a business. He is definitely one of my guys.

Guy Number 2

Guy Number 2 was a young woman with Coopers & Lybrand when they merged with Price Waterhouse in 2000. I was asked to run the combined Technology, Infocom, Entertainment, and Media practice. Guy Number 2 was identified by me as an up-and-coming young partner from the C&L side. I set up a meeting. We discussed career and life matters, hit it off, and the rest is history. I followed her career closely, and she would consult with me whenever she wanted to by telephone, meeting, lunch, or long dinner. My role as mentor was to advise on career moves and to be her supporter when needed. In this particular case, my help included guiding her through parts of PwC, particularly in connecting and collaborating with some of our partners and leadership whom she did not know. She was and has been very successful, and is definitely one of my guys.

Guys Number 3 and Number 4

In my last seven years with PwC, I was asked among many other things to stabilize certain matters in Russia. As part of that undertaking, I met and befriended many partners in our Russian firm. I mentored and helped many of them, but I had significant involvement with two of them who were Americans. I certainly helped their careers in Russia, and I worked closely with both: one with their business in the Russian market, and the other with the Olympic Movement and specifically the Sochi Olympics. In both cases, I was instrumental in getting them admitted as partners in the PwC U.S. firm and getting transferred back to the U.S. They were both my guys.

Partner Candidates

A significant area where my mentoring had a particular impact was with our PwC staff who ultimately got admitted to the PwC partnership. I mentored many of these staff members for years, before *and* after they made partner. Many were females and/or minorities. Most were gathering extensive experience (including international experience), and I was active in consulting with them and then assisting in making opportunities happen. Most that succeeded were those who seized the opportunities when they arose.

One interesting aside is that generally most mentees grossly exaggerate the help their mentor has given them, in some cases claiming to be "blown away" by the help they're given. That said, the right help given at the right time can certainly change their careers and maybe their lives.

As is readily apparent from my discussion of the people who were instrumental in my success in business and my life more generally, most of my mentors were men. When I was coming up in the business world, few women were serving in executive roles at PwC and the C-Suites of our clients. While there is still a long road ahead and I know many challenges remain, I am thrilled to have witnessed and to have been part of a sea change in this regard during my career. The reason for this is simple: many of the best and brightest in any field are women, and given access and opportunity, they succeed. All they really need are opportunities to gain necessary experience and help in building their networks.

In my quest to build and lead high-performing teams over the years, I recognized the presence of some incredibly talented women and I worked to include them on my teams. I was never disappointed. A key to truly high-performing teams is diversity—of background, culture, experience, thought, skills, and perspective—and this includes gender diversity. As more and more women joined the ranks of our firm and our clients, they added immeasurably to the strength and success of our collective work. I was glad for the chance and proud to mentor and work alongside many enormously talented, high-performing women, and to see them flourish in their business careers.

In fact, some of the most successful people I have known in business happen to be women, and many of them remain friends to this day.

The world keeps turning. Now, when I lecture to undergraduate and graduate business students at Fordham University, over 50% of them are women. These smart young people—women and men—fill me with optimism for the future.

Let me flip the mirror now.

How do you get a mentor?

Identifying someone who you think would make a good mentor and then getting introduced is always a good way to do it. If done this way, it will either stick or not stick; there is a bit of chemistry needed to make it work. It always helps to try to begin the relationship as soon as possible. Going back to how I selected a mentee, I strongly recommend that you do a great job for the person you are working for and show a high degree of motivation. In my experience, once you get their attention, the rest will happen naturally.

If you're consistently focused on putting your best foot forward, you will more than likely find yourself in a mentorship situation. This occurs most often through working together with a prospective mentor, but also by meeting and interacting in some other setting. In most of my relationships, I personally chose the person who I would later mentor, but in some cases, people came to me with introductions: "Martha told me I should speak to you," "Gabriella told me I should try to get you as my counselor," "My father who worked with you told me I should connect with you," "I heard you were a good guy to know to get advice"—you get the picture. As I mentioned earlier, I am of the belief that people are naturally inclined to want to help those they can, and so simply approaching them with the aim of learning is a good place to start.

Also, getting a good reputation for being a high performer or an "up-and-comer" tends to draw people to you, some of whom may become mentors. When trying to identify those who would be good mentors, you will usually be led to certain leaders or executives who are known for this skill. Once you identify them, try to get their attention—either directly or through your network. I also recommend you be direct about wanting to connect: you're selling yourself in these exchanges, and if the sale isn't going to work, you'll want to know sooner rather than later so that you can move on and try someone else. This said, if you're direct, motivated, and authentic, few will turn you down.

Chapter 17

WORK-LIFE BALANCE

Work-life balance is a very complex but important area. It is one that will have a significant impact on your career and your life, and thus, an area that needs your attention. Understanding it and dealing with it will be critical to a happy life and a successful career. This chapter, like all of them, reflects my experience and my views based on the evidence I have seen. This topic, however, is the kind of stuff that psychologists and psychiatrists counsel on often, and I am not one of them.

I started at PwC as an intern in 1972, and then went full-time in 1973. Jobs were difficult to come by, and I didn't come from money. As a consequence, I was not very focused on work-life balance; I was more or less just focused on work. There actually was a saying back then—"You worked hard, and you played hard." It was kind of a Wall Street thing, but it also described how I lived.

As times and priorities change, I learned that one's view of work-life balance changes too. This is 100% true. What is not 100% certain is how and why it changes.

Work-Life Balance for Me

Work-life balance is a really personal thing. It is different for each and every person, and changes for that person on an individual basis over time. This is to say what one person considers a healthy work-life balance is not what another person considers a healthy work-life balance. Said another way, the same work-life ingredients can mean balance to one person and imbalance to another.

I remember that years ago, models of work-life balance were published and disseminated to employees by organizations, including PwC. I don't know for certain, but I bet they were based on academic studies that were flawed. I remember us all being encouraged to take weekends off and to make sure that our people did as well. We were encouraged to take our vacation in the summer and to take full advantage of national holidays. To the same point, overtime was not considered a good thing.

There were even things that "everyone knew," such as how long was too long to be away from home, or other more personal things that were kind of decided for you because "everyone knew" they would cause imbalance.

Let me start with myself. Balance for me had five distinct areas, each applying in force at different points during my career and based on major developments in my life. The first applied during my early days before I was married, the second was when I was married with no kids, the third was when I had my kids, the fourth was when I was working while the kids were in college and out of college, and the fifth was post-PwC. Each of these was also defined by high-level goals that I had, and later, that I'd agreed upon with my wife. An example of this was when I decided I wanted to be a partner at PwC. We discussed the pros and cons of that journey and agreed to go for it.

Early Days – 6 years

My focus was on doing well in my role at my firm, making a name for myself, learning as much as I could as fast as I could, meeting and connecting with as many people as I could, and getting promoted as fast as possible. Overtime and hard work didn't bother me, and in fact, I viewed the tough stuff as giving me the best experience. My view was to never say no to an opportunity, and I tried to get as much experience as I could as quickly as I could. In my opinion, my personal life was great, although looking back, I think I was probably a bit sleep-deprived, but I didn't know it.

Married, with No Kids – 8 years

This period was similar to the early days, except it started with a three-year tour in Milan, where both my wife and I had a great time. We were both really busy for different reasons, though despite that, we saw most of Europe and Italy over the three years, were visited by family and friends constantly, and became even closer to each other. This last point was the result of being each other's go-to person. This remained true even after we came back to the U.S. Obviously, my definition of balance took into consideration what was important to my wife. It also, however, included what we both decided I needed to do to achieve our joint objectives.

Married, with Kids – 18 years

Kids really do change everything. At this point, work-life balance was determining what I needed to do for my wife and kids, who came first above all else. That said, I then had to work around those things to get my job done. If you can picture 24/7 with spaces for wife, kids, sleep, and a little bit of personal time, you will get a good picture of how I managed it. It was important to me to make it to most of my children's games and important events. I didn't care that I had to do work at five a.m. on Saturday or Sunday as long as it meant that

I had time for the personal stuff. Also, both of my children greatly benefited from international travel as a result of my job, which somewhat compensated for some of the games and events that I was forced to miss.

Kids In and Out of College – 9 years

I remember learning quickly that while your kids are away at college, they really don't want you to visit every weekend; once or twice a year is fine. I also found that after college, they will visit you more often for various reasons. By the way, as my kids were growing up, we created reasons to get together as a family. These included visits to Disney World, ski trips, trips to the Caribbean, a family beach house in Rhode Island, and New York Giants season tickets.

During this period, finding balance became much more flexible for many reasons. I did have two very demanding jobs, but also world-class teams to support me. It also was a period when I traveled more than 70% of the time, but I got to bring my wife (and in a few cases, even my kids) with me. I also was able to occasionally mix business with pleasure, and tack a personal vacation onto a business trip.

Post-PwC – 10 years

Post-PwC, my work-life balance is completely different. I am involved with several companies and not-for-profits, but I have a significant amount of flexibility in my time, location, and the types of things I am doing. I can often work from home or the beach or NYC or wherever I want. I don't travel the way I used to, but I still travel a fair amount, usually for a week or more, and to places I choose.

Final Observation

I outlined my view of balance to allow you to benchmark yourself against me. I know your view of balance will be different. I know my children's view of balance is different from their father's. My point here was actually to raise it as a topic for you to focus on, and to focus on what it means to you and your family, how it fits into your career plans, and how it is likely to change over time.

An Almeida Point: Nothing In Life Is Free

EVERYTHING HAS CONSEQUENCES. FOR EVERY PRO, THERE IS USUALLY A CON. WHEN YOU SET YOUR OBJECTIVES AND GOALS, THERE WILL BE REWARDS IF THEY ARE ACHIEVED, BUT ALSO SACRIFICES YOU WILL HAVE TO MAKE. IT IS UP TO YOU AND YOU ALONE TO DECIDE WHAT CHOICES YOU SHOULD MAKE. EVERYTHING IN YOUR LIFE AND CAREER WILL COME AT A COST, AND I URGE YOU TO CONSULT WITH THOSE CLOSE TO YOU AS YOU CHOOSE WHICH ARE WORTH PAYING.

One more story...

For whatever reason, I know several up-and-coming executives who are both triathletes and also married with young children. For the record, I work out regularly, and exercising to maintain a healthy body and mind is something I believe in. Every day, I do an hour-long workout or a round of golf, and sometimes both.

I have discussed with these up-and-coming executives that they essentially have three full-time jobs: their career, their spouse and young family, and their triathlon preparation. The career is extensive and six to seven days a week, the triathlon preparation is six to seven days a week for months before each event, and time dedicated to family can be a range of 24/7 to zero—your choice. I have counseled each of them that if they want to excel at any of their aims, they need to pick just two. Doing all three will almost guarantee that you will fail, or at least sub-optimize one or potentially all of these commitments. I have seen this happen many times.

I use the triathlete example here, but it can be almost anything. If you are career-minded and have a family, your third and fourth priorities need to be carefully selected. Some can fit into your schedule almost anytime, like golf, tennis, running, fishing, etc. Even these, however, can become your triathlon. Some golfers I know play all the time and travel around the world to play.

HOW TO BE THE BEST: ADVANCED CONCEPTS

Chapter 18

LEADERSHIP

"Leadership is not about titles, positions, or flow charts. It is about one life influencing another."

— John C. Maxwell

This is a very big and important topic. There have been many books written on it, and I will only devote a chapter. Interestingly, I have found that many of these books were written by academics who themselves are not great leaders or even leaders at all. Some of these books were also written by businesspeople who were notoriously bad leaders. You can take this fact or opinion for what it's worth.

There is a view that leadership can be learned, but not taught. I strongly believe that this is true. I also believe that, for whatever reason, there is a relatively small percentage of true leaders. The quote about leadership not being about titles is so very true. Over the years, I would promote people to leadership roles, and I would always say: "I can put you in the job, but the people who you lead will determine whether you keep it." In a few cases, this was followed by a long conversation about what I meant, and at that point, I had the first indication that I may have made the wrong choice. I almost never had.

Leadership is a key component—and a *very* key component at that—to being the best. It is often the thing missing in many that are good that prevents them from being truly great. Unfortunately, many cannot, for whatever reason, become great leaders, and some cannot become leaders at all; the qualities that make a leader are simply not in everyone's DNA. The reverse is also true; I'm sure you have heard yourself or someone else described as a "born leader." I have seen this many times, and it often becomes evident in people at a young age. In *Building Your Experience and Profile (and Resume)*, I gave examples of leadership positions that could differentiate you. These most often occur with born leaders. If you are a born leader, you naturally have many of the core components of being a great leader. It does not mean you *will* be, but that you *can* be—usually with a lot of hard work and experience.

When I look back, I can think of many examples of times that great leaders helped me in my journey. They taught me much about life and leadership, both as mentors and friends.

I also see examples of non-leaders: typical managers, micromanagers, and bad managers, and I've even learned from them. Most were good people who were doing their best in a difficult world, focused on working to live and support their families. I supported them in every way I could. Luckily for me, in most cases, I observed from afar and did not have to work for them. We all know what they are like; they tended to focus only on themselves and their immediate area of responsibility. If you put together the list of attributes of a true leader, they might have some, but not many. They typically do not view their jobs as supporting the people who work for them, instead treating them exclusively as means to their own ends.

The worst of the worst are the micro-managers. They need to make every decision—because no one can do it as well as them—and usually surround themselves with "yes people." On their teams, they take credit for every positive development while blaming others for every setback, and in either case, are likely to belittle the other members of the team—progress is made "despite them," and shortcomings occur "because of them." This model, in almost all aspects, is the opposite of the true leadership model.

In my case, I believe I was fortunate to be born with leadership genes (thanks to my parents). I was also fortunate to be presented with opportunities (in leadership roles and otherwise) that both honed my leadership skills and taught me new skills. What *really* elevated my ability, however, was the influence of the true leaders who mentored and worked with me throughout my career. These were people at PwC, as well as those I worked alongside at clients thereof. At PwC, the list includes many of the partners I reported to and worked alongside, whom I cannot name. They also included many members of my leadership teams over the years, as well as my peers who were the lead partners on the major PwC clients globally. I had the honor and the privilege to work for them and with them, and I learned a lot from each of them. I owe each of them a large measure of gratitude.

I have thought long and hard about the attributes of all great leaders. So, here it goes. All great leaders have the following seventeen attributes: they are trustworthy, confident, generous, focused, passionate, inspiring, authentic, open-minded, decisive, people persons, able to empower, optimistic, persistent, insightful, good communicators, accountable, and restless.

I have tried to put these attributes in order of importance but cannot decide what order is best, though I'm sure that honesty, confidence, and generosity are high on the list. Regardless, it is of critical importance that an aspiring leader demonstrates all of these qualities, and they each have nuances in how they apply specifically in the context of leadership. So, how to start? I decided to begin each section with one of my favorite quotes to introduce the topic. These quotes will, I hope, frame my view of the very complex art and science of being a leader, and each of the qualities and skills thereof. I may not agree 100% with every word of the quote, and I may not even be a fan of those I am quoting. I do strongly believe, however, in the substance of each quote.

TRUSTWORTHY

"There is a difference between being a leader and being a boss.
Both are based on authority. A boss demands blind obedience; a
leader earns his authority through understanding and trust."
— Klaus Balkenhol

Being trustworthy is at the core of all great leaders. It is imperative that the members of a team trust the person who is leading them, and thus leaders must be honest and have high integrity. This is non-negotiable. The bottom line is that someone is either honest or they are not—*period*—and everyone will quickly draw their own conclusions as to whether he/she is trustworthy or not. As such, it is imperative that leaders are honest *always*, even when honesty means being blunt, or might create less-than-comfortable situations.

If you are not trusted, no one will follow you. If you are, your team will follow you even if they do not know exactly where you are going, and even if they don't believe the goal or objective is achievable. If they trust you, they will put their careers in your hands; they will put themselves in unpredictable situations if you tell them it will be ok; they will be willing to take a risk because they believe you when you say "We're in it together."

CONFIDENT

"Sooner or later, those who win are those who think they can."
— Richard Bach

All great leaders are confident. The dictionary defines "confidence" as *"the state of feeling certain about the truth of something"* and *"a feeling of self-assurance arising from one's appreciation of one's abilities."* Being meek, mild, and insecure are not attributes of great leaders.

When I look back on my career, I remember facing significant challenges at just about every stage. That said, I cannot remember ever thinking I could not do it—whatever it was. Never once! I had faith in not just my own ability, but in the world-class resources and teams I had at my back. I am pretty sure most viewed me as confident, both within PwC and while working with clients at all levels. There were definitely some who viewed me as overly confident, but I never viewed myself that way. Maybe they were right and I was wrong, but what I've learned from decades of experience in and under leadership roles is that teams will not follow you unless you are confident and have proven your confidence is well-placed by prior successes.

GENEROUS

> *"Real leadership is leaders recognizing that they serve the people they lead."*
>
> — Pete Hoekstra

Generosity is an interesting attribute, but it is one that all great leaders have. Great leaders focus on their people, and in particular, on making them successful. The significant nuance here is that true leadership is not about managing the people who report to you, but uplifting those you have been entrusted to lead so that they may find success individually and as a team. To be successful as a leader, you must take care of your team first, and in every sense of the word. Generosity—and that which is viewed by the team as being generous—is in fact what creates great teams, and even contributes to the construction of high-performing teams. As a leader, you must ensure that as the pie gets bigger, each team member gets a bigger slice.

FOCUSED

"Leaders think and talk about solutions. Followers think and talk about the problems."

— Brian Tracy

I used to (and still do) say "Focus, focus, focus." All leaders have objectives, but *great* leaders are those who continually focus on achieving them. It is then the responsibility of the leader not to simply possess this focus themselves but to share it in a way that is well-communicated and well-defined, such that it is in turn well-understood by the team and thus becomes the foundation for a sense of purpose shared by all.

PASSIONATE

"Average leaders raise the bar on themselves; good leaders raise the bar for others; great leaders inspire others to raise their own bar."
— Orrin Woodward

When I was leaving PwC, some twenty-five partners from around the world were asked on video to share one word that described me. About twenty of them said "passion" or "passionate"—one actually said "passionate about everything," though what I think he meant to say was "passionate about everything Don thought was important." Regardless, I believe this word describes me well: if I thought something was important, I went for it lock, stock, and barrel. This could be people-related, client-related, or firm-related. I was on a mission to get it done or get it fixed, and you could see and feel the passion.

I also learned early on that passion can be contagious, and further, that passion coupled with generosity, confidence, and being trusted was magic. The bad news is that the opposite of passion—indifference—is equally contagious. If you are passionate about something, you are positioned to get others on board. If you and your high-performing team are passionate, then great things can happen.

INSPIRATIONAL

> *"A good leader leads the people from above them. A great leader leads the people from within them."*
>
> — M.D. Arnold

All great leaders are inspirational. In many cases, this is achieved by way of the leader sharing their vision with their team in a compelling way. This can be through their words in one-on-one conversations or larger meetings, or through their action and conduct in directing the team and pursuing their overall objectives, but always with confidence, passion, and a good measure of optimism.

We have all heard inspirational communicators at one time or another, and know what impact they can have.

AUTHENTIC

"Leadership is not about titles, positions, or flow charts. It is about one life influencing another."

— John C. Maxwell

Authenticity is an important trait of being a great leader. To me, being authentic is a way of life: either you are or you are not. Some find it easy to be, and others find it impossible. I always got the feeling that everyone thought they were authentic even if they were not, but where a team is concerned, let there be no doubt about it: everyone knows whether you are authentic or not, especially those you work alongside. Authenticity, I believe, also helps you be trusted.

OPEN-MINDED

"The greatest leader is not necessarily the one who does the greatest things. He is the one that gets the people to do the greatest things."

— Ronald Reagan

I will say upfront that I believe I am truly open-minded. That is not to say that I do not hold strong and, in some cases, passionate opinions—I do. That said, I am always in search of a better way, a smarter way, or a quicker way. If we disagree (and I respect you), I will listen to you explain your position for as long as it takes to reach a resolution. As I've mentioned, I was in charge of PwC's technology practice for a number of years (pre-bubble and post-bubble, for the history buffs or those old enough to remember), and so I come from the tech mindset: change is inevitable, and it's better to be a leader than a follower. In today's world, you are either a disrupter or you are disrupted.

Leaders for many reasons need to be open-minded and need to be viewed as such. Making sure your team feels like their ideas will be heard and respected leads to more new ideas from your teams, and may even develop a reputation of you being progressive or a "change agent."

DECISIVE

> *"Indecision and delays are the parents of failure."*
>
> — George Canning

Being decisive means being able to make decisions quickly and effectively. This attribute defines a very small part of the population. It is, however, key to all good leaders. In my experience, there are two types of people at the extremes. On one side are those who, having 95% of the information, are in continual search for the remaining 5%. They can never make a decision. At the other extreme are those who make a decision when they get 51% of the information. I am much closer to the second group than the first.

For those of you in the first group: not making a decision is deciding to do nothing. This is, in and of itself, a decision. In my experience, not making a decision is usually viewed by the indecisive person as lower risk. In actuality, depending on the circumstances, it may not be.

In my career, I would tend to make decisions quickly. Despite not having all the information, in my view, they were informed decisions based on experience. I would always consider the risk of being wrong alongside our ability to quickly pivot if we were wrong. I also had the view that we should always try new things. If they did not work, we could change and not do them again. Obviously, the order of magnitude needed to be considered. I remember calling things "pilots"—a seemingly simple label that made it okay to fail, as we were only trying it out.

PEOPLE PERSON

"You manage things; you lead people."
— Grace Murray Hopper

It's always all about people, so naturally being a people person is a big advantage. Why do I say it this way? Well, I have found there are different types of "person people." There is the one-on-one, the one-to-a-few, the one-to-many, and in a few rare cases, the one-to-millions. While there is some overlap between these, each of the four constitutes a unique communication skill (set) in and of itself. I have found that the best leaders align with at least the first three—most don't actually get the opportunity to practice the fourth. I, for one, am pretty good with the first three. I have never actually tried the one-to-millions.

I also believe that some of the other seventeen attributes also connect here, and in a big way: certainly, being passionate, inspirational, generous, and authentic do. Being a people person is also all about soft skills like empathy and compassion.

I know great leaders who are uncomfortable one-on-one and even in small groups. I view this as a disadvantage to being a great leader, but not necessarily a deal-breaker. One or two of these individuals rose to high levels because they had most but not all of the seventeen attributes and were very good communicators to big groups. For them, their style worked and was effective.

ABLE TO EMPOWER

> *"I start with the premise that the function of leadership is to produce more leaders not more followers."*
>
> — Ralph Nader

All great leaders pick great teams, empower each member, and stay out of their way unless they ask for help. A team made up of empowered individuals is key to exceptional performance and contrasts sharply with the management style of the dreaded micromanager.

In my career, I found it very easy and natural to empower great people and great teams—I knew empowerment would always make the result better. Whenever anyone would want my opinion on the best way to go about something, I would give some high-level guidance and maybe point out some pitfalls, but would always end up saying "Never give me what I ask for, give me what I want," and thereby give my team license to deviate from any specific instructions in pursuit of achieving the goal to the fullest. In some cases, I was not sure what was in the realm of the doable, but I was never disappointed.

Also exemplary were the instances when leaders who were on my teams wanted to go in a certain direction, and came to me for approval, support, or funding. I always said yes, and almost always on the spot. I might have asked them to reduce phase one or take a little less funding, but I always said yes. Why? The fact was that in every instance I knew they had done their homework and had put together a conservative business case. I also trusted their judgment. My saying "yes" on the spot was empowering for them: they knew that I trusted their acumen, and it also made them 100% responsible for the results.

A key to empowerment is that you do not get in the way of the team's efforts, but it is clear to everyone that if they need help, you will give it no matter what.

Also, a prerequisite of empowerment is the alignment of expectations between the leader and the team. Ironically, teams that are not empowered will usually report bad news only when there is no other choice. Empowered teams will ask for help before it is too late, and in my experience, often before they need it.

OPTIMISTIC

> *"Don does things that are not possible to do. When we tell him it's impossible, he says, 'I know it's impossible, but if it were possible, how could we do it?' And then we just do it!"*
> — a global government leader at PwC, speaking at my
> retirement party.

I'm sure you have heard the adage that some say the glass is half-empty and others say the glass is half-full. I am a "half-full" guy. Always. I have a sales and client service mentality. I learned years ago that there are very few problems that cannot be solved if you put enough smart people in a room. I also worked with several clients over the years with CEOs who were "can do" types—I once heard the phrase "blacken the skies with airplanes if necessary" when I told the CEO that the planned project may not be able to be done in the hoped-for timeframe.

The quote above is from one of the most global people with whom I've ever worked. His words resonated with me for two main reasons:

The first is because I believe what he said about me was true, and maybe even funny in an ironic sense. Obviously, I did not personally or with a team "perform the impossible." That cannot be done. What I *did* do, however, were things that others *thought* were impossible. In the end, I was right and they were wrong. An example of this was getting something important changed in our organization—a modification that had been attempted multiple times before without success. How did I do it? By getting the key decision-makers to change their views, and see that change was necessary. This required them to take a risk, so I needed to convince them that the risk was manageable and the potential reward was significant. I also had to have their trust. This last point was the key.

The second is because I really did not like people telling me why we could not do something that I viewed to be in the best interest of our people, our clients, or my firm. Not a day went by that I did not hear "This is impossible" or "That is impossible." It drove me crazy, and everyone on my teams knew it. This was generally the result of managers looking out for their parochial interests without seeing the broader vision for the organization—the greater good, so to speak. This dynamic is true most of the time and in all organizations. It is also supported by the chain of command: "My boss says it's the way it is, and therefore, it is the way it is."

Optimism in a leader is a stabilizing and motivating force. Pessimistic people are "downers," as they say—no one wants to be around pessimists, let alone led by them. All high-performance teams are led by optimistic leaders.

PERSISTENT

> *"It's not that I'm so smart, it's just that I stay with problems longer."*
>
> — Albert Einstein

Persistence is a trait of all good leaders. One of my qualities is that once I decide to do something, I become laser-focused on the target. I am, as I would say, on a mission. I have found that this quality of focus is how big things (and little things, for that matter) get accomplished. Persistence is particularly important (and beats out pure focus) when the objective is to be pursued over a longer period. The team needs to see the leader focused on the stated objective and "staying on message" until the aim has been achieved.

INSIGHTFUL

"A leader takes people where they would never go on their own."
— Hans Finzel

Great leaders have a vision and see things before others, even those on the team, can see them—I call it being "visual." They consider questions like "What will it take to get there?"; "What will success look like?"; "How will we run it?"; "Who will be on the team?"; "What skills will be necessary?"; "How long will it take?"; "How much will it cost?"; "What is the revenue potential?"; and "What industries will benefit most?" without being asked, and think about how these variables will interact with the team's strategy at a high level.

This is a trait not unique to leaders: very often team members can be just as insightful as their leaders.

GOOD COMMUNICATOR

"The challenge of leadership is to be strong but not rude; be kind, but not weak; be bold, but not a bully; be humble, but not timid; be proud, but not arrogant; have humor, but without folly."
— Jim Rohn

Good communication skills are important in life and business, and unsurprisingly, they are also critical for a leader. On the subject of effective communication, I tell my students to "keep it simple" and "make it clear." For leaders especially, transparency and inclusiveness are important in communications. Be transparent with your team or constituency: make sure they know what is going on in real time and seek their input often. Make them part of the solution—always. Also, make the message honest—don't sugarcoat the problems or difficulties. Even if the situation poses major challenges, the message should be "It's hard, but we will get there as a team."

ACCOUNTABLE

> *"A good leader is a person who takes a little more than his share*
> *of the blame and a little less than his share of the credit."*
>
> — John C. Maxwell

I agree with this quote, except I would say "a lot more of the blame." In my experience, great leaders shoulder the blame and give the credit to the team. What goes around comes around, as they say, and everybody knows who the leader was and what they have done. A key attribute of a bad manager (and certainly not a leader) is that they blame the team when it does not go well.

RESTLESS

> *"Restlessness is discontent, and discontent is the first necessity of*
> *progress. Show me a thoroughly satisfied man, and I will show you*
> *a failure."*
>
> — Thomas A. Edison

I was known for having the patience of a gnat when it came to how fast something could be done. I heard the phrase "do it instantaneously if not sooner" early in my career, and this more or less describes my view of time. One thing I learned in business was that different people in different industries, in different geographies, or under different time pressures would take dramatically different amounts of time to do the same thing. For example, when a proposal came in for new work, we would assemble a global team and put together our proposal in a matter of days. If handled by a different team with different leadership, this process might take weeks or even months to complete. "Faster, better, cheaper" is the direction in which the world is moving, and this is also representative of how great leaders think.

These are the elements that when taken together make for a truly great leader. I have seen each of these qualities in the many great leaders I have been fortunate to encounter in my life and career, and I have tried to embody their values myself. This said, a great leader *does not* need to possess every single one of the above to qualify as "great," but I have found (as I'm sure you will too if you have not already) that they all demonstrate a majority of these qualities.

As I said at the beginning, entire books have been written on the topic of leadership. Here, I have tried to deal with the topic in a more condensed way. I have also tried to give some insights into areas I think are important. It is obvious even in this short chapter that leadership is a complex area with a number of moving parts. I have tried to highlight only those that I think are mission-critical.

An Almeida Point: Measuring Your Leadership

HAVING CONFIDENCE THAT YOU ARE A GREAT LEADER IS IMPORTANT, BUT IT IS NOT THE BENCHMARK BY WHICH LEADERS ARE JUDGED. THE BENCHMARK IS WHAT OTHERS THINK OF YOUR LEADERSHIP, AND HOW YOUR TEAM VIEWS YOU. IF THEY VIEW YOU AS A GREAT LEADER, THEN YOU MUST BE. IF THEY DON'T, THEN HOW COULD YOU POSSIBLY ARGUE

OTHERWISE? THE NUMBER OF GREAT LEADERS YOU HELP CREATE, GUIDE, AND MENTOR IS ALSO A BENCHMARK OF YOUR LEADERSHIP AND A KEY PART OF YOUR LEGACY.

Chapter 19

RELATIONSHIPS

TRUSTED RELATIONSHIPS

Trusted relationships are the most important, impactful, valuable, powerful, empowering, reliable, transformational, and helpful relationships you can have either in life or business. They are the ones you can count on, and that you can forecast. That is to say that you know they are 100% reliable, and if you come to them with questions or for support, you know what the answer or action will be. These relationships very often exist between family members and between friends who have known each other since childhood.

To have a trusted relationship, you must be trusted. To be trusted, you must be trustworthy, and demonstrate it all the time—no exceptions! I would say this in business, and many times it would get a laugh and a sarcastic "Oh yeah, right!" After some discussion, however, it was clear that this standard is very often not met by those who think they should be trusted. This is to say that many people—maybe even most—cannot be trusted using this definition.

There are many examples of this, but most revolve around people not doing what they say, or even what they promise to do. It also takes the form of people doing the things that they promise *not* to do. This includes things like when you were looking for a job and they offered to help but did not even try; when they offered to write your son or daughter a letter of recommendation to a college they were involved with but did not; when they offered to make an introduction for you to someone they knew well, but did not; or when they guaranteed their A-team would be put on a project you gave to them, but it was not. Even worse, when you called them out on it in any of these cases, they still did not hold up their end.

I talk about trust in connection with building high-performance teams and in creating networks and global networks—it's a key element in both. Trust is also key in leadership: your team and networks need to have a high level of faith in what you say and what you will do. This always starts with you, but over time—and not a long time—it transfers to them. They trust you. They see what that means. You in turn learn to trust them. This is at all levels—in your relationships with those whom you report to, your peers, those who report to you, and those whom you lead but do not report to you, trust is *always* key.

To gain trust is difficult, but to lose it is easy. Said differently, to gain trust takes time and clear demonstration of why you should be trusted, but to lose it takes only one mistake. Once trust is lost, it can (almost) never be regained. That said, if you are trustworthy, this one mistake will never happen.

One other important concept on this topic is that trustworthiness is not something that can be taught—except maybe at a young age and typically by your family. It is either built into your DNA and a core value or it is not. If it is not, I can only recommend you try to change. I, however, cannot help you.

So why have I included this topic as a chapter? Because it has a huge impact on being the best, in creating networks, including global networks, in selling and delivering big deals or transactions or making big sales, in building, sustaining, and leveraging high-performance teams, and ultimately in being a true leader.

If I look back on my career, at the core of my success was a small group of attributes, including being trusted. I was (in my view) trustworthy: it came across quickly in everything I did, and it quickly became an attribute I was known for all over the world. It was not something I thought about or prepared for or worked on—I just was! I think I owe this to my parents and how they brought me up, and it has served me well. Some may not have liked me, but I believe even they trusted me. This may sound odd to you, but even those who did not like me knew I would keep my word and do what I had committed to.

I have mentioned that I teach at Fordham and lecture on Global Business. At every first class and lecture, I will mention at some point this concept of trust. I will also lead a discussion of what it means and how you get it. When I talk about my global network, I reference trust and I always say that I have concluded that "gaining trust may require some different approaches based on local customs, but after you have trust, everyone's the same." This is to say that the starting point for developing trust may be different in each country—and even with each person—and that local customs may slow it down or accelerate it, but in the end, all trusted relationships operate in the same way.

To pick an extreme, there are countries where trusted relationships outside the family are rare, or even nonexistent. This is typically due to historical reasons, usually related to poverty and/or the "everyone for themselves" mentality which existed in the country. In these situations, I found that the skepticism goes away after two or three promises are met. After you demonstrate that you are worthy of their trust, you are trusted for life. You also usually gain an ally and a friend, and a strong one at that!

In these cases, I can remember doing business in a country and having a trusted friend there to explain to me over dinner why I could not trust someone we were about to do business with, citing this person's country of origin. I was surprised by this, and remarked to my friend that he himself was from the same country as the person he was warning me about. His response was "Yes, but I am different." I often wondered whether my friend considered *me* an exception to his rule. Said differently, if *I* could trust him, but other people could not. I knew at least three countries where this was true.

Let's also look at the outcomes of being trusted.

Any good salesperson can sell a product or service that costs $100. They may even be able to sell ones that cost $1,000. This usually does not really require trust, but trust does help even here. On the other hand, to sell a product or service for $1 million, $20 million, $50 million, or $100 million requires trust, and at a high level. If I buy a service for $20 million, I have to have 100% trust that the seller will deliver on all promises and that all the expectations that have been set will be met—all the time and every time. In many cases, someone's position or job may be on the line should things go south. If the project is not delivered on time, or if a mistake is made, there will be consequences.

If you offer someone a job on your team, they will usually say yes if you are trusted. If it is risky—like a position that operates in a new division of a company or even a new company altogether—and you recommend it, they will take it nonetheless. This is because they trust that you would not recommend it unless you thought the venture would work out, and that you also thought the position would be good for their career. Further, their faith in you means that they know that if things don't work out, you will help get them another position.

When I was putting together my core team after I was asked to lead our technology practice, I approached a number of people with offers for very specific roles. I approached one by saying "I need you as a key member of my team, but I don't know yet what the exact position will be. We'll work it out, and all I can tell you right now is that it will be challenging and we'll have fun." Despite the glaring lack of information, the person took the offer on faith. They became a key member of the team and got promoted to managing director.

Being trusted is just as relevant when dealing with members of your global network. Take the proposal process for new work, for example: even if the economics of the particular deal you're offering initially appear not good for them, they'll still engage immediately because they trust that you will make it fair. No lengthy negotiations, just action. To maintain this level of trust, you then need to make it fair. In my experience, that could be done on the current deal or the next deal—having a relationship that was built on trust meant that each party was confident that everything would be made right when all was said and done. In this way, you are actually making your global network stronger than the local group that comprises your primary reporting line. This is very difficult to do and requires the highest level of trust.

I hate to say this, and you can judge for yourselves, but I found that an outcome of being trusted is that you tend to be considered the exception, not the rule. I never really understood why this was the case, but I found it to be true. It was even true when I was giving negative feedback. This was normally done in a way where the other person could make changes and push back if they so chose. In many, if not most cases, what was initially a negative reaction to "criticism" turned into a satisfied "thanks for being candid," or even "thanks for helping me get promoted" when the advice I'd given led to advancement or similar outcomes.

This concept of trust seemed to make me a magnet for those who wanted trusted advice. Whether they liked what I had to say or not, they trusted that I was being honest and that I was trying to help them.

In business, if you are known for being good, knowing your business, making good decisions, taking reasonable risks, and you are trusted, then anything and everything is possible.

LONG-TERM RELATIONSHIPS

I should have said this before, so let me be clear now: you cannot have a relationship with someone you have never met! I already know your reactions. One-third of you thought, "Why say that? It's so obvious!" One-third thought, "Of course you can! Why would anyone think you can't?" And one-third thought, "I think in some cases you can and in some cases you can't."

A quick aside: I have witnessed over the last twenty-plus years, as the internet and social media have taken off, that more and more of the younger generations communicate in every way possible except face-to-face. They are even moving away from voice communications—i.e., they do not make very many phone calls. This is a pet peeve of mine and has been for a long time. It is also an area that I have discussed with my kids (young executives). Why send a series of text messages (or whatever) instead of just calling and having a one-minute conversation? It is so much easier and can get you the answer more quickly. I feel better now, so let me move on.

Let's say that a big problem occurs between you and your client (or customer, or friend, or relative, or business associate). The client will generally have one of two reactions:

First reaction: "I can't believe this happened. What a major problem. You took your eye off the ball and weren't paying attention. You used to consider us important and a priority. Obviously, that has changed. This is the last straw. It's time to pick another firm."

Second reaction: "It's certainly a big problem, but anyone can make a mistake. You have been so good for so long. I think we should give you a pass on this one and just move on."

What is the reason for the difference in reactions to the exact same situation or problem? Simple—long-term relationships.

To be clear, I am not speaking here of only social or personal relationships. A long-term relationship in this context is a long-term business relationship, which is a trusted relationship founded on a record of high levels of customer satisfaction. Said differently, the client has very high regard for you, your team, and your firm based on past performance. In many cases, this is also a personal relationship, however, the personal side evolved from the business relationship.

An Almeida Point: Transactions vs. Relationships

WHEN YOU CONSIDER A BUSINESS'S CUSTOMER- OR CLIENT-FACING PEOPLE, THEY CAN USUALLY BE IDENTIFIED AS EITHER "TRANSACTION PEOPLE" OR "RELATIONSHIP PEOPLE." I WAS A RELATIONSHIP PERSON. THESE TWO DESIGNATIONS ARE NOT EXACTLY WELL-DEFINED, AND IN MANY CASES, THEY ARE MORE REFLECTIVE OF A STATE OF MIND THAN A SPECIFIC SET OF CRITERIA.

A **TRANSACTION PERSON** GOES CUSTOMER-TO-CUSTOMER AND SELLS A PARTICULAR PRODUCT OR SERVICE. VERY OFTEN, THEY ARE SELLING THE PRODUCT THEY ARE RESPONSIBLE FOR OR THE SERVICE THEY DELIVER. THEY MAY THINK IN TERMS OF COMING BACK AT A LATER DATE TO SELL ANOTHER PRODUCT, OR EVEN ASKING THE BUYER TO INTRODUCE THEM TO OTHER PEOPLE AT THE COMPANY SO THEY CAN SELL THEIR PRODUCT TO THEM TOO. THEY ARE OBVIOUSLY A REPRESENTATIVE OF THE FIRM THEY ARE ADVERTISING, BUT THEIR FOCUS IS ON WHAT *THEY* SELL, NOT WHAT THE BROADER FIRM SELLS.

A **RELATIONSHIP PERSON** TYPICALLY REPRESENTS THE WHOLE FIRM TO THE CLIENT. THIS PERSON USUALLY SELLS A SPECIFIC PRODUCT OR SERVICE, BUT THEIR JOB IS BROADER THAN THAT, AND THEY, THEIR

CLIENTS, AND THEIR FIRM VIEW THEIR ROLE IN A BROADER CONTEXT.
THEIR RESPONSIBILITY IS TO DEVELOP RELATIONSHIPS WITH ALL KEY
EXECUTIVES ACROSS THE ORGANIZATION, IDENTIFY THEIR PRIORITIES
AND ISSUES, AND DETERMINE HOW THEY AND THE FIRM THEY REPRESENT
CAN BEST HELP.

Now, back to long-term relationships.

Long-term relationships comprise a series of interactions—usually surrounding projects, events, or problems—where value is brought every time and where expectations are always met or exceeded. The strength of the relationship is usually dependent on the significance of the value delivered, the importance of the matters to the client, and the period over which the relationship has lasted thus far. Put plainly, if you are viewed as "the guy who I call when I have a life-or-death problem because I know they can help me fix it," then you have a very strong long-term relationship.

Long-term relationships are also always mutually beneficial. This mutual benefit is usually based on fairness. I remember talking to the CEO of one of our large clients—a relationship that happened to be very profitable for us. This client used our firm for almost everything important to them. Why? Because they knew we would always deliver, and if something was breaking, we would fix it. Period!

In any event, we were talking about the relationship, and he mentioned to me that he knew that his company was a profitable client for us and that that was the way he wanted it. I smiled and asked why that was important to him. I will never forget what he said:

I know you only put your best people on our account, and you do it all over the world. Most of these people ask to be on our account based on our reputation within your firm, and many of these people get promoted quickly. Your best people bring great value for money for us—not just because they are your best, which they are, but also because they have been on the account for a while, they know our company and our people, and they go out of their way to make a difference. If you were losing money on us, you would not be putting your best on the account and the value would not be the same.

This was an extremely insightful comment made by a very smart executive. Although it may not have been 100% correct (we likely would have put the same level of effort forward even if the relationship was not as profitable), it was a good illustration of the mutuality of benefit that existed between our organizations.

I would like to discuss two real-life examples of long-term relationships and real-life examples of what happened. So, let's go.

Example #1

The first was a client of my firm who will remain anonymous—but if I said the name, you would know it. It also involves a chairman who will also remain anonymous, but you would know him too. This was a longstanding client of the firm; over many years, we had collaborated on numerous projects, effectively resolved a variety of issues, and overall, had established a great relationship based on strong mutual respect. As an aside, this was and is a very highly respected company with a very highly respected management team and board. Up until this event occurred, I'd had no personal contact with this client or their management team because the relationship had been handled by other partners in my firm. They get the credit for the long-term relationship.

One day, shortly after I had gotten the position of Vice Chairman, my phone rang, and I was asked to review a major issue that had arisen at this client and to see if I could resolve it for the firm. Suffice it to say that the issue in question was of the "life-or-death" type, and needed to be resolved "instantaneously, if not sooner." It was the type of issue that people got fired over, and one which is hard to fix. I also knew that tensions were high with the client as a result of the issue.

Through our team, I set up meetings with key management at the client's headquarters for the next day. My preference was to meet at the lowest appropriate management level first and work upwards. This was so I could better understand how the issue was being viewed and to get a better feel from my team and the client as to what the viable options might be. I also needed to get a better understanding of where the relationship stood and if there were relationship issues, what they were, and between whom. Unfortunately, I was forced to meet with their chairman first, which I assumed was due to scheduling issues.

We did a team call that night and then had a breakfast meeting the following morning to discuss our view of the situation. I remember being concerned that my meeting with the chairman was a signal that we were going to be fired. I got the impression that we had a huge relationship issue, and my reading of the tea leaves told me it was over communication or lack thereof with our lead partner on the account. It was one of those "and then" conversations: I would ask my team what the worst thing that had happened was, and someone said "Well, there was issue number one... And then there was issue number two... And then there was issue number three..." And then, and then, *and then*. After we'd finished, I couldn't help but conclude that if I were the client, I would fire us!

At nine a.m., I went to meet the chairman. Remember, this is someone fairly famous and probably twenty-plus years my senior. To say I was a bit apprehensive would be an understatement. I had already concluded that we were wrong and that I needed to figure out how to fix it.

His assistant escorted me into his office. I was about five minutes early, and he was on the phone, sitting at his desk. His office was roughly divided into three sections: he had a sofa and two chairs, his desk and two desk chairs, and a conference table with six chairs. He apologized for being on the phone, said he would be right off, and pointed me to the sofa (not at the conference table or in front of his desk). There was a chair to the left of where I was sitting, which is where I assumed he would sit.

Thirty seconds later, he told the person on the phone that he had to go, and that he had a very important partner from PwC who he could not keep waiting. He asked if he could get me some coffee—which I politely refused—and then sat down *right next to me* on the sofa. Remember, he and I had never met before. He started by saying "Don, thanks so much for making the time for us. I know how busy you are. I have heard great things about you, and congratulations on your recent promotion." He then puts his hand on my shoulder and says "Don, my great company and your great firm have been together for years through the good times and the bad. You guys have always been there for us when it counted. Don, you and I have to fix this darn thing, and I know we can." We then went on to discuss what he needed to do and what I needed to do to work through the issue. It was clear he wanted to meet with me one-on-one first so that we could be aligned before I met with his management team.

I have told this story often, and have named names where I could. It's one of those events that you never forget. It was a classic story of a long-term relationship, which can weather the periodic storm.

Example #2

I had a client once—a household name. This particular client and my firm and I shared a long, impactful relationship, which had included ownership changes and complex transactions. Over time, my firm—and particularly myself and my team—had forged a close professional relationship based on the consistent delivery of our commitments. I personally had a trusted professional relationship with all levels of management, including the CEO and CFO. The CEO was a marketer, and the CFO was an operations and finance guy.

One day, I got a call from the VP of Tax informing me that the client had a major tax problem in a large foreign country which would result in the premature payment of a significant amount of tax. He also informed me that the problem had been caused by PwC. He went on to also give me some color around the reaction at the company up to the highest levels, and it was not good. I quickly got the facts: failure to make a certain tax filing had caused tax to become due, and the issue was not whether the tax would ultimately be paid or not, but rather that this error was making payment due five years earlier than it needed to be.

Within an hour of the call from the tax director, my assistant got a call from the CFO's office asking that a lunch be set up for that Friday (two days away) and that the CEO would be joining the CFO and me at lunch. This was extremely unusual, since lunches were typically set up a month or more in advance. Also, it was rare that the CEO would join us for lunch: the normal protocol was that I would visit briefly with the CFO, then meet with the CEO, and then the CFO and I would go to lunch.

This call and its accompanying request certainly got my attention. It triggered a two-day review with our tax experts and the foreign firm involved to do our homework and make me an expert in all available options. I was certain that this was the topic of lunch, and that the size of the pending cash payment had gotten even the CEO's attention. We were able to identify a possible alternative treatment, but it needed more research, so I could not yet hold it out as a solution. Yes, I was a little tense in getting ready for our lunch.

On the appointed day, as was protocol, I went to see the CFO. After normal hellos, he and I went to pick up the CEO and headed to lunch. At that point, I had been in each of their offices for a few minutes and we had been together in their car for the ten-minute ride to the restaurant, but there had been no mention of the tax issue. We had a cordial lunch, and the topic of discussion was not anything related to the error but instead focused on other matters altogether. The urgency of the lunch was not because of a mistake that urgently needed fixing, but because the CEO would be away for a month and wanted to connect with me before he left. We talked about how I could help, and they were both happy with what I could do.

At the end of the lunch, as was customary, the CFO said, "Don, anything on your list?" I said, "No, not really, except I thought you might want to talk about the tax issue." The CEO asked, "What tax issue?" and the CFO said, "No big deal, it's just a timing difference."

Lunch was over, and we went back to the company. As usual, we went to the CFO's office for a final discussion. When his door closed, he looked at me and said "It may be 'just a timing difference,' but it's a big deal. Don't let it happen again, otherwise you guys have a problem."

The point of this example is that the fact that we had a long-term, trusted relationship made the issue not a deal breaker.

I think you get a sense of how important being a relationship guy is to me, and more importantly, how relevant long-term relationships can be to one's success. Just remember, they are based on bringing value every time and always. You want to be the person they call when the chips are down because they trust that you can and will help them fix it.

THE ART OF MANAGING COMPLEX RELATIONSHIPS

All relationships in life are complex. We all intuitively understand this. All relationships are based on personal factors and motivations, the nature of which can vary wildly from person to person.

Qualities of a relationship—things like trust, respect, caring, and mutual benefit—are improved by positive experiences and hurt or even destroyed by negative experiences. If I've said it once, I've said it a thousand times: it takes a long time to gain trust, but trust can be lost in one moment.

In my experience, one's ability to manage complex relationships is very often a significant key to their success. In most cases, one actually must undertake the management of an interconnected series of relationships, all complex, that make up one macro complex relationship.

There are endless examples, but the common thread is the management of several different individuals who make up a group. This could be your family, your bosses, your peers, your team, your client or customer, the C-Suite, a company, or an even larger group like a country, territory, or the whole world! Some of these may seem outrageous at first, but I will give real examples to demonstrate what I mean.

A Goal or Goals

To manage a relationship properly, and certainly in managing more complex relationships, you need a clear goal or a very small set of goals.

The goal may be short-term, or it may be a series of short-term goals to achieve a larger goal. A simple example of this could be establishing a trusted relationship with one person.

More often, however, the objective is to establish a relationship with a group of people, and over time, develop trust between the individuals and the group. Goals may also take the form of steps or building blocks. If your goal is to form a relationship with a specific person, step one might simply be to meet them. From there, two would be to get to know them, three would see you building a relationship, four is establishing a trusted relationship, and finally, five is establishing a trusted long-term friendship.

Simple to write, but *very* difficult to actually do. This is why establishing and managing a complex relationship is so very, *very* hard. That said, if you know how to do it and can execute the process, it is an incredibly valuable strategic skill set.

A Strategic Plan

Establishing and managing a complex relationship requires a clear strategy, and thus, a strategic plan. I refer you here to Chapter 23 on *Strategy And Strategic Planning* for a more robust discussion of the formation of a good strategic plan and the elements necessary for execution. That said, the strategy you need here begins with clearly identifying what success looks like. It needs to identify with a high level of specificity the people who are critical to achieving that success: who are they, what do they do, and how are they connected to each other and potentially to you? Once this is done, individual strategies are developed for each person, leaving you well-positioned to build the relationships necessary to help achieve the goal.

As a real-life example, in my career, I would take on a client (new or existing) as the lead partner. The client represented the opportunity for a potentially complex relationship between themselves and me and my firm. The first step was to put together a strategic plan for the client. This was done with the help of my core team and maybe some subject matter experts. As outlined above, this plan always started with clear objectives. These typically included client satisfaction targets, relationship targets (e.g., who we wanted to know, how did we think we could help), and oftentimes revenue and profit targets as well. I want to be very clear here: establishing and managing complex relationships is all about *the relationships themselves*, not about the potential for revenue or profit!

I had a number of clients throughout my career where the relationship had forged a very high level of trust. This trust was reinforced daily in our interactions, and across the entire organization from the C-Suite to the mailroom. These clients generated a large amount of revenue and profit for my firm, the result of our ability to consistently meet their expectation that we would identify and solve complex problems for them. Because of our track record with the client, they trusted that we would deliver on our commitments and promises 100% of the time! These clients had an initial plan, and that plan was periodically updated and critiqued (what's working or not working), but the real keys to success were the high-performing team and its ability to execute daily across the organization, and in many cases, across the world.

Win-Win

A key element of successfully managing a complex relationship is ensuring that value is delivered to the person with whom you are establishing the relationship. This can be done in many ways. Some have short-term impact, some have long-term impact, and some can last forever. "Forever?" you say! Example: help someone get a job when they are unemployed! This is something they will never forget.

When developing a new relationship, I always tried, including as part of the plan, to identify personal areas that were strategic to the person in question. As an example, I would ask executives (including CEOs) what the objectives were in their personal plan for this year. When they asked why I was asking, I told them so I could identify areas where we might be able to help them personally. This always seemed to get their attention.

Long-term relationships are at their best when they are win-win. This can be accomplished in many ways based on the specific facts and circumstances. Long-term partnerships where they benefit both sides are the best. This can take many forms, from formal partnerships to helping both sides expand relationships. For example, I very often would offer to make introductions between parties using my global network. I connected them to the network of high-value people I had assembled, offering valuable access for them and creating another contact for myself in the process—a win-win! This was generally easy for me, and high-impact to one or both of the other parties.

Stay In The Moment, But View Everything As Long-Term

Two mistakes that are often made are that one either plans too far ahead, or conversely, makes decisions only on a short-term basis rather than with a long-term view. In reality, one must strike a balance between the two. It is important that you stay in the moment, but also that you continue to keep an eye on what's ahead. By this, I mean being laser-focused day in and day out on bringing value, but also making decisions that ensure a long-term relationship. Very often this idea is maximized by your ability to supercharge the relationship by bringing value first and often.

Strive to Communicate

Good, timely communication is imperative to all good relationships, even more so when the relationship is a big and complex one. You can never over-communicate. Constant communication can give rise to leads as to how you can bring value. It also sends the message that the relationship is important to you. One area to pay special attention to is communicating bad news. Some put off communicating bad news, which often makes the situation worse. I always tried to communicate bad news quickly, and hopefully with a solution or partial solution to the problem. Fixing a problem very often has a greater impact than if there never were a problem, and thus presents an opportunity to bring value to the relationship that should not be overlooked nor shied away from.

Be Honest, Be Transparent

When I talk about building your brand, I often emphasize being known for honesty and transparency. Successfully managing complex relationships requires that you be honest and transparent 100% of the time—You MUST be! Unfortunately, these are traits that you either have or don't have—they cannot be taught.

Stay Relevant

Staying relevant in a relationship requires work. Staying relevant in a *complex* relationship requires work, constant planning, and assessment and reassessment. Relevance is critical to success and continued success. As they say, if you are not relevant, then you are irrelevant and therefore useless. Also, to truly maximize the relationship, you must stay relevant to *all* parties in the relationship, not just those at the top.

Play Big

Someone once said, "If you are going to do it anyway, you might as well do it big!" I agree with this premise, and I've found that it also applies to managing complex relationships. If you are going to bring value to the relationship, try at times to "play big." A big idea that brings big value can earn favor that lasts a long time. When I, together with my firm, was able to help a major client sell one of their very large global businesses, they never forgot it. They concluded that they couldn't have done it without us or me. True or not, that's what they thought, and perceived value is just about as good as the real thing.

Surprise Often – Strengthen Your Brand

When I talk about "surprising" someone in a relationship, I'm referring to times when you bring value, deliver a solution, or solve a problem when the client or other party was not expecting it or hadn't asked for it. Pleasantly surprising your relationships is a very good thing and helps to significantly strengthen the relationship. Doing it often establishes a stronger and stronger personal brand, and the stronger your brand, the better. Sooner or later, there will be a problem or an unforeseen issue. When your brand is strong, most problems are considered small because they are taken in context of your reputation and the relationship, as a small part of a long list of positives.

Be Global

For over forty years at PwC, I always found that being global had the biggest impact. Most U.S.-based relationships have their biggest, most difficult-to-solve problems occur outside the U.S. As a consequence, some of the greatest value you can bring to the table is in helping to solve them. Being global and having a global network helped me assist in solving many of these problems: knowing international customs, regulations, players, and precedents—or knowing someone who does—puts you in a position to find solutions that non-global people will likely miss. Even today, my global network brings the most value to my personal relationships. This is true whether it is business-related or personal. I often get calls from friends asking about specific countries they are going to visit. This includes what to see and where to go, but also matters of security and safety.

Grandstand, But Be Modest

I always found it strategic to make sure my relationships knew what I/we had done for them and what the impact of our actions was. In some cases, it made sense to be modest, but in other cases, I found it more useful to grandstand. If my client had concluded that what I/we had done was above and beyond and was already impressed, I would usually be modest. However, if they didn't truly appreciate what had been done, then grandstanding might be appropriate.

Always Be Supportive

Not a lot of complexity to this. It's all about bedside manner and sincerity. You must always be supportive of your relationships, and be viewed by them as being supportive.

Never Do It for The Money

Long-term complex relationships, especially mutually beneficial ones, are almost always money-makers. That said, money is always an output of the relationship, and should not be a requirement going in. Also, as I mentioned before, it is always better if the other side benefits first—in fact, bringing value to the other party first and early is the best way to supercharge your relationship.

Be the *Go-To Person*

If you manage a complex relationship well, you will become one of the "go-to" people (or even the only one).

This is a very special relationship, but one that carries a lot of responsibility. When this happens, it often supersedes specific skill sets. In my case, it meant hearing comments like "Don knows everybody" or "Pass it by Don and see what he thinks" or "Have you gotten Don's view of this?" Sometimes, being the go-to person means becoming one of the most important advisors. Very often, this is the result of the perception that you are knowledgeable, smart, serious, independent, and a friend.

This is meant to be a discussion of factors to consider in managing complex relationships, especially in business. It clearly is an area which requires hard work and experience. In my experience, long-term relationships are extremely valuable in business and in life. Global long-term relationships are generally at the higher end of value, in part because they are so hard to get and keep. When it comes to your network, networking and the benefits that these things accrue are the most beneficial—and to *both* parties.

What I have spoken about here deals with managing relationships and managing complex relationships. In my case, my relationship management experience not only included the examples I have given but also all my interactions with members of my teams, my executive assistants, the support staff, people in the mail room, and on and on. I have many stories of trying to help someone who needed it, and often asking them for help myself. As I've said, relationships must work both ways to be considered long-term.

Chapter 20

CREATING AND SUSTAINING HIGH-PERFORMANCE TEAMS

Being a high performer as an individual and being part of a high-performance team are two very different concepts. The first is difficult, but the second is almost impossible.

In my experience, there is no strict definition for what a "high performer" is, and in many cases, it can be applied to very different types of people with very different skill sets and even major flaws or weaknesses. The term "high performer" is typically used to describe someone who does one thing or a small group of things very well. A high performer can be a great student, or a great tennis player, or a great running back, or a chess master, or a great actor, and so on—the only core criteria is that high performers are very good at what they do. They may even be the best in the world, or even the best there ever was.

When you try to select for these same criteria in creating a high-performance team (HPT), you'll find this logic doesn't apply in the same way: a high-performance team is not simply a team made up of high performers. You may think this sounds odd. Well, the principal reason for this is high-performance teams require team members with skill sets that are different from those of individual high performers. The classic example of this is a professional basketball team that has only all-stars on the roster, but is not high-performing as a team and may even find it hard to win games.

Let's start at the beginning. In business, it is not always about the team, but it very often is. You win as a team and you lose as a team. This is true if you are the CEO, the CFO, or Senior VP of Marketing of a company, or a partner at PwC or McKinsey. It takes definite skills to create and lead a high-performance team, and a high-performance team can do things that other teams cannot do.

A high-performance team delivers extraordinary results, exceeds expectations, and generally has high value—which in business, usually results in high profit. Most teams think they are high-performing, but ALL high-performance teams never think they are good enough; the constant and maniacal motivation to get better and better is a fundamental attribute of all high-performance teams. I would go so far as to say that if this is lacking in a team, then they are not a high-performance team.

High-performance teams come in all sizes and can be global or local. Small teams are easier to create and lead than larger ones. Global teams have certain complexities, which make them more difficult to create and sustain.

So, after years of field research, what do I believe are the attributes of high-performance teams? The leader is always high-performing; all team members are valued and they know it; there is trust throughout the team; they have a deep sense of shared purpose; they set ambitious goals; they exhibit creativity and innovation; they are diverse by nature and design; there is always shared ownership and mutual accountability; they have multiple complementary—and often interchangeable—skill sets; there is always opportunity within the team for learning, growth, and advancement; and there is a commitment to all team relationships, and to making them personal.

Let's discuss each of these:

The leader is always high-performing.

A high-performing leader does not necessarily make for a high-performance team. This is true most of the time, which is why many high performers work by themselves or on low-performance teams.

That said, a high-performing team MUST have a high-performing leader. A key detail here is the word "leader": high-performance teams must be led by a *leader*, not a "manager" (see *Leadership*, Chapter 18). Said as simply as I can, the high-performing leader has to be a true leader, and either exhibit or create the environment for all of the attributes listed above.

The team operates around the leader similar to the way an orchestra operates around a maestro. Orchestra members execute their performances by excelling at their instrument and responding to the direction of the maestro, who in turn coordinates each musician, blends the tones of each instrument together, and delivers the group to a successful performance.

Great leaders always give credit to the team, and in rare cases, to specific members of the team—never to themselves. Success belongs to everyone in HPTs, and even the latter situation usually only occurs when something truly extraordinary happens or when someone is getting ready to succeed the team leader and has the unanimous support of the team.

I remember early in my career being on a client where the PwC manager was extraordinarily smart and an expert in auditing and accounting. He was also well respected by the client. That said, he managed our team "by the numbers," so to speak. We each were given individual objectives to complete and a time budget for each. If we had questions, our manager was available to answer them, but that was about it. I didn't really feel like I was on a team, but rather like I was on my own. I can remember over time that certain members of the team would get together for drinks or dinner, but our manager did not join, and it was not ever a team get-together. It's interesting, because despite not having an HPT, the job got done and the client was happy. At the time, I did not realize it could be different. I now know that an HPT would have exceeded the client's expectations, not just met them, and that there would have been a real team feel that made the job fun.

Another time, also early in my career, I worked on a PwC team of about ten people with two leaders—a senior and a manager. This team, however, was high-performing from the start. The manager—a true leader—with the assistance of the senior, organized the team on day one. Not only did we know our areas of responsibility, but we also knew the high-level objectives of our team and how we were expected to interact with each other and with our leaders. There was open communication, and we met often as a team to assess progress. A high level of collaboration among the team was expected. The manager and senior were true HPT leaders and led by example. Everyone was encouraged to help each other, and this help made it possible for everyone to perform at a very high level. The difference was obvious, and the team's performance was dramatically better. It also became personal and fun.

All team members are valued, and they know it.

All team members being valued and knowing it is one of the most difficult but important attributes to create in the team. This starts with the HPT leader, and is evident in how he or she begins the process of selecting members and creating the team. The leader goes out of their way to meet one-on-one with each new team member on day one. This meeting—and the many thereafter—is meant to communicate that the leader specifically picked the member for the team and that his or her top priority is to make the new member successful. In these meetings, it becomes evident to team members that the leader believes that if they are successful as individuals, then the team will be successful overall. If the team is successful, then the leader will be successful. Everyone wins. Also, this first meeting is intended to clearly set the ground rules: things like "if you need help call me"; "if you don't like something I am doing, come see me"; or "if you have a personal problem, don't hesitate to see if I or the team can help." Value as I describe it here means that the individual is highly valued, both personally and professionally. At its core, a high-performing leader knows that it needs to be understood at the outset that they value each member of the team, and that team members not only feel this but see tangible signs of it over time. Tangible signs are things like rewards, recognition, promotion, advancement, and the like.

This attribute is driven home by the team leader and permeates the team. That is to say that team members value each other, recognize one another's successes, and help each other succeed. Making this environment a reality must be treated as a constant point of emphasis until it becomes part of the team DNA, and thereby automatic. You'll know you've succeeded when new members joining the team are immediately embraced by the other team members; the culture of HPTs is such that if a new member fails, then the team has failed.

To this point, I have intentionally placed moderate performers whom I thought had untapped potential or needed mentorship on high-performance teams and witnessed them change into high performers, in some cases even becoming leaders of high-performing teams themselves.

A marketing manager joined one of my global teams. The team in question was clearly high-performing and had been working together for a few years. Two things quickly happened to her. First, she was immediately embraced by the team, and this was by people who had been together for a while and had strong bonds with each other. They went out of their way to help her. Second, she promptly felt valued as a member of the team. After a month or so, she came to see me. She wanted to thank me; she really liked the work she was doing, but more importantly, she knew it was valued by me and the partners she worked with.

There is trust throughout the team.

This is a really tough one! "To be trusted you must be trustworthy"—an adage I've used in discussions about team building for more than twenty-five years, and one that I've found to be integral to creating high-performance teams.

The team members need to trust their leader, the leader needs to trust each team member, and all team members need to trust each other.

Each team member needs to trust and believe that the leader has their best interest as his or her number one priority—that the leader is doing everything within their power to make the team successful and see it rewarded, and perhaps even get members promoted. This connects to the earlier note that all members of an HPT are in constant pursuit of higher standards of success: each member needs to believe that the leader (a) wants the team to succeed in its objectives; (b) wants each team member to succeed individually; and lastly, (c) wants to succeed themselves. If any of these elements are in doubt, then the team is not truly a high-performing team.

I have many examples of this in my career, but one stands out to me:

I was a manager up for partner and I was working on three different clients. I found one of them in particular to be extremely challenging, because the client decided to sell off a number of its pieces that roughly amounted to half the total company. This meant finalizing financial statements, SEC registrations, and assembling extensive due diligence and other such deliverables necessary to push through a number of billion-dollar transactions. It was a lot of work, and my team and I worked 24/7 to get it done. The partner on the team was a high-performance leader and so was I (or at least I thought I was). In any event, this was one of those projects where the team grew even closer, forming deep bonds of camaraderie and trust. Team members also got big bonuses in recognition of their efforts. The big surprise was so did I. It was unheard of to get both admitted to the partnership and also a big bonus. Our partner made it happen, putting his all into ensuring that every member of our team was rewarded for the great work we'd done, and I have never forgotten.

The keys to the success of this project were many. One was that trust among the team had to be established very early on. The team had members who already knew each other, but also those that did not. Each team member (myself included) was also working on other projects at the same time. For these reasons, it was important to clearly define the project plan and each team member's specific responsibilities, and get buy-in on all of it before we could function as a true HPT. Getting buy-in required gaining the trust of each team member and fostering trust across the team. As a leader, this meant assuring team members that they could trust that I would help them succeed, that I would have their back, that I would facilitate their success on their other accounts, and that all would be appropriately rewarded for their extraordinary efforts. It also meant creating a team culture that saw each member committed to uplifting one another, which is cultivated by way of leading by example.

They have a deep sense of shared purpose.

All HPTs have a deep and shared sense of purpose. It comes from wanting to be the best at something—individually and as a team—in connection with an objective or mission that all team members support. At PwC, the objective or mission could have been connected with a client, an industry group, a business unit, or the firm as a whole, as well as any subgroup within these.

I will tell you that the team leader plays a major role in emphasizing the importance of the mission, and can influence perceptions within the team in many ways. This is easy when the mission is clearly set in connection with strategic imperatives, like a key industry or important client. It becomes more difficult when the importance of the mission is not so obvious. In these cases, the leader needs to elevate the perception of its importance. This is often true in the startup areas of most organizations. The leader talks about the team's area of focus being "the future, not the past" and "cutting-edge," where the investments will be made and where all the smartest and best will want to be—you get the point.

When I refer to "startup" areas, I'm referring to initiatives that are small now, but strategically planned to grow significantly in the future. These are strategic imperatives to the organization, but the issue is that they require long-term management buy-in and support to realize the aforementioned potential for growth, which in turn requires high performers. Incentivizing outstanding performers to join these areas requires clear and consistent communication of the strategy and the assurance that appropriate rewards will be there. While one is best served by being persuasive in the drafting of high performers to their team, this is not so much a sales undertaking as an exercise in clear communication to people who believe in the strategy and trust you as their leader to help make them successful in executing it.

They set ambitious goals.

This is one of my pet peeves. I have been told it is "human nature" to set goals that are achievable, and very often in business, people set these same safe, facile goals. I understand why this is, and I understand why it works in most organizations, but this is not conducive to creating a culture of high performance, and thus, is counterproductive in forming a high-performance team. Let me explain:

I once had a boss counsel me on my annual personal plan. I put it together in a way that I thought reflected my level and compensation, and in such a way that I thought the goals I'd outlined could be achieved, provided I put forth maximum effort—in other words, a significant stretch. I also thought—with some luck—I could even exceed them. My plan was aligned with our strategy and objectives. The counseling I got was that my plan had too much stretch and that I should make my goals easier to meet. I made the proposed changes to my submitted plan, but kept my plan for myself the same. By the end of the year, I'd exceeded my submitted plan by 50%.

So, what's the point? The point is that for most of my career, I did the opposite of what my boss counseled me to do that day, and consistently set very high objectives for myself and for my teams which could only be met to the fullest extent if everything went right. In some cases, for this reason, they were not totally met, but what this did in almost every case was assure that our results would be better than the results from an "attainable" plan because we'd set our sights on achieving something more. I proved this time and time again.

I remember starting a new global practice that was strategic to the firm. I selected a global leader, who in turn put together a fantastic plan with a revenue target of $100 million after five years. After significant back-and-forth, I made the target $1 billion. We then had to present our plan for budget funding. As was my practice, my global leader presented his plan to our leadership group. When he got to the revenue goal, he pointed out that the $1 billion was my number, and that he thought $100 million was more attainable. Of course, I knew he was going to say that.

I was asked where my $1 billion came from. I explained that it was based on data from clients in similar industries—historical revenue numbers that would get us to that goal or even higher. I had made an aggressive estimate, yes, but in the context of these figures, it was reasonable. Everyone agreed with my higher number. I then got asked what I thought the worst case was. I said $500 million. My point here is we could have targeted the easily achievable $100 million and exceeded it by say $50 million, or we could have targeted $1 billion, fallen short by 25%, and "only" achieved $750 million. Which is better? I always thought the latter.

They exhibit creativity and innovation.

Members of HTPs think outside the box, and they each expect their team members to do the same. Old thinking and old ways are always questioned, and concepts that are newer, better, and faster are the concepts that drive day-to-day decisions, often resulting in higher efficacy, better efficiency, higher quality, and more value added across the board. No idea is stupid. Concepts once universally agreed on are debated. Plans are challenged. "Not invented here" syndrome does not exist. Everyone is always in search of best practices, striving to answer the question, "How do we become the best?"

High-performance teams actually get more creative over time, and when you look back on their progress, it can be almost unbelievable. I used to say, "Never give me what I ask for, give me what I want." This was because I knew that the team would be way more creative than I alone could be. This was true 100% of the time.

I remember many times when the recommendations we made to clients—for example, as to how to improve their core business models—were luminary and, in most cases, came from the team—not from me.

They are diverse by nature and design.

HPTs are ALWAYS diverse, and the more diverse they are, the better. A team of look-alikes will generally think the same and have similar experiences. In order to get diverse ideas, what you want to create is a team that is diverse in all ways. At my firm, we included gender diversity, ethnic diversity, geographic diversity, core skills diversity (e.g., finance, marketing, engineering), age diversity, and so on. Throughout my career, I got a reputation for being a strong supporter of diversity and pushing our diversity agendas. I did this for many reasons, but I also did it because it was good business.

One thing that always amazed me was how diverse teams can bond and form trusted relationships. When I lecture on Global Business, I talk about cultural differences and give examples pertaining to different countries. One of the points I make, however, is that while there are different ways to get a trusted relationship depending on the culture, once you have it, most everything else is the same.

At PwC, I would often get my global teams together to develop strategy and align the teams around it. There were usually more than thirty countries represented at these meetings, and there would always be an informal welcome dinner on the first night and a more formal dinner on the middle night of the meeting. The formal dinner had assigned seating. I would always sit at a table for twelve with partners from eleven different countries. They were each members of my global team, and I was one of them. The language being spoken was English, but the conversation and laughter were amongst twelve friends and colleagues. The culture at the table was my "global team culture," not anyone's local culture. I was not primarily an American, but rather a fellow industry leader, a fellow lead client service partner, or a fellow global leader.

Shared ownership and mutual accountability.

Everything is owned by the team, and by every individual equally. This is either true in all circumstances, or, in cases involving very large teams, at least true for all key objectives. You win as a team, and you lose as a team. If a single team member fails, the team has failed as a whole. Everyone helps each other "do good." Team members even help team members who are competing with them for the same promotion. When you see this happen, you know you have a high-performance team.

I can remember being told by a manager that their objectives had not been achieved because the team had let them down, or even worse, that a particular member of the team fell short. This told me immediately that the manager was not a true leader, and that they did not have a high-performance team.

Whenever I would interview a potential new team member, I would ask what their biggest failure or shortfall had been in their career so far. After they told me, I would ask what the principal cause had been. If they told me it was a failure in their leadership, they were in. If they told me the team let them down, they were out.

They have complementary (and often interchangeable) skill sets.

Think of a baseball player who can play multiple positions. Think of an orchestra where instruments play together to make and maximize beautiful music. HPTs are most often composed of really smart people who can do multiple things well. They may speak multiple languages, they may be math whizzes, they may be computer programming experts, they may be good at strategy, project planning, and execution. In many cases, they have these skills in addition to those relevant to their primary role.

Team members of HPTs have different years of experience, different subject matter expertise (they may be currently responsible for one area, but have prior experience in others), different industry experience, different people/management skills, etc. These different skill sets mean that one member's expertise can compensate for the shortcomings of another, and vice versa, such that the team is well-rounded and equipped for just about anything.

High-performance team members always want to have specific skills where they are really good (or even the best) so they can bring value to the team. With experience, they want to have multiple skill sets that are ever-expanding. Remember: no matter how good they are, they are never good enough.

They are also always assessing the skills the team needs and the skills of the future. They are in constant pursuit of improving themselves and their team.

There is opportunity for learning, growth, and advancement.

Fostering learning and growth in team members is a key job of the team leader and the more senior members of the team.

On client teams, we spent a lot of time planning for the next steps of each team member. This included input from each team member, and knowing them well enough to know what challenges they were ready for. In most cases, the challenges exceeded what they thought they were ready for. In all cases, we knew they were ready, but we gave them a safety net to assure success—most often in the form of another team member to fall back on, though this was almost never needed.

This planning also included going onto different projects with different challenges to broaden team members' experience, and sometimes even included sending U.S. team members to foreign countries and bringing foreign team members to the U.S. so they could get global experience.

Also, many of my larger accounts over the years were known to help accelerate a person's career. This was principally due to the challenges and experience involved and the prestige of the client. A foreign tour to Japan or China was definitely viewed as accelerating promotions.

Advancement is key; the promise of being rewarded by way of a promotion is a huge motivator. As such, the potential for advancing at an accelerated pace is a supercharged motivator. HPTs having a high-performing team leader who is generally highly thought of makes this all possible. Added to this is the reputation that many HPTs get for having effective and talented team members—and they are becoming more talented all the time! Soon enough, everybody wants them!

There is a commitment to making all relationships personal.

I am not a psychologist, so I do not know the scientific reasons behind it, but what I do know is that almost all members of HPTs become close friends. In my mind, this is not too dissimilar to the classic story of a military group that fights together, has each other's backs, and remains close friends for life. Why is it that two teams—one high-performing and the other not—can work on the same type of project—long hours, weekends, hard work—and in one case, they are friends forever, while in the other case, they never want to see each other again?

I spoke earlier about the overlap of business and personal lives. Never is the overlap more significant than on a high-performing team. High-performing team members like being high performers, and even more, like being part of a high-performing team. By supporting one another in pursuit of doing good work, all team members grow to like and respect each other, and in many cases, become close friends. As a consequence, they socialize together in- and outside of work. The line between business time and personal time blurs. Even their significant others may also become friends, and I've seen many cases of significant others forming groups to support the team.

I remember back to the NASA days when not only were the astronauts close friends, but so were their significant others. The bonds in business are more or less the same.

Obstacles To Creating an HPT

There are two major obstacles to creating a high-performance team:

- First, in many cases, you cannot pick your team. This can present a major challenge, depending on which team attributes either do not exist or cannot be created.

- Second, a fact of life is that all team members may not survive the high-performance culture—I used to say, "The treadmill started moving too fast for them." In these cases, team members may need to move on.

I have tried to explain what makes a high-performing team work, although as with all things in life, it is easier to explain than it is to create or execute. It also requires that all eleven components work together and that each is made a focus every day. In my career, I worked with many different teams from all around the world. Some were high-performing, and some were not.

Creating and sustaining high-performance teams and a high-performance culture was an extraordinary experience for me. The level of satisfaction gained is immeasurable. The results in terms of performance improvement of the team, performance improvement of each team member (many of whom became great leaders themselves), and delivery of extraordinary value to our clients were simply outstanding. Further, HPTs and their culture very often made for a fun working experience, even if under great pressure. It was a real privilege for me to be able to work with these teams, and I thank all the various team members all over the world for being such key components to each team's success. We always did it as a team.

Chapter 21

THE VALUE OF TENSION AND CONFRONTATION

Though internal conflict tends to get a bad rap in business, tension and confrontation are actually good qualities in an organization and on a team, and are indicators that it may be a high-performing team or organization. REALLY! High-performing organizations have a number of attributes as described in the chapter on high-performance teams. Because they are constantly in search of how to get better and are never satisfied, they create an open and candid environment where everyone's views are valued and discussion and debate are encouraged.

This type of environment is conducive to a degree of confrontation, and by extension, does cause some tension. This is to say that while ideas are openly shared, they are also openly challenged by those who disagree. This environment results in the best ideas being identified within the team, and in many cases, is ultimately constructive in getting group support and buy-in. When all members of the team are able to challenge any ideas that they disagree with, they come to a better understanding of why certain elements of the plan are necessary and have some input as to how the strategy might be changed, and thus, they are more likely to agree to the plan. Remember that the group believes that no matter how good they have done, it can always be better and they expect to make it better. Over and over again.

To cultivate this kind of confrontational-yet-collaborative environment, the group must select members who are not "yes men/women" and who are generally smart and creative, as well as set the expectation that they are to participate in these types of strategic forums. Putting these types of people in this environment actually causes them to be more creative than normal. They tend to thrive.

Now some bad news: most organizations and teams do not handle tension and confrontation of the nature described here well. Instead, any internal disputes ultimately hinder progress rather than galvanize it. In my experience, many of these organizations fall into one of two categories, as follows:

The Dominant Environment

These organizations or teams have a very dominant leader who generally surrounds themselves with "yes people." This leader determines the strategy alone and puts it into action by themselves or with a very small inner circle. When they seek input—and they normally do—they want answers such as "Yes boss," "Great idea boss," or "Way to go." In my experience, these individuals actually think they are smarter than everyone else. They also typically don't see themselves as doing what I just described—they consider their plans faultless, and themselves effective leaders.

Let me be clear here: there are many great companies and teams with assertive leaders who *do* foster open environments, and thus allow room for the tension and confrontation described above. These dominant leaders, however, surround themselves with strong people—usually those they consider to be smarter than they are themselves—who are expected to challenge them and one another.

If I use myself as an example, I have a very strong personality and I form opinions quickly. That said, I surrounded myself with diverse, very smart, and creative people. I expected those team members to put forth their own ideas, voice opposition when they disagreed with something, and work as a team to make us better as a unit. I always loved the debate because I knew it would help us get to the best answer. I also loved passionate debaters strongly putting forth their ideas and the bases for their conclusions. The tension—or as I used to call it, the "heat in the room"—was a good thing. Team members were always respected and treated respectfully. There were never any "stupid ideas," and many times the ideas voiced with the least confidence ended up being considered brilliant by the team at large.

The Collegial Environment

Another example of a lower-performing environment is one where confrontation is unacceptable, and where any degree of tension needs to be defused immediately. This is what is known as a "collegial environment," where leaders attempt to ensure that every member of the group is supported and valued. In reality, this systematic pacification of all conflict actually prevents the team from realizing its full potential and strips the value of any one member's individual contributions or opinions in pursuit of a frictionless workplace. In these settings, the leader and the team generally think most everything is okay and going well, and anyone introducing confrontation into this group is considered to be acting inappropriately and regarded as out-of-line.

This group usually remains silent at meetings. They also become passive-aggressive: they look like they agree, but they don't, and as a consequence, they do not support the agreed action and instead try to silently undermine the agreed action by phoning in their part in it or not doing what they committed to. This usually results in the plan not being executed, or at least not executed on time. The company or team tends to see maintenance of the status quo as good, and incremental improvement as good progress. This may have worked in the past (although I doubt it), but it is dangerous now with the rapidly changing world. I think I have already mentioned my view that if you are not a disrupter, then you should expect to be disrupted.

These are but two examples—there are many others.

In my experience, ideas tend to get broadened and expanded. That is to say that the original idea (and someone may have thought it stupid, though never me) gets debated, and the debate adds modifications to the original idea. The discussion also usually adds implementation dynamics and other dynamics that may take the idea to a new level. I can think of many ideas that went from good to great, and from "do it when we can" to "do it immediately."

Also, the debate would usually include "what-if" scenarios that caused the group to not only discuss the idea in different contexts but also change basic assumptions. You are trying to fix one problem, but you conclude the problem is much bigger than you thought; or you are trying to fix one problem and conclude there is a completely different and much better way to do it.

I have tried to articulate the benefits that can come from selective tension and confrontation. I use the word "selective" here because in high-performance environments it is not *always* tense and confrontational—this only happens when needed. To be effective, all team members need to understand and feel comfortable with elements of confrontation and tension. This happens only when a high-performance leader has communicated the "rules of engagement" to the team, such that team members clearly understand that selective confrontation is expected (and, in fact, fostered where necessary). It can never be personal. It must be respectful. It can't be constant. It can't be targeted (i.e., A goes after B at every meeting). Also, for it to work really well, the team leader must referee the proceedings/meetings. In my own experience, I would on occasion stop the discussion and ask that everyone sleep on it and reconvene in the morning. If we had drinks and dinner that night and the topic was discussed, the discussion the next day might be quick. In very rare instances, I as team leader made the call (i.e., the decision).

Utilizing tension and confrontation does not and will not work for everyone and every team. As I have mentioned in the chapter on creating and sustaining high-performance teams, not everyone can be a high performer or work comfortably on a high-performing team. If they can't, they will probably hate working in an environment that has confrontation as a working element. There are whole industries that thrive on it and there are whole industries that find it offensive—compare the investment banking sector to academia, for example.

One last comment: in my experience, the high-performing teams that included selective tension and confrontation have been some of the most successful teams I have ever seen. They have also been fun (at times "leave the room" funny), and they have been teams whose members (including me) became and remained close friends for decades.

Chapter 22

BUSTING THE MYTH OF COMPETITION

C ompetition is a topic discussed fairly often in business. In these discussions, it's usually implied that there are two or more parties competing against each other to win. It engenders a vision of someone climbing a ladder by beating the other person to the next rung. I have certainly seen organizations where this was more or less how it worked. These kinds of organizations were usually light on leaders and nowhere near being high-performance cultures.

When I think of high performers and high-performance cultures, I always think about the performance of the high performers and the performance of the team. I always viewed the "winner" or "winners" as being those who performed the best. "The best team always wins" was one of my sayings.

Those who focused on the other guy were focusing on the wrong thing. When you did that, it was easy to think that the other guy's poor performance would make you a better performer by comparison—a winner. I never saw it that way. My focus was always on being the best I could be, and making sure my team was the best it could be. Our competition was not important, because I thought if we were the best, and our team was the best, then we would win every time.

When you are focused on the other guy, you tend to do only well enough to beat their performance. If their performance is mediocre, then yours will tend to be just better than that, meaning mediocre plus a little. Not only does this obstruct your ability to do the best that you can, but it also opens you up to being outperformed. If the other person or team does better than you predicted they would, then your performance presents as mediocre by comparison, and you're likely to lose. This is really important, because great performances are usually the result of competitors trying to be the best they can be, and they "win" by being the best there was. This is certainly how I lived my life, in business and beyond.

When I was in charge of the PwC technology practice, I met with my team of about 150 partners and we talked about strategy. I am an "output guy," which means I measure performance by outputs like client wins, revenue generated, projects won, profits, and the like (the other side of this comprises input measures, like hours worked, people hired, proposals executed, etc.). I remember two strategic targets were owning the market and being number one. As I was known to do, I remember saying, "We want to be number one by such a margin that number two can't catch up, and they know it."

As I mentioned, I was always focused on my own personal performance—on my level of expertise, on my experience, on building and maintaining my network, on how to do better, on how to *be* better—never on anyone else's. If I lost, I blamed myself—I fell short because (in my mind) I didn't know enough, or didn't know the right people, or wasn't well enough prepared.

My view was molded from a very early age. In every situation where I was trying to achieve something, there were always other people trying for the same position. I felt that the best candidate would always get one of the open positions, so my objective was to be the best. If I was the best, then it didn't matter what anyone else did. I also felt that if I didn't get the position, then I needed to try harder next time.

A great example of this occurred both in 1985 and 1986, when I wasn't admitted to the PwC partnership. In 1985, I thought that I was ready, and I thought there was a real chance I would be admitted. This was and is a decision voted on by the partnership, and a number of the partners told me at the time that they thought it would happen. When it didn't, I was very disappointed. In whom? In myself, for not doing enough to *make* it happen. In 1986, I was again denied admission to the partnership. I was angry with myself again, but this time for underestimating how well I was known across the partnership. By then, I had believed myself and my credentials to be generally known across the partnership, but after my second denial, I concluded that this could not have been the case. I undertook to change that, and in 1987 I was admitted. At the time, I was the only audit partner admitted in the New York metro region.

Never during this two-year-long period of seeking partner did I ever feel like I was competing with someone else. Certainly there were other senior managers up for admission, but in my view, if you were the best qualified, you would get in. I viewed myself as highly qualified, and I was admitted.

I know that judgment and subjectivity—and in many cases, who you know—also have their parts to play in a selection process. If it is a close decision, these elements will always influence the final verdict. What I have found, however, is that more often than not it is not close when all the facts are known and evaluated. There are usually clear choices. Thus, it's incumbent on you to make sure the decision-makers know all the facts and that when they do—provided you are focused on being the best you can be—you stand out as the most qualified.

There are organizations where what I talk about here does not broadly exist. These are organizations that are known as "cutthroat," where coworkers step over each other to get ahead. In many cases, they are managed by using fear and intimidation as a weapon. This is not the kind of organization you want to work for. One of the things I tell my students is that when you take a job, make sure the organization aligns with your values. What I describe here—a work culture that sees its team members cutting one another down in order to get ahead themselves—probably does not. Also, if the organization is a true meritocracy—as I have described PwC to be—it will likely have the attributes described in this chapter.

In my career with PwC, we competed with many other organizations. The Big Eight, then the Big Six, then the Big Four and others. We competed in different countries and industries. Our objective was not to show that we were better than anyone else, but to prove we were the best, and therefore that we were better than all of them no matter who they were. We did this by industry or country, and we always tried to demonstrate we had the best team and that our experience was better than anyone else's.

Our proposals always focused on the prospective client and our capabilities to help them execute their strategy—never once can I remember drawing focus to the competition with the intent of making them look bad or incompetent. When you are the best, you really don't care who the competition is. It doesn't matter.

In client situations—and with high-performance teams in particular—it was always about the collective success of the team. Staff members working together would go out of their way to help each other, even when they were seeking the same promotion. In some cases, one got the promotion and the other didn't. If this happened, the one promoted worked to get the other promoted the next year. Usually (in my experience), both were promoted at the same time because they were both extremely qualified.

I also remember a number of times being a manager on an account with more than one manager. We each had our own responsibilities and had to focus primarily on our own areas. That said, we always helped each other where we could. This often happened when one of us had experience in an area where the other did not. It also happened when the workload was greater than expected and one of us needed help from the others.

I can only remember two cases in my experience with PwC where someone did something that seemed to undermine me. I thought it was odd, dismissed it, and just moved on without saying anything or confronting the other person. It was so counter to how I operated that it surprised me. In both cases, sooner or later the truth came to light, and neither perpetrator got promoted. I believe this was because this "antagonistic" approach was exhibited elsewhere and had been routinely frowned upon by our organization and its partners at the time.

Chapter 23

STRATEGY AND STRATEGIC PLANNING

D eveloping a strategy, formalizing a strategic plan, and then executing that strategic plan are three of the most difficult undertakings in business and life. I am devoting a chapter to these topics and will try to outline the areas within each that I think are most important. I have developed and executed strategies on businesses I ran, on multinational client teams that I led for PwC, and with a number of clients directly. It was never easy, and in all cases required smart people who were committed to an open (sometimes heated) debate and discussion to get to the best answer.

If you search the words "strategy" or "strategic plan" online, you will get hundreds of hits with courses and templates and experts to consult with. There are many types of processes that can be followed. What I will discuss in this chapter are what I view the key elements of strategic planning to be, what works and doesn't work, what helps and what hurts, and how the best outcomes are achieved.

What I will discuss can apply to any organization of any size and of any complexity. It can apply to a candy store or to a multibillion-dollar global multinational. It can also apply to one's personal strategy development and decision-making. Some of the elements and their execution may be different or more difficult, but the overall approach and outputs will be the same. The process will also apply to almost any problem or issue of almost any kind. Good strategic thinking functions as a perspective on things, and you'll find that it applies often.

———————

So, what is "strategy?" One high-level definition I found from Oxford Languages was "a plan of action or policy designed to achieve a major or overall aim." Here, I will discuss strategy in the context of organizations; later, I will deal with it in a broader context.

The most effective strategies start at the end, not at the beginning. The first step—let me say it again—*the first step* is defining the endgame. Some call it a mission (as in a mission statement), some call it a goal, some call it an ultimate objective, and there are other names I have heard. I say, "What do we want to end up looking like when the strategic plan is finally executed?" This could be after just one year, or five years down the line. Your endgame can be even further out—some strategies are for life. These kinds of targets will be incrementally executed over a lifetime, and are things like building a network, expanding your knowledge in certain areas, or becoming global. If it's a comprehensive strategic plan based on a real strategy, then, by definition, it represents big change— "big" like paradigm-shifting or game-changing. It's building something new for the future, not tweaking the methods of the past.

When working with a team, the endgame I speak about here is one that is arrived at after significant debate and discussion. Before it's agreed upon, its results need to be measurable. In the chapter on branding (Chapter 13), I reference making the PwC Technology practice number one in the U.S. This was a decision consciously made at high levels of my firm, supported by a strategic plan and planned execution over a specific period with very specific goals.

One key to top-level strategy is that the strategic priorities and strategic areas (see Pyramid on page 217) need to be crystal clear, such that they are able to be precisely communicated across the organization. By this, I mean clearly communicated to everyone in the same way one delivers an elevator speech. I recommend creating a strategy on a one-page document that clearly sets out the strategy. It also needs to be evident that the strategic priorities are supported at the highest level of the organization, and that this support is long-term. Most strategies that are unsuccessful are unsuccessful because they were not clear, not well communicated, not supported by top management, or all three. Yes, some strategies are flawed or not attainable, but in my experience that was almost never the real problem.

Strategic planning is the process of determining the strategy, developing the sub-strategies, drafting the plan of execution, and executing the strategic plan. All four major steps are critical to success, but are almost never carried out correctly. I used to always say that putting together the plan was easy, and its execution was always the problem. I now know that I was wrong. In a high-performance culture, what I thought and said was true, but in regular cultures, it is not. Developing a strategy requires skills that many do not have, like vision, knowledge of the industry, and knowledge of the organization, as well as the ability to think broadly and boldly, understand what is doable, deal with and drive change, take risks, and have the ability to understand what must be done.

I always viewed determining the strategy to be a multi-step process. I will attempt to outline the steps here:

Step 1: *Determining the High-Level Strategy*

The first step must always be looking at what you are or where you are and identifying in crystal clear terms what you want to be or where you want to go. As I've already mentioned, this must include a vision for what the endgame will be, including objective measures of what it will look like when the vision is achieved. Ideally, these are quantitative things, like $100 million in revenue, or 1,000 customers, or 2,500 students, or $50 million raised from donors, or a cure for a specific disease. We should be able to argue over whether the objective is worthwhile or even attainable, but not over what it is. Also, there can be more than one top-level objective, though not many—I always say three.

In many organizations, they supposedly put together a "Strategic Plan," but it has many, many, many objectives—I once saw one with 150. This is NOT a strategic plan! Strategic plans must target only a few high-priority objectives and set clear blueprints for how and when their aims will be met, otherwise, nothing will ever get done, and no one will take responsibility for its execution. In cases like these, most of the 150 objectives are not strategic imperatives, but disconnected ambitions—frankly, a bunch of meaningless BS. With plans like these, there is no prioritization (how could there be with 150 aims?), there is no assigned responsibility, there are no timelines, and there are no strategic targets. As I'm writing this, I don't even know what to call plans like these, but I know that they usually have zero value. This particular instance reminded me of the "all work and no play" scene in The Shining: page after page of useless points and unimportant goals.

An Almeida Step — Building Your A-Team

What I always did was put together a group of very smart people with diverse backgrounds to discuss and debate the potential strategy. These people included subject matter experts in certain key areas. The areas depended on the organization developing the strategy but would include visionaries with vital knowledge on the industry in question, or on technology that might have an impact, or on the competition.

Broad areas could include macro trends like globalization, technology, geopolitical changes, demographic changes, economic changes, etc. Interestingly, all of these can impact an organization's strategy, but can also impact your personal strategy. As you put together a personal career strategy, you should be considering the same macro trends that organizations deal with. For example, today, the impact of artificial intelligence (AI) will impact the strategies of all organizations, and thus experts in this sector will likely have a seat at the table in the years to come. In turn, this might motivate you to educate yourself on the subject as it pertains to your focus areas, and eventually, to seek relevant job placement as you achieve expertise.

I would assemble the group (usually between ten and twenty) to discuss and debate what the strategy should be. This process included two broad steps.

The first step is **strategically defining the endgame**. What I always tried to do was to get the group to settle on a number of strategic priorities. I made sure that no idea was off the table, and no idea was stupid. I always wanted this effort to result in ten to fifteen different visions of success. We then would spend significant time discussing, debating, arguing, challenging, pushing and shoving, sometimes raising voices, laughing, acting, playing devil's advocate, etc. In the end, we tried to prioritize the strategic priorities from best to least best—none were bad!

There are many ways to do this, but the one I used most often is called the "nominal method." I had used the nominal method throughout my career to help prioritize and allocate resources, but I didn't know it had a technical name until years later, after I became a college professor. To utilize this approach, you present every idea to the group, then have each member vote for the best idea, but they can't vote for their own. If you start with twenty ideas, after the first vote you drop the bottom 25%. Then you vote again, and again drop the bottom 25%. When you get to the top five ideas, you prioritize the five in descending order from number one to number five. This process ultimately formed a kind of pyramid, where each idea was ranked (see page 217).

At this point, I would always revisit all twenty of the original strategic priorities one by one to make sure they should be dropped. In some cases, this resulted in strategic priorities being moved to the middle or bottom of the pyramid. Finally, we decided on the strategic priorities that would determine our strategy. Remember, this must also include the key indicators of success—some use the title "key performance indicators," or KPIs. The KPIs also require discussion and debate, and they are absolutely key to having a chance of success. At this stage, a high-level timeline should also be agreed upon, along with a five-year plan. This is typically when we define what deliverables, accomplishments, or progress is planned by the end of year one, year two, and so on (the "To Be" vision).

The second step starts with what some consultants call **an "As Is" analysis**. This meant that we'd start the discussion by clearly defining where we were today relative to each strategic priority. This must be factually correct, and in many cases, it will be surprisingly negative. This means that many think the organization is doing better than it really is, but the analysis demonstrates that this is measurably false. In my experience, this happens almost 100% of the time. This analysis must include clear metrics in defining where you are, and in most cases, these will be the same metrics used to determine where you want to go with each strategic priority (the "To Be" vision).

Additional Resource — **The Strategic Planning Pyramid**
I have written about the concept of core competencies. Here, I will use a slightly different concept—one which I always used in any strategic planning exercise, especially those that pertained to an organization's efforts to establish or modify its overarching identity. This concept takes the form of a pyramid with three segments.

The bottom segment is what I call "**Core Values**." These are key values to the organization that cannot and will not change, no matter what the strategic changes are. They are intrinsic to the organization at its core and are the essential values that permeate the organization and its strategy. They can be aspects of identity, like "honesty and ethics always," "helping the underrepresented in all we do," and so on.

The middle section of the pyramid represents the **Strategic Areas** we want to be good at. A few examples of this are being global, being diverse (which could also be a core value), being technology-focused, etc. Because these are areas the organization has concluded they want to be good at, and therefore known for to some extent, it would not be unusual for there to be five to fifteen strategic areas. Although important, most if not all of these areas would not be differentiators (things that make the organization one of one or one of a few).

The top section is for the **Strategic Priorities** that you have determined are key to your determined strategy. They are what you want to be known for. Of the ten to twenty ideas that you have debated, these are the top three to five—they are the things that are crucial to the strategy's identity, and the things you want to be famous for.

In my experience, many of the strategic areas are actually core values. They also are things you want to be known for, but in many cases, they are not differentiators. This is also true for the bottom two sections of the pyramid. My view was always that areas in the middle of the pyramid were critical to an organization's identity, as were the core values, but not unique enough to truly make you one of one or one of just a few.

Step 2: *Determining the Sub-Strategies*
For each strategic priority, there will always be three to five key sub-strategies that need to be executed over the strategic plan period (though there could be more). These areas are in essence the requisite steps (building blocks) needed to achieve each of your strategic priorities in pursuit of your overall goal. Let me give a simple example to illustrate this:

A New York City high school decides its overall strategy includes four strategic priorities: (1) to be a top ten academic high school in NYC; (2) to be a nationally-ranked sports school; (3) to be number one in NYC in educating the underserved community with learning disabilities; and (4) to be number one in NYC in teaching financial skills and partnering with Wall Street.

Each of these strategic priorities must have defined KPIs, which when achieved will indicate that the strategy was successful. Achieving these objectives requires deploying sub-strategies. The high-level strategy of becoming a nationally-ranked sports school, as an example, requires sub-strategies in identifying what sports are in scope, what the measures of success are, and over what timeline this aim will be achieved. This area is very specific to each strategic priority and can be very subjective and debatable. That said, the sub-strategies are just as important as the strategic priorities and are key to execution.

While developing the sub-strategies, the middle and bottom of the pyramid are often refined or even changed. In one case, I saw the middle of the pyramid split in two, with the top of the middle being more important to the overall strategy than the bottom. This may sound minor, but at the end of the process there must be timelines and KPIs for each element, which includes the matter of critical asset allocation—how many people and of what experience, how many investment dollars, and generally what kinds of resources should be put toward each item of the strategy. As such, each aspect of the strategy is "competing" for the best resources, and determining priority, while necessary, means that some efforts may wind up underserved— something that becomes even more true when you have to split priority across more categories.

Step 3: *Developing the Plan for Execution*

The execution plan is often where things start breaking down. It requires clear timelines for the overall strategies and all sub-strategies and defines each step that needs to be executed under each of those. For simplicity, I will refer to these collectively as "key steps." Each key step must be crystal clear. It must have a five-year timeline with checkpoints along the way. My recommendation is to set annual targets with checkpoints that occur even more often. Each key step—as well as each sub-strategy—must have an "owner" with clear responsibilities. These owners manage each key step, are answerable for the progress of their respective executions, and are tasked with making any necessary course corrections along the way. All targets must be quantifiable and able to be measured. In the end, this is very similar to the development of almost any base-level project plan, but in this case, it covers very strategic priorities.

Step 4: *Executing the Strategic Plan*

My recommendation here is that the overall strategy and strategic plan has a clear leader and a high-level steering committee. These positions need to be filled by senior people in the organization, very often including (and as I'd recommend) the CEO. The strategy needs to be communicated across the organization with as much early buy-in as possible (the more buy-in, the better). As dealt with in the chapter on leadership (Chapter 18), true leaders can communicate their strategies effectively, and have built them in a way that assures buy-in has already been acquired by the time the strategy was finalized.

When execution begins, it is imperative that progress be closely monitored, and that action is taken quickly when necessary. In my experience, you will face many types of personalities throughout the plan's execution. Two to look for are those who are passive-aggressive and those who strongly disagree with the strategy. The passive-aggressives are those who say all the right things but are always trying to torpedo the strategy behind the scenes. They are usually easy to find and must be dealt with quickly. On the other hand, anyone who strongly disagrees needs to be counseled—after all, these types are just telling the truth as they see it, and so it's usually worthwhile to try to reach common ground before taking action—but ultimately, they too need to be dealt with. "Dealt with" here means doing whatever is required to move the strategy forward. This could mean a demotion or even an outright firing; no one person or small group can be allowed to hinder the execution of the strategy.

Step 5: *Funding and Return on Investment (ROI)*

Funding of the strategy with both dollars and people will be critical to success. These costs relate to both the development and execution of the strategy as well as the funding of the strategy and its related components. The strategy not only includes what we will do, but also very importantly what we will stop doing. This step is critical to success and will hopefully free up needed resources.

In a business context, a proper ROI analysis needs to be done. This is a separate topic, but it will include an analysis of future revenues and expenses related to the strategy. It needs to make sense that the expected revenue growth warrants the added cost related to the development and execution of the strategy.

In not-for-profit organizations, this analysis can be more difficult. Generally, these organizations are funded at least in part by outside donors. The analysis here needs to consider the impact of the strategic changes not only on the organization and its mission and profile (and revenue sources), but also the impact on the donor base. This is to say that the analysis must ask if the changes will resonate with donors and potential donors, and if they are likely to generate incremental donations. This is absolutely key to concluding the strategy.

Step 6: *Funding Plan*

Part of the overall strategic plan is how it will be funded. In typical organizations, this requires an allocation of resources from operations or capital raising. For not-for-profit organizations in particular, this is its own "sub"-strategic plan. Also, as organizations change in strategic ways, the need for clear funding or fundraising plans is critical. As new areas are implemented and expanded upon, so too must funding and fundraising strategies evolve.

There are many obstacles to success. Let me note just a few:

- **Change** — most people and most organizations do not like and do not deal well with change.

- **Candor** — getting the strategy correct as described above requires candid conversation about what we are and what we want to be, which cannot happen in many organizations.

- **Vision** — many organizations and people do not have the vision to see what is possible.

- **Commitment** — most people and organizations do not have the staying power to complete execution over a three-to-five-year period.

- **Determination** — most CEOs and companies won't do what is necessary to successfully execute the strategy. They will not deal with the passive-aggressives or the strongly-disagrees.

- **Shiny Objects** — the strategy drifts or fails and is replaced over time by a "shiny object" (i.e., a new idea).

After I retired, I remember a time when I was helping with the development of a strategy for a $600 million organization. This was post-PwC and not a PwC client. At my first meeting, the CEO informed the group (including me) that the strategy was almost done, and that he had gotten total alignment across the organization. After some discussion, it quickly became clear that the strategy was nowhere near done, and I informed him of the following: implementing a strategy, by definition, means making big changes to various areas of the business, and thus they will never get total alignment. When he forcefully challenged this statement, I further said "On average 30-40% are aligned at the start." Why? They have determined that they are "on-strategy"—their job is part of the strategic plan (e.g., they work in AI, and AI is a key element of the strategy), and so they'll adapt to the changes in their sector as the plan progresses. On the other hand, 20-30% start as not aligned. Why? They have determined they are "off-strategy"—their job is not part of the strategic plan, and so they are made to feel detached from the organization's new direction and may even worry about their job security. Self-preservation is human nature, and sometimes strategic changes mean that people will be displaced or even removed. This is a critical fact that needs to be dealt with head-on in order to be successful. I dealt with one organization where they loosely referred to this counterproductive group as the "cement layer" of the organization—immovable, and in the way of progress. The remaining 30-50% will declare their support or lack thereof once they know if they are on- or off-strategy.

This chapter details my view on what is important in developing and executing a strategic plan based on my various experiences with the practice of doing so. Is it the only way? No. Is it the best way? I don't know. Will it work if executed as described? Yes, I'm sure of it.

Chapter 24

HOW TO ADDRESS AN OBJECTIVE (A.K.A. PROJECT IDENTIFICATION AND MANAGEMENT)

I n life, we are always running into problems that need to be solved or targets that need to be met. This holds true in business, too, and objectives can range from becoming number one in a market, to getting to know all the right people in a certain country or company, to fixing a certain problem. In my career, these types of things were faced fairly routinely. In almost every case, the route to success was directionally the same.

The first step is to clearly define success. In many cases this is a matter of opinion, not necessarily fact, and is therefore subject to debate. Great minds don't always agree. Nonetheless, this step needs to be completed before you can effectively proceed.

Step two is defining the steps necessary to achieve success. This is usually more difficult than step one and typically requires careful thought and planning to identify all the key components. Step two also usually explores multiple different paths or ways to get to success. That said, there usually is a preferred way that emerges because it makes success more clearly achieved, or because achievement is more assured, or it gets you there quicker.

The third step is identifying the various parts of the ecosystem that you need to engage with. This almost always includes recognizing the people you need to get to know or the organizations you need to connect with.

The fourth step is committing to a timeline to get there and delegating people to spearhead the completion of each step. This is both a method to ensure that progress is made and also a way to measure progress. Measuring, assessing, and reassessing progress is key to success. In my experience, the discipline of doing this is lacking in many organizations.

Last is identifying key metrics and indicators that prove success has been achieved. The metrics need to be objective and not subject to interpretation, and the indicators have to be independent and preferably outside indicators. These metrics are very specific to the objective and could take a number of forms—like reaching $1 million in revenue or completing the project by December 31st, for example.

The road to success is essentially tantamount to hard work in executing against the plan and measuring completion as efforts progress. There will always be course corrections along the way as learnings are evaluated and circumstances change. Achieving success can take weeks, months, or even years, and in some cases, it may never be fully realized.

I know what I have just described sounds very simple and basic, and to some extent it is. That said, maintaining the effort and discipline needed to pursue an objective from start to finish is usually really difficult for a number of reasons. In most cases, succeeding requires a team effort and, in some cases, that could mean coordinating a large team of hundreds of people if not more. Let me give you some real-life examples of how I've used this process to achieve some specific objectives.

How to win and maximize a new account...

1. **Defining Success:** To win an account, we first had to define what winning an account means. It's relatively easy to get a small one-off project somewhere at a company, but cultivating a sustained relationship is much harder. Usually, this meant setting a revenue target—one that was large enough to represent a long-term commitment, and thus, winning an account. These types of revenue targets would typically increase over time to a theoretical level of sustainability.

2. **Defining The Steps:** This meant identifying areas where we thought we could bring value to the client. If it was acquisitive, then acquisition services would be on the list. If the company was global, then international tax or foreign assignee services might be on the list. This was done by gaining an understanding of the company and its needs. This list was also ordered based on what we thought was the highest priority for the client, the second highest, and so on.

3. **Mapping Relationships:** We then set to identify all the key executives and employees we needed to meet over time, as well as any organizations that we both belonged to, or maybe organizations that we needed to join to make a connection. This list typically included top executives who were not the economic buyers in addition to the economic buyers. This list could quickly get complex, because it also needed to include any and all stakeholders, including those beyond the economic buyer. These connections were used as the basis of a relationship map, which detailed all the relevant relationships we'd already formed, relationships that we were pursuing with respect to the objective, and how each of the entities therein was connected.

4. **Committing To A Timeline:** Next was our construction of the timeline. I typically would target specific projects in specific

timeframes, and each project would have its own sub-timeline and a team that was tasked with completing all steps necessary to get the project introduced. The relationship map identified in step three would also be created and monitored down to the project level, as well as for the company as a whole.

5. **Measuring Progress:** As we made progress toward our ultimate goal and the sub-targets thereof, we were constantly analyzing the metrics and monitoring success at the company level—typically in terms of a revenue target—and at the project level—typically in terms of achievement of certain steps in the journey.

The relationship map referred to above (step 3) had key company executives listed, as well as our designated contact person or people. The relationship map also had a designation of how well we knew the executive on a five-point scale: "zero" meant we had never met the executive, and "five" meant we had a long-term trusted relationship. The relationship map typically had the areas of responsibility listed and included targets using the number scale for the following year.

Progress against the metrics was monitored periodically to measure progress. Changes were made as needed and based on changing circumstances.

How to become number one in an industry...

1. **Defining Success:** We'd begin by defining what it means to be number one and determining the indicators of that. For argument's sake, let's assume it includes having the most Fortune 500 tech companies as clients, measured in terms of number of companies and revenue. In addition, this could include having the greatest number of tech public company clients, as well as doing the most IPOs and having the largest share of venture-backed clients among our contemporary firms. As you can see, this definition is somewhat arbitrary and can be

defined by any number of factors. That said, if you had all of these components, you would have a fairly strong basis to say you were number one.

2. **Defining The Steps:** As expected, this took the form of a fairly detailed list of steps or sub-targets to make progress toward and ultimately achieve the goal. It would include targets by geography, and in the context of this example would include Silicon Valley, San Francisco, New York, Boston, etc. It would include targets by category, in addition to objectives pertaining to specific Fortune 500 companies, venture-backed companies, public tech companies, and so on.

3. **Mapping Relationships:** This was the formation of a long list of people and organizations we needed to target across the country—organized by geography, company, organization, etc.—and then have our people assigned to each. How this would work from a practical standpoint was that each subcomponent—for example, a geography—would have an individual action plan, devised by carrying out all five overarching steps as they applied to the relevant objectives in the area, and then linking these comprising elements to the whole. This was usually a top-down, then bottom-up exercise. Accountability was very specific at all levels and across all the metrics.

4. **Committing To And Delivering On A Timeline:** This timeline was again organized by geography, company, etc. This also was done at different levels of detail: at one (more detailed) level, you might have very detailed targets and measure progress empirically against them. At the top (summary) level, you might simply choose to track progress via color designations, using red to indicate that you are not on schedule, green to indicate that you are, and yellow to indicate somewhere in between.

5. **Measuring Progress:** At this point, we'd begin the analysis of the metrics that determined success, which again were monitored

periodically and more detailed at each level.

This example, I think, shows how large and complex a plan can be, as well as the difficulty in execution that comes with a large, geographically dispersed team. It also would require a number of years to execute and re-execute. That said, I have been involved in the execution of many such plans in my career and believe the above framework is effective. Steps 1 through 5 represent in totality a major project plan, where every step and data point in each of the five steps needs to be completed in the planned time frame to meet the predetermined target. The execution of some steps will be firmly under your control. Others will not. The execution of the five-step plan will need to be assessed and reassessed periodically to ensure all steps are on track or completed. When they fall behind, course corrections have to quickly be put in place. In my experience using this strategy, step 2—**Defining The Steps**—is the most critical to success, but step 4—**Committing To And Delivering On A Timeline**—will always be the most challenging.

Despite the complexities that might arise in specific circumstances, I have found the process described here to be conceptually simple. The keys are reevaluating the components in the model over time, assigning responsibility for execution down to the lowest level, and constantly monitoring progress.

Chapter 25

SETTING THE BAR HIGH

T his is a topic that is part of my DNA. It separates a relatively small percentage of the population from the rest. In business, it separates the high performers from the average performers. It is a mindset that can materially change the answer or the outcome, and this proves true time and time again, over short periods of time like months or years, or over extended periods like a career. Needless to say, it is an important concept.

When I look back at my career, I cannot believe the experiences I had or the things I was able to achieve. If I told someone what would happen, they would have thought I was crazy in 1973. Hell, *I* would have thought I was crazy. In fact, I *would have been* crazy to believe any of it at the time. That said, what happened was in no small part the result of setting the bar high over and over again, and almost always. One of my partners once said, "Don always thinks big, he makes you think big. He has the confidence to think big and he gives you the confidence to think big." I'm not sure that this comment is exactly correct, but I do know that I've always tended to think outside of the box and generally big. It's just what I do.

The path I took over my career certainly included some big steps, many of which were the result of setting the bar high. Reaching that bar—and in many cases, even exceeding where the bar was set—was always owed to the team I had at my back. I think in my early days, my teams may have thought I was crazy. After reaching or exceeding the bar that I'd set, the next time I was not so crazy. It may sound strange, but I can remember a number of times when my targets were considered impossible by many of my colleagues and were achieved nonetheless.

The effect of setting a high bar for oneself can be understood using simple math. If you have a 10% growth target and you reach it every year for five years, you will have grown about 61%. On the other hand, if you set a 20% annual growth target and meet it consistently, after five years you will have grown almost 150%. I know that these are just numbers, but it's helpful in setting up the concept.

With regards to setting the bar, these are several tenets that would appear to be true.

One: The bar should not be set at an unattainably high level, so as to avoid failure to meet expectations.

Two: If the bar is set low, then it is likely to be exceeded.

Three: People tend to set the bar to stretch themselves a little and achieve the maximum possible outcome.

Four: Most people will tend to come to the same conclusions regarding where the bar is being set (i.e., as being high or low).

While all of the above may present as downright obvious, the truth is that each of them varies from case to case, and their accuracy is beholden to a whole host of different factors and circumstances.

In my experience, many people set the bar so low that meeting it is practically guaranteed. At the same time, they may exceed it, but usually only by a little. While on paper this makes for consistently meeting or exceeding expectations, these outputs fall well below what maximum performance could have been. Also, sometimes the bar is not met, but it is *almost* met, which comes close to being "a success." Not good in my view: it's fine to fall short of reaching your goal if the bar for success was set high, but failure to reach a low bar evidences not only a lack of vision but also a lack of drive. Also, people who set the bar low usually don't build in any stretch. They intend to put the bar only where they can reach it. My personal view is that in many cases these people tend to recalibrate their assessment down over time. This is to say that the bar is set lower and lower with each future objective.

The exceptional performers, on the other hand, set the bar as high as it can reasonably be set. They build in a large amount of stretch, and may actually set it so high that it can only be met if everything goes right (which it never does). Some—maybe most—view this as crazy, but these performers are focused not so much on where the bar is set, but on getting exceptional results. In my example above, they may not achieve the 20% growth target, but even if they achieve only 18.5% they have still doubled the result set by the low bar.

It's interesting to me that many would focus on the fact that the exceptional team missed their target of 20% whereas the other team met their target of 10%. This view was always contrary to how I viewed the world and how I calibrated success. To me, the 18.5% was a home run, and maybe even a grand slam compared to 10%. The irony here is that in my experience and using this example, the exceptional performers usually exceeded the 20% target. They did this by constantly working the issues and fixing what did not go as planned. They work like a world-class tennis player plays tennis: they start in first gear, and as the game gets away from them, they take their game up to a higher gear, and they keep doing this until they win. Exceptional performers do the same. It is also common that a commitment to a 20% growth rate would actually result in the team setting an even higher target for themselves, say 22% or 24%. This is to help ensure that 20% will be met.

Now let me say that I am well aware that a target, no matter what the area, requires a detailed plan with a series of steps that need to be executed in order to achieve it. It also usually requires a team to be aligned on the target and in their execution of the steps. There also are usually budget or funding issues that need to be addressed, and that may be negatively impacted if the targets are not met.

I realize all of this. The point I am making—and that I have seen work time and time again, in many different circumstances—is that setting the bar high will dramatically change the outcome. I have seen this in growth rates, in timelines (i.e., how long something will take), in expected promotions—I've even seen this happen with respect to SAT scores and grade point averages!

As I mentioned, setting goals this way is part of my DNA—to do otherwise does not compute. What's more, I firmly believe that my career would not have gone as far as it did without this mindset. That said, this was not always a popular strategy: there was no shortage of pushback along the way, though I never allowed that pushback to change my mind.

I remember dealing with client satisfaction on our large global accounts. When we started, we were not number one, but we were very close. The question was "What would we have to do to be number one by a convincing margin, and what steps would we have to take to get there?"

We had a world-class team, including teams on all of these global accounts. We agreed on a plan and started focusing on execution and monitoring progress. Our overall strategy hung on two key questions—one answered by our clients, one answered by our teams internally. Externally, companies were asked which firm they would recommend. If they said us, that meant that they considered us the best. The threshold question for us internally was what could or should the margin be—what percentage of these companies needed to pick us as number one before it truly meant we *were* number one? There were essentially four firms at the time, so if we each got our pro-rata share it would be 25%. As I recall, our survey efforts determined that we had 33%.

The answer to this question was hotly debated. Many believed the target should be capturing just enough of the market to get to number one. To do this would take a 1% or 2% increase. My vote was 50%, which all things being equal, would have given us a sixteen-point advantage over number two at 34%. I remember this being considered by many to be impossible. Also, it wasn't a target that would be published, but one that was put up as an aspiration. So, the bar was raised from 33% to 50%, and all 150 teams raised their bars.

We had decided to survey a number of executives at each company using an outside firm so that the companies didn't know who was conducting the survey. Our primary targets were CEOs, but we surveyed other C-Suite executives as well, and recorded the results for all. Some teams were already at number one, but some may have been between two and four. Remember, to have 33% considering us number one also meant we had 66% who didn't.

The teams were energized and the objective was clear. By the way, this was happening on some 150 teams in twenty-five countries. After three years, our satisfaction percentage (i.e., being rated number one) rose to 66%—a 35% margin over number two. Which is better: being number one by two points, or being number one by thirty-five points? I think the answer is clear.

The focus here is not the thirty-five points. It's that putting the 50% target in place signaled a *very* high bar, not just a normally high bar. Where the bar was set signaled how high we had to try to jump, and how hard we had to work to get there.

I set a bar once for the market share of one of our industry groups. The target I set was 100% market share. I remember speaking to about 200 of our industry partners and putting up a slide that targeted 100% market share. The room erupted in uncontrollable laughter—I know they all thought I had finally lost it! I went on to tell the group that I knew we could not ever get 100% market share. I told them, however, that what I did not know was how close we could get. In addition to my own projections, I had partners from about fifteen cities across the U.S. put up our estimated market share in each city. It ranged from very low to almost 70%. The laughter, as you can imagine, stopped.

I then asked the partner in charge of the city with 70% market share to explain to the larger group how they had been able to get there. His presentation was all around "basic blocking and tackling," as they say in football. Everything they had done and were doing could be replicated across all fifteen cities. Also, there were best practices across the other fourteen cities that could be replicated in his city, which might actually increase his market share further. Obviously, this initiative required increased resources, and also some resource reallocation. That said, however, the power of the bar and where you put it was clear. The 100% got their attention, and the 70% said it could be done.

I have one last example of setting the bar. I was asked to lead an account where the client was extremely unhappy with our services. They were so unhappy that they were going to fire us on one or two projects, and even threatened a lawsuit. This was a large multinational company, and our fees at the time were around five million dollars a year. I remember meeting with our core team and also with management at the company to assess the problems. It was a very complex set of issues, which it always is, but the overriding issue was that the client thought we took them for granted.

I'll never forget the words "house account." At PwC, this was a term I used to denote one of our most important clients: a marque company that we were proud to serve and have on our client list. A client that warranted our best people and our best teams. The client in question knew the term house account because it was also used by the previous partner on their account, however, they believed that the term referred to a client that we'd had for a long time and thus took for granted. Wow, some difference—and a perception that would be really hard to change.

So where to set the bar? I set the bar at being their number one preferred supplier in all the things we were doing and could do for them. I had to convince my team (that had a few new members, but only a few) that I was serious, and that we could and would get there. I not only set the bar there for our teams internally, but also at the client. That is to say that every executive I met with all over the world heard that this was our objective. "I want us to be your number one preferred provider all over the world." Period. Over and over and over. I only asked that they give us a chance. I guaranteed that they would get our best people and that we would deliver on our promises 100% of the time—no exceptions!

It took about six months of really hard work to start to see some small signs that the relationship was changing. It took another six months to get a big chance. After we delivered on that opportunity and exceeded their expectations, it took another year to become a preferred provider. A year later, we were their number one preferred provider.

Three years from start to jumping the bar. Attaining the goal was a huge team effort, requiring leadership and experience from both myself and the other leaders on my team. The raw energy that we needed and the constant focus that honed it came from where the bar was set. This was one of my high-performing teams, and they were laser-focused on where the bar was set.

Chapter 26

RISK

The dictionary defines the noun "risk" as "the possibility of loss or injury." As a verb, it is "to expose to hazard or danger." To be "at risk" is to be "in a state or condition marked by a high level of risk or susceptibility." Synonyms are "danger," "threat," "hazard," "pitfall," "gamble," and "trouble."

In business, risk is not so easy to define. Instead, it's a complex topic—a very relative term that means different things to different people. In some cases, these differences are dramatic.

In life, nothing is without risk, and almost anything can be at risk of failure. The key is to first ensure that you understand the risk—that you are able to quantify it, put it in the context of any relevant industries, assess its probability, and minimize it if possible—before you deal with it. This is much easier said than done.

It also requires multiple steps as described here. Each step has its own inherent error rate, that is, the rate at which you would be wrong. In order for the five steps to result in a good outcome, each step must be executed correctly. If you do not adequately understand the risk, or you cannot quantify it, or you cannot assess its probability, your ability to even *try* to deal with it will fail.

Assuming you get all steps correct, you still need to assess whether the risk is worth taking at all. In many cases in life and business, the answer is no. When it is no, it is because the loss, should it occur, is more significant than the gain.

In assessing risk there are multiple considerations, but they are usually weighed across the same two axes. The first axis is the order of magnitude from small to big. The second axis is the probability from low to high. For example, let's say I'm assessing the risk of investing in a company, with the goal of exiting the position with the most money I can. Somewhat obviously, if there is a high probability that I will lose a large amount of money, this is likely a bad risk to take. Alternatively, if there is a low probability that I will lose money, this risk is usually worth taking—makes sense right? Taking it one step further: if there is a high probability that I will lose money, but the size of the investment necessary to see significant returns is small (order of magnitude), this could very well be a risk worth taking, as the potential for gain outweighs the potential for loss.

This type of assessment is called a "risk-reward analysis." Said differently, is the reward worth taking the risk? This is a very personal decision, and usually is based on factors unrelated to the core decision. An example of this is if you are worth five million dollars and you are betting five dollars. You will likely take the risk of losing it all if the reward is high enough. Similar is buying a lottery ticket, where you spend five dollars and can win fifty million. You have almost no chance of winning, but you might still make the bet. This example gets ridiculous when the potential jackpot goes up and the amount bet also goes up. The betting increases even though the odds of winning go down as the jackpot goes up as a result of more people betting.

In my life, I have seen many people make bets which I believed were crazy—almost none of them were relatively small bets like the lottery ticket example. Lottery tickets are in the category of what I always call "excess disposable income"—if you have it, you can do with it what you want, be it jewelry, wine, cars, trips, or gambling in Las Vegas. The relatively big bets are what concern me here. I have seen too many examples of people who risked most of their net worth—even some who risked *more* than their net worth—and lost everything.

In 100% of the cases, these were extremely smart and experienced business people who thought the risk of failure was almost zero when in fact it was not. In many cases, it was starting their own business after working for someone else in that same type of business. In some cases, it was starting their own business when they had watched from afar and concluded it looked easy, so they wanted to do it themselves. In other cases, it was a newer, perhaps unproven business that they "knew would be successful."

In each case, when failure happened and they lost everything, they essentially started over with nothing. This is always a life-altering experience! I give these examples only to illustrate that the determination and assessment of risk is not only empirical but can also be influenced by emotion. My rule is generally only to invest what you can afford to lose, even if you assess that the odds of losing are low.

I have worked as a mini venture capitalist for about ten years, and I have worked with many venture capitalists over my career. What I can say with 100% certainty is that on the day of the investment, all venture capitalists believe that their investment will be successful. On average, about 90% fail. There are many reasons why they fail, but they fail.

The best ways to minimize risk and maximize reward are to **be an expert** in the area you are taking the risk in, to have the ability to **change the risk profile**, and to have the ability to **increase the reward potential**.

Be an Expert

By being an expert in the area of risk you will be dealing with, you will not only increase the probability that your risk assessment will be correct, but also increase the chances that you will be able to see the challenges coming and manage them. Although a somewhat obvious concept, I can't tell you how many people I see taking risks that they know almost nothing about. Just because you like to eat or even cook does not mean you know how to run a restaurant. I find it laughable how many failed restaurateurs thought they knew what they were doing because they had great interpersonal skills and would be good at greeting customers as they arrived. Similarly, if you are a real expert at something you may be able to lower the risk and increase the reward because most others don't have your expertise. An example of this could be a specialist foreign exchange trader who knows when to make the trade before anyone else, and thus they could be making more money on the way up and losing less money on the way down.

Change the Risk Profile

Changing the risk profile is one way to maximize the outcome. There are many examples of how this is done, but they all include certain expertise or connections. I saw this done often in my career when an American company sold a company, subsidiary, or asset to a local country buyer (say, in Brazil). The seller sold a high-risk asset, which usually means it was sold at a discount. The local buyer, with their local country expertise and connections, could dramatically reduce the risk of loss and at the same time maximize their upside. I also saw this done often in Asia, and in fact, I had two clients who specialized in these types of transactions across many asset classes. They bought high-risk, discounted assets and sold or operated them as low-to-moderate-risk assets. Another way to change the risk profile is to ensure that local experts are put in place to run your business or manage your asset base. Again, in this situation, the risk profile goes down as the level of experience of the operators goes up.

Increase the Reward Potential

Increasing the reward potential can occur in a number of ways. The last paragraph offered an example of this in its mention of the utilization of local experts. The broadest way, however, is typically referred to as "synergies." There are many situations that result in synergies. In an acquisition situation, often when you combine Company A with Company B, the resulting Company C can be run for less cost than A and B combined. This increases the reward. This situation can also increase revenue when Company A's sales force sells Company B's products to A's customers. Often in the startup space, many develop products or services that can work with or even improve other companies' products. This can and does give rise to acquisitions that in many cases increase the value and reward for both selling and buying stockholders.

Managing risk in business and in life is a critical skill set. Taking no risk is not possible. Taking appropriate risks can be a game changer.

Chapter 27

ENTREPRENEURSHIP

E ntrepreneurship is not a job title: it is a mindset; it is a group of characteristics; it is a perspective; it is a way of life; it is an essence; and I think it is genetic. Entrepreneurs are very unique people. They can be found as CEOs of startups in Silicon Valley or as CEOs of huge multinational companies headquartered in New York. In my experience, those at both ends of this spectrum—from lower-level novices to high-level pros—have very similar characteristics.

I have met and worked with many entrepreneurs in my career and life, and I see myself in many of them. Being entrepreneurial does not mean you need to start a business, although many do; it means being innovative, creative, resourceful, and adaptable. These qualities can help in most aspects of a career, whether you want to work for yourself or someone else, in business or academia. Let me try to describe what I think it means to be an entrepreneur.

Risk-Taker with Confidence

All entrepreneurs are risk-takers at heart, but not all risk-takers are entrepreneurs. What differentiates them is that entrepreneurs are also very confident—in some cases, overly confident—that the risks can be overcome, and that they will succeed. In some cases they are right, and in some cases they are wrong. As I discussed in the chapter on *Risk* (Chapter 26), an acceptable risk is defined by not only the probability of success but also the order of magnitude of the bet itself.

Supremely Confident

Many entrepreneurs are supremely confident: to them there is a zero chance of failure, and they are 100% confident that they will succeed. This is an interesting attribute which can be very good or very bad. At the extremes—and I have seen this often—they seem to believe themselves capable of willing success into being, even when failure is all but assured. As the situation gets worse and worse, they hold onto the belief that a miracle will save them, and they'll be able to "snatch victory from the jaws of defeat." They believe they will win even though it seems they are certain to lose.

In my case, I tend to be supremely confident, but only after assessing it can be done. If I believe it can be done, then I am 100% sure I will succeed. This is clearly an entrepreneurial trait that I have, but one which is tempered with reason and logic.

Bet The Ranch

As referred to above, entrepreneurs are risk-takers and so am I. We can debate what a "big risk" is, but I will tell you that in my life and career, I have taken big risks. The size of the risk I was willing to take has evolved over time, and so too has the size of what is "big." As we've already discussed, entrepreneurs tend to be both risk-tolerant and supremely confident in their own success. As such, you'll often see them take on massive risks in the hopes of massive rewards—in other words, "betting the ranch" on their success. A given entrepreneur can have any number of reasons for taking such chances, but in most cases, it ultimately boils down to their belief in themselves in the face of any odds and aligns with their passion for whatever aim they're undertaking (as I'll discuss in the next section). The other end of the spectrum is a small bet on something that has a high probability of success. This latter bet would not qualify you as entrepreneurial. I have worked my entire career in the technology and healthcare fields—two areas that are known for entrepreneurs and entrepreneurship. That said, the highest percentage of entrepreneurs I have ever seen are New York City restaurateurs. I am not an expert on the restaurant industry, but I do know that more than 80% of restaurants fail, and most restaurateurs have staked their life savings on the success of their ventures. Don't get me wrong, these are real entrepreneurs, but I wouldn't try it myself!

Independence

All entrepreneurs are independent in thought and action. This does not mean they do not collaborate and team well, but rather that they always have their own ideas. They also are self-starters and do not need direction. In my experience, they also do not take direction well, especially, from people whose opinions they do not value. You see this often in interactions with board members, especially those who are venture capitalists, who often think they know better when they don't.

Passion

Passion is a universal trait of all entrepreneurs. They have a lunatic passion for the company they have started or the job they are doing. It is usually obvious to all around them. It is not that they do not have a personal life—in most cases they do—but that they are so zealous in their pursuit of success that they have a hard time stepping away from their work. If they can separate business from pleasure, fine, but in most cases, they cannot. Many of their close friends are friends from work. Many of their parties are with people from work. In my career, I was passionate about everything that was important to me. I also socialized with my partners, my teams, and my clients, many of whom were friends.

No Attention Span

Many entrepreneurs (like me) have a very short attention span. I always said that I had "undiagnosed ADD." I've also always said that I had "the attention span of a gnat." One of my character traits, which I've found in most if not all entrepreneurs, is that I can be "a little curt." This is to say that I and those like me change subjects while you are mid-sentence or interrupt you often. It is an impatience that derives from being entrepreneurial—we think ahead, think quickly, and act even more quickly. This is what I do to a tee and always—I cannot help it. When I understand what you are saying and I agree, then there is no need to talk about it any further, and I'd rather move on to the next thing than belabor the point. This trait pisses off many people I deal with, but it is one which I cannot change.

Decision-Maker

All entrepreneurs are decision-makers, and they make decisions quickly. All their decisions, however, are not necessarily good. Also, many of their decisions are clouded by their passion, confidence, independence, and assessment of risk or lack thereof. Somewhere in this book I say that all great leaders know how to make decisions and make them quickly. Although I believe this is true, I caution against making a decision without objective facts. I also said that I make decisions with 50-60% of the information—I do not wait to get 100% (which never happens). I stand by this statement as well, with the caveat that the 50-60% must be correct information.

Oversimplification

I oversimplify everything, and so do most entrepreneurs. I have learned from working with many of them that they make everything sound easy, fast, and doable with minimal resources. I tend to do the same. One thing I will tell you, however, is that in a world where most people make simple things complex, this trait gets things done. I remember a meeting where the presenters were talking about a six-month timeline. Given the project, that was way too long. I challenged them and said it could be done in one week. When they laughed, I explained that when we, as a firm, were in proposal mode (i.e., proposing on a new account) and we only had one week, we always finished in one week. I further explained that a week could be five eight-hour days (forty hours), seven eight-hour days (fifty-six hours), seven twelve-hour days (eighty-four hours), or seven twenty-four-hour days (168 hours). 168 hours in normal day terms is 4.2 weeks. They got the message, and we got it done in one month, not six months.

Simplicity

Keep it simple. Simple is usually quicker, cheaper, and better. Complexity is bad, except maybe in areas like science or math and the like. Most entrepreneurs like simple, repeatable, and reliable processes, and businesses will almost always opt for simplicity over complexity. I personally love simplicity, and I actually "majored in simple" as part of my consulting mantra. I would consult with CEOs and CFOs and would often say, "If it's that complex, it must be extremely inefficient and costly." They always agreed.

Work Ethic

All entrepreneurs I have met and worked with were workaholics. This was always true: their focus was constantly on their business or their company. It was their passion twenty-four hours a day, seven days a week, fifty-two weeks a year, and anywhere in the world. They were always working—on holidays, on vacation, at the beach, in the mountains, wherever, whenever.

Mission and Focus

All entrepreneurs have a clear mission, and they are focused on it day after day. They usually wake up in the middle of the night thinking about what they need to do to complete the mission. Like high performers—which many of them are—they get closer and closer, but will never reach their ultimate goal. That's because their goal will always keep changing, with the bar being constantly raised.

Formality

Most entrepreneurs do not respect formality. It tends to slow things down, which they hate. Most of them accept necessary evils like lawyers and accountants only to keep them out of trouble. They also usually only defer to their board (if they have one) on formal, non-critical, non-business matters.

Creativity

Most entrepreneurs are exceptionally creative. They tend to think outside the box, and they always think big. Most, if not all, are trying to do something that has never been done before, or if done before, then they're trying to do it their way. They have identified a problem and are refining a product or service that will solve it. Some of these solutions are fairly simple, but some are extraordinarily complex and sometimes involve technologies or components that don't yet exist.

Hear The Train Coming

One thing that all entrepreneurs need to watch out for is that they may not "see or hear the train coming"—a major problem is about to happen, but they don't or can't anticipate it. If they do not hear it, or hear it too late, it can be fatal from a business perspective. I have seen this happen on multiple occasions. The most common example is when they run out of money unexpectedly and are unable to raise new funds.

In this chapter, I have tried to articulate what an entrepreneur and entrepreneurship is. As I noted in the beginning, it is a state of mind and not a job position. Many of the qualities I have included can be improved and refined. Some are intuitive and maybe even genetic.

Chapter 28

HOW TO MEET (FAMOUS) PEOPLE – HOW TO WORK A ROOM

B eing able to meet people is key in business and to some extent life. Meeting famous people from all walks of life is exciting and can be tremendously rewarding. Knowing influencers, famous or otherwise, is not only rewarding but also good for business.

I had my first experience with celebrities when I was pretty young: I met Hume Cronin and Jessica Tandy, whom we built a pool for when I was seventeen. For those of you who don't recognize the names, they are theater royalty, and she won an Academy Award for Best Actress in 1990 for Driving Miss Daisy. They were really nice people, and really appreciative of the pool we built for them.

My first *illuminating* experience, however, was in 1976. I was a very young staff accountant at PwC, and one of my clients was an organization that was trying to save New York City from financial ruin. At the end of year one of this mission, a group of bigwigs threw a celebration party for the expanded team. This was about two or three hundred people, mostly from the political and business world. There was every living New York mayor, governor, senator, congressman, etc.; there were the New York and Washington financial and legal elite; and there were many other famous guests. Every relevant person on the team (and then some) was in attendance, all the way down to me—I was probably the last invitee.

What I learned that night is that famous people do not know who they know. This is generally because they meet so many people that it is hard to keep track of names and faces. So why is this relevant? Because if they don't know who they know and you act like you have met them before, they will assume that they have and act like they know you. They also have what I call "event memories," meaning if you introduce yourself at an event you're both attending, they will remember you for the next two or three hours while the event takes place. In the case of this organization's event, I can remember to this day the various governors, mayors, and the like that I had spoken to at the event saying "Goodbye Don, and take care of Gail" or similar goodbyes as we left. I also remember some of my colleagues asking how I knew Abe (as in Beam—NYC mayor), or Hugh (as in Carey—former NYS governor), or Felix (as in Rohatyn). I really didn't answer, but the truth was I didn't—I had only met them that night.

I built a very large global network over forty years by combining three complementary skills.

First—I found it easy to talk to people about many topics, not just about business, although in some cases talking business was key (remember what I learned as a taxi driver).

Second—I found it easy and somewhat exhilarating to go up to important and famous people and start a conversation. After a while, I'd find I knew some of the same people they did, or that I knew people they would like to meet.

Third—I was always focused on trying to meet everyone, and later in my career, giving them my business card so we could stay in touch. Interestingly, many will either give you theirs back or email you later with a thank you. Most people stand around and talk to people they already know and, in some cases, see every day. Not me! Some would say "I had a terrible time because I didn't know anyone." I would say "I had a great time because I didn't know anyone."

This may sound funny or strange, but the attitude encapsulated by that last point was a game-changer for me. Over time, I got a reputation for "knowing everyone," which was not true—obviously, I didn't know *everyone*. Many of the CEOs and CFOs who were my clients would say that—the result of being together in larger groups like fundraisers or industry meetings, where I guess they noticed me speaking with a lot of different people. At my retirement party, one of my British partners said, "Don is different. He has no fear. He doesn't just stand around. He goes and meets and talks to people." This seemed unusual to my British partner, and maybe it was, but it was not at all unusual to me. It was what came naturally.

A little story: it was the opening night of the season at Carnegie Hall. I was with some of my partners at cocktails, and I had just excused myself so I could "work the room." One of them made a point to everyone as a joke that "Don thinks there is no one here he can't meet." At that very moment, the elevator doors opened, and a very famous actor and his girlfriend came into the room. They were about fifty feet away, with many people between them and us. I turned to my joking partner and the rest of the group: "Watch this."

I looked toward the actor, called him by his first name, and waved my arms to signal him to come over to our table. Surprise!—they walked right over. I shook his hand, said his first name, then said my full name and that I was glad to see him (NOT glad to "*meet*" him). He said "Great to see you, Don. Where did I see you last?" I said, "On the island." He said, "Oh yeah, right." I then introduced him to my wife and partners, and we chatted with him for fifteen minutes about his then-current TV show.

When dinner started, I was hosting a PwC table, and the actor came back my way just as we were sitting down. We said hello again, but this time we "knew" each other. He says "Don, can you introduce me to your friends?" I introduced him to everyone at my table, which were some of our most important PwC New York contacts and names you would know. This, I am sure, helped get his attention. In any event, he came by another three or four times during the gala, and by the end, was sitting with us and calling me "Donnie Boy."

I gave him my card, and we have loosely stayed in touch since. "Loosely" means I have invited him to a number of events, and he has said yes to the invitation. By the way, this was not an isolated example—once you understand how to work a room, you'll find yourself in these sorts of situations often.

Whenever I was invited to an event, business or otherwise, I would try to determine who might be at the event and which of those attendees I really wanted to meet. This is something I learned from my not-for-profit work, where the focus was on identifying who among the guests might be interested in becoming a major donor. In any event, I viewed these events predominantly as work and networking opportunities, with the possibility of maybe landing a client or two. My conversational focus was on whatever the event was for, but also on personalizing the conversation to whomever I was speaking with. This meant finding out what was on their mind and trying to help them with whatever issue or issues they might have. Once you get into the issues, then you need to employ some skills to take it to the next level. This requires critical thinking and analysis on the spot to react to the conversation and hopefully give some value-added feedback. It requires understanding things the other person might be interested in. It requires trying to determine who each of you might know, and how you might be connected via your respective networks—an example of this is if he/she is a banking CFO, do you know any banking CFOs, and might there be a connection? Above all else, the key is to try to bring value that they appreciate and remember.

As I traveled around the world and tried to replicate what I have just described, I found that in many cases it worked the same way. I learned, however, that it could be very helpful to have someone I called my "strategic advisor" or "handler" with me at events. My strategic advisor in a given country had a different role depending on the country, but they always accompanied me to major events. At these functions, their job consisted of just two elements: first, to introduce me, and second, to pull me away. The introduction part involved telling the person I was meeting who I was and why they should meet me. This was essentially an elevator speech, but more flattering than someone could do for themselves. This gave me the opportunity to downplay what my strategic advisor had just said, maybe get a laugh, and many times supercharge the conversation. The "pull me away" part was put in motion after a certain amount of time spent in a single conversation, taking me away so that I didn't spend too much time with any one person. If the person I was speaking to got annoyed by this, it was usually not at me but rather at my strategic advisor. This becomes even more useful when speaking to someone one-on-one and leaving the conversation leaves them alone. I also used these encounters to elevate the stature of my strategic advisor, who typically was a local partner. These interactions tended to go a little something like this:

My handler begins by saying something along the lines of "I'd like to introduce you to Don Almeida, the PwC Global Vice Chairman. He visits here often and is on the foreign investor council. Part of his job is to meet and connect with CEOs around the world."

As the CEO is saying hello, I say being a Vice Chairman is greatly overrated, and certainly nowhere near as challenging as being a CEO. He'll tell me not to be so modest, and ask me what exactly it is that I do.

From there, I immediately started talking about PwC, my connections with other CEOs, and how I/we might help his company. I also connect the dots to his company in the country we are in and also to the global network.

In business, as in life, you need to decide what you are going to do and how you are going to do it. As I have said often, every interaction is a test or an interview. For better or worse, people begin drawing conclusions about one another from their first meeting: Is he or she impressive? Are they smart? Do they bring value?

Are they someone I want to connect with? In terms of what has been discussed here, making a good impression needs to be a focus, and there needs to be a plan or a strategy whenever you meet someone new. After execution, there should be a postmortem—how did it go?

At a macro level, this is also connected to an overall strategy that broadly determines what types of people you are trying to meet (like CEOs in a specific industry or country, for example) and how you are to execute your plan (what exact people at which events and at what times).

For several years, in connection with PwC's business in Russia, I would go to the St. Petersburg Economic Forum. This tended to attract the who's who of global business from many countries around the world. With the help of my global and local teams, I would participate in a significant number of panels and events over the three days and nights of the Forum's duration. I used to describe this event as condensing months of work into three days. It was a way of seeing many people you knew and meeting many more you did not. It also combined pure business with social interaction. This was true at APEC, Davos, and a number of other venues around the world.

I always found that these events provided a way of supercharging your network. By being on stage as a panelist or moderator, I was exposed to hundreds of people in a value-added context. They were there to hear from the experts on a topic they were interested in, and I was one of the experts. Later, in more informal settings, it was easier to meet them: either they remembered me right away, or I introduced myself alongside the panel I was involved with. Being a member of the panel held a certain cachet, and so not only was I "soft introduced" to those at the event, but they also automatically assumed that a relationship with me was valuable—which, for networking purposes, is nearly as useful as actually demonstrating value. In most cases, leveraging this perception could get me an "in" with just about anyone at the event, and from there it was much easier to have a meaningful, fruitful interaction.

An Almeida Point—In the Kingdom of Networking, Value is King

WHENEVER YOU ARE MAKING NEW CONNECTIONS, YOU HAVE TO ALWAYS THINK VALUE! IF YOU ARE ABLE TO BRING VALUE, THE RELATIONSHIP IS LIKELY TO CONTINUE. IF YOU DON'T BRING VALUE, MAINTAINING THE RELATIONSHIP WILL BE MUCH MORE DIFFICULT. ALSO, WHEN YOU MAKE A POINT OF BRINGING VALUE TO YOUR RELATIONSHIPS, YOU START TO GET A REPUTATION FOR DOING SO, WHICH IN TURN MAKES IT EASIER TO MAKE NEW CONNECTIONS GOING FORWARD: SOMEONE YOU'VE MADE A POSITIVE IMPRESSION ON BECOMES MORE LIKELY TO TELL ONE OF THEIR FRIENDS OR ASSOCIATES TO SPEAK TO YOU, AND SO YOU BEGIN THE RELATIONSHIP WITH A FOOT IN THE DOOR.

Chapter 29

HOW TO DEAL WITH CHIEF EXECUTIVES

When I refer to chief executives, I am really referring to the "people who run things" who usually sit at the top of an organization. They are usually very busy, know what they run very well, tend to want to deal primarily with people in similar positions to them or people they think can help their organizations, and hate wasting time. These could be CEOs, university presidents, union leaders, small business owners, large company divisional presidents, and so on.

Getting the first meeting with a chief executive may be difficult, but getting the second meeting can either be easy or impossible. Within two minutes of meeting you, a chief executive will have concluded whether you are relevant to them or not. If you are, you will get a second meeting—which may even be scheduled before you leave in the case that you are *really* relevant. If you are not considered relevant (I hate the word "irrelevant"), then there will be no second meeting. Not next week, not next month, not next year—never.

Chief executives are very often leaders. They are generally very smart and experienced—even experts in one or more industries. They usually are decision-makers, and generally present as impatient with a clear aversion to "wasting time." Many of them have a sales gene: they gravitate towards customers and they can be "person people," but will only act as such if they want to (i.e., see it as in their interest).

In my career, I learned over time how to deal effectively with CEOs and the heads of organizations. I even, in my later years with PwC, had to deal with high-level government officials (and in some cases, the highest level). The most important thing I learned was that to be effective, you had to bring value, and you had to do it each and every time—a strategy that applies in dealing with chief executives of all descriptions.

Whenever I got a new client and was going to meet with the CEO for the first time, I always did two things. First, I would learn his/her top five priorities. This was usually not difficult, as they are generally known in the organization and sometimes are even published. Knowing these, I could then research and prepare so I had a view as to how PwC and I could help them in these areas. Sometimes this was the first time this kind of discussion had taken place with a PwC partner.

Second, I would listen to customer calls to see what the issues were. In the old days, this meant actually having to go to a specific location; now you can use a call-in number. I would listen to about an hour of calls and put together a summary list of issues and my insights related to them. When I met with the CEO, I would do a one-minute introduction covering why I was there, and then mention the customer calls. I told them that I had listened to their customers and asked them whether they wanted to hear what they'd said. As you might guess, they always said yes.

The issues were different depending on the company, but always interesting to the CEO. Also, if you heard the same issue multiple times in an hour, you knew it might be systemic. My insights were usually very well received. They were things like the customer didn't know who to call for their problem, or a problem required three different touch points to solve, or certain people were more concerned with selling an add-on product than fixing the customer's problem, or the very common issue of the organization seeming to be too complex, with the different parts not working together.

All CEOs gravitate to their customers, and I found that all of them wanted to discuss my findings. Also, it clearly signaled that I was a customer-facing person like they were. An interesting fact to me was that some of these CEOs had never listened to customer calls. After our meetings, I believe many of those who hadn't started to.

My experience with CEOs cemented another common theme: CEOs want to deal with people who tell them things they need to know and who bring value. They also want to deal with decision-makers like themselves. If you are not the decision-maker, then they will want to meet the real decision-maker—not you.

When it comes to bringing value, the highest on my list was any important or insightful information related to their business that they may not know or may have been misinformed about. The reality is that many CEOs, especially those of large companies, can be shielded from bad news. The reason for this is that "the troops" may not raise issues until they absolutely have to be raised. Platitudes like "Boss, it's going great" were commonly heard.

What my teams and I would do was plan to become very knowledgeable about strategic issues, strategic businesses (especially of the future), and strategic geographies (especially emerging ones). We would then determine how we could help the company—and by association, the CEO—in these areas. When I finally met with the CEO, a topic of discussion was always these strategic areas and how we were helping create value therein, along with any observations we had that might be of interest to them.

I can remember a list of areas by client over the years where we made a significant impact and brought significant value to the organization. Interestingly, many of these areas became core competencies of mine, which I then utilized in my service to other clients. These were geographic proficiencies, such as operating in India, Russia, China, and Brazil; how to deal with certain regulatory bodies in

Washington; strategies surrounding change management; how to effect a major ERP implementation; or, particularly for new CEOs, how to deal with their boards of directors.

At most of my clients, my team and I got a reputation for being experts in certain geographies or subject matter areas. This always started by telling the CEO something he or she didn't know about their business. Often, when we shared this kind of information for the first time, their reaction more or less boiled down to "you can't be right." Once we were able to prove that we were, however, we were in. Sometimes this information could be facts that were not known, sometimes it could be insights that were not focused on before, sometimes it was risks that had gone unassessed. In every case, we proved our value clearly and quickly, in most cases from our very first meeting.

Some real-life examples...

A client had a number of fairly autonomously-run global divisions. At the same time, there were some emerging markets that were becoming increasingly attractive due to low labor costs. Each division was making decisions to add people in those emerging markets. As it turned out, each of their analyses pointed to expanding opportunities in the same country. Over time, each division increased its headcount in that same country. This caused the accumulation of a fairly large percentage of the overall company's employees in that country—in fact, this amounted to about 20% of the entire staff. When I mentioned to the CEO that I considered this 20% to be a fairly high concentration that certainly presented unique risks, he told me it couldn't be that high. It was. The result was a companywide review with specific risk minimization strategies employed.

Another client had a subsidiary in a highly regulated business that was unrelated to their core business. To make matters more complex for the CEO, this subsidiary reported up through a finance company subsidiary, so it was one level removed from his line of sight. There had been recent rule changes that negatively impacted the subsidiary, and that had heightened the risk related to it and its industry. When I asked the CEO and CFO for their reaction to the recent regulatory change, they were hearing it for the first time. The aftermath of this is a long story, but the result was ultimately selling the subsidiary.

***

One very specific thing I would try to do early on in a CEO relationship was to identify three to five objectives that were in the CEO's personal plan for the coming year. This is even more personal than the top five priorities referred to above, and can change each year. This is typically the plan they are reviewed and compensated against. My purpose was to try to see how we could help. I remember once having a CEO say, "Why the heck do you want to know that!?" When I said, "So I can see how we can help," he smiled and said, "Sounds good." We then discussed what they were. This was a little risky, but it always seemed to work, and it sent a number of messages that were good to send.

I will never forget a video recorded for one of my retirement events, wherein a CEO of a major corporation said "Don was different. Whenever we would meet, he always wanted to talk about my problems and how he could help me fix them. In many cases, he and PwC did." This was emotional for me because the CEO's comment reflected exactly what I was always trying to do: make them feel like I was there to help them, and that I cared about them as a person and not just as a client. The fact it was mentioned meant they appreciated it, and also found it different in a very positive way.

CEOs also like to deal with "players," and usually view themselves as "players." Some of the characteristics of players are they are generally authorized to make important decisions, they know other players, and they generally speak with confidence. Whether or not you believe yourself to be a player, it will help your relationship to be perceived as one.

Let me start with speaking with confidence. You need to be confident and speak with confidence, but this can't come across as being forced. You need to be relaxed. You need to act naturally. You need to act like you're authorized to represent the firm, and that you do this sort of thing all the time. This effect can be accomplished in many ways. Very often, I did it by starting with a funny comment, or even a joke. I might start with a comment about a family picture in their office, like "Looks like he's a good football player." I might even start with a marginally off-color comment. I remember once visiting a female CEO shortly after she got the job, and starting by saying I thought that "Women don't get the corner office." This was referring to a recently published book with that title. She laughed, and I went on to offer to make introductions to other CEOs if she had an interest—and she did.

Knowing other players is also key. I was lucky that over time I built a network of CEOs, CFOs, and other C-Suite contacts. In discussions, I would mention companies and executives who naturally fit into the conversation. It was sort of "name-dropping," but didn't come across that way because the other person expected that I would know them. This was also an area that can bring real value if leveraged correctly—making introductions has the potential for considerable value, and executives will treat you much more favorably if they think you can connect them to other relevant parties. One example was introducing U.S. CEOs to CEOs of non-U.S. companies and vice versa. Also, sometimes a CEO would be new to the industry and didn't know their counterparts. Making these types of introductions could also be very helpful.

Lastly, players are authorized to make important decisions. On this point, you are either so empowered or you need to make it look like you are. Later in my career, I was so empowered. Earlier in my career, I did my homework before these meetings so I understood what might come up, and I got whatever clearances I needed to be able to make the decision. I will tell you that I did take risks at times. Most consistently, the risk was that I would have to go back later and change my view—although I can't remember ever actually having to do that. I credit this fact to my world-class teams who prepared me well.

As I said before, CEOs want to deal with decision-makers. If you can't make the decision, you are dubbed "not relevant." With this in mind, let's close with a hypothetical...

Bad Scenario

You walk in to meet the CEO. You are visibly nervous and your speech is unnatural. As the conversation starts, he/she asks you if you know one or two of their counterparts. You say no, or even worse, you say you don't often get the chance to meet a CEO. The CEO raises an issue that the company is dealing with and asks for your view, or perhaps even for your advice. After a brief discussion, you tell him/her that you need to check with someone, but that you will get back to them shortly with an answer. Conclusion: the CEO now understands that you are not a player, and consequently, you are done.

Good Scenario

You enter the CEO's office relaxed and natural. When they mention some names you don't know, you shift the focus to the names of other relevant people (players) whom you do, indicating that you are used to dealing with people at their (*your*) level. When issues are raised, you respond clearly and concisely with your opinion on the situation, and if possible, offer a solution. As you do, you might suggest consulting with other experts to broaden your answer and advice. You take the initiative, you guide the conversation, and you come up with the next steps.

Chapter 30

BEING GLOBAL

Traveling extensively overseas was an area I got experience in early on. In my first six years with PwC, I went on more than ten international trips—the result of being put on a client where the U.S. team did work overseas. It is also important to remember that foreign travel was not routine in the 70s—traveling for business was a big deal. To say this changed my life forever would be an understatement; this was the start of my becoming a global businessman, and when my on-the-job learning was supercharged. I got to see some really neat places and do some really neat things. I was getting a reputation because of these trips and how unique each of them was.

As I write this chapter, I think back over sixty years ago to a time when what I am about to write would have sounded like Star Wars. Now, it is mandatory and virtually commonplace. In this chapter, I want to discuss the importance of being global, how you become global, and what it means to be global.

Being global is a mindset that involves doing everything with a global view—thinking, acting, speaking, interacting, and dealing. This comes at the end of an extensive process, which for me evolved over forty-plus years. In my early life, I did not really appreciate that there was life/business outside the United States. As I began my career, I first understood that there were companies with overseas offices and businesses. As I recall, they had limited foreign operations, say between one and five subsidiaries. I then began to think in terms of international operations—businesses with subsidiaries in many countries. The first of these I was exposed to were U.S. companies operating in many countries outside the U.S., then it was foreign companies operating in various countries including within the U.S. I was then exposed to certain companies based both in the U.S. and outside the U.S. that operated in many countries—*global* companies. Today, most companies are global by virtue of the internet and many other such enablers. This is an outline of the U.S. and global environment that I grew up in. The world as a whole was constantly becoming more and more global, and I was adapting to it, being influenced by it, and taking advantage of it to broaden my experience and to differentiate myself as a professional in my field.

From 1965 to 1969, I would go to southern California each year on a mini vacation to visit my aunt who lived there with five of my cousins. For a kid from New York, it was an exciting trip for many reasons. Principally, because of all the new and neat things we did and saw. In 1968, four of us drove to Baja California for the first time. This was the first trip I'd taken outside the U.S.—well, technically second: I had been taken to Mexico by my parents when I was six years old. That trip to Baja, which I remember as if it were yesterday, opened my eyes to how other people live. It was my first taste of the international scene, and I was hooked. I later discovered that I was a flexible, easy, and adventurous traveler, and therefore I was able to recognize, appreciate, and enjoy all the differences between our respective ways of life: the food, the language, the culture, the customs, and so on.

During my college years (1970-1973), I traveled to a number of countries, mostly in the Caribbean. These trips built on my experience, and reinforced my desire to see more. It was during this time that I also took my first trip to Europe—Portugal. This was also a great experience.

It's interesting what you remember. In those days, even taking an airplane was a big deal. Getting a passport and a visa was a big deal. In those days, the drinking age was still eighteen, and as a consequence, it was normal for college students to drink. I remember flying to Puerto Rico for spring break one year, where the center cabin on the airplane was a stand-up bar with seats in case it got turbulent. Can you imagine that today?! No way.

When I joined PwC in 1973, my life changed forever. I had a number of clients, all with international operations. One in particular had very large operations in Ireland, and those operations were audited by a local firm, not PwC. As a consequence, and even as a first-year member of the staff, I was sent to Ireland three times a year to review the work of the local firm. Because I was already going to Ireland, I was also asked to go twice a year to the client's foreign headquarters in Geneva, Switzerland to review the consolidation of their international operations. I made these trips, no kidding, for six years in a row—eighteen trips to Ireland and twelve trips to Switzerland. Also, every so often during these trips, I was able to add on an outing to London or Paris or Milan. Do not misunderstand, this was hard work and long hours, but the side benefits were fabulous.

Whenever I went to Ireland, I always stayed at the Shelbourne Hotel on St. Stephen's Green in Dublin. Many times, I arrived on Saturday morning so I could sightsee on Saturday and Sunday. In those days, most restaurants were closed on Sunday, but one—Shanahan's on St. Stephen's Green—was always open. It had a downstairs bar and a separate steak restaurant called the Oval Office. The owner, an American of Irish heritage, had purchased President Jack Kennedy's rocking chair and displayed it prominently in a glass case inside the restaurant. I ate there many times on every trip to Dublin, which as of today totals some thirty trips. By the way, this was when I learned to love real Irish coffee. It was usually made with Jameson whiskey, but at Shanahan's it was made with Shanahan's own Irish whiskey. At the Shelbourne, it was made with Irish Mist. Whenever I had one at Shanahan's, I would ask for Irish Mist. For years, they had two Irish coffees on the menu: Shanahan's Irish Coffee and Don's Irish Coffee. No kidding!

I was promoted to manager in 1979. This was also when I took a three-year assignment to Milan. I was newly married, and my wife and I headed to Italy.

It was another life-changing experience. Over the three years, we took the opportunity to travel all over Italy, as well as throughout most of Europe. We had a myriad of incredible experiences, from skiing in the Italian, French, and Swiss Alps to swimming in the Mediterranean from shores on all sides—in Italy, France, Greece, Spain, Portugal, Turkey, and Malta. Not bad for a kid from Yonkers.

Milan at the time was a very diverse environment. It was not dissimilar to New York City, though with the difference that, as an American, I was in the minority. It was very interesting to be part of an expatriate community that included thirty to fifty other nationalities, many of whom bonded together on the basis that they were not Italian. Strange as it might seem, southern Italians were also included in this group: they were considered different and were treated differently by the Milanese. The common languages were English and Italian, but if you were out to dinner, there might be five or more languages being spoken at the table, with English or Italian being the only two that were broadly understood. Looking back, it is interesting to see how many Italian (and non-Italian) friends we made. These are friendships that continue today, fifty years later.

Two things that years later I still cannot get over: going out for Chinese food in Milan where the waiters only spoke Chinese and Italian (no English), and speaking to dogs in Italian to get them to respond to commands because they did not understand English.

From a business standpoint, I worked primarily on large multinational Italian companies that were being required to register with the Italian Stock Exchange, as well as with the Italian—and in some cases, the European—subsidiaries of American and other companies from the U.K., Ireland, Japan, and Sweden that operated in Italy. The experience was tremendous, and it felt like I was working 24/7. This included not only the company audits in Italy but around the world, along with the Italian registrations and acquisitions, and also meetings upon meetings with visiting executives. Because I was the only American on tour in

Milan, I was also often asked to meet with visitors representing clients who were not mine. You can only imagine the breadth of experience that I got doing this.

An Almeida Point: Being Global is a Must

AT THE TIME, MY ASSIGNMENT IN ITALY WAS A MAJOR DIFFERENTIATOR CAREER-WISE. THIS IS TO SAY THAT IN MY DEALINGS WITH U.S. CLIENTS, MOST TOP EXECUTIVES HAD NOT HAD A FOREIGN ASSIGNMENT; IN FACT, MOST PwC STAFF AND PARTNERS HAD NOT HAD ONE EITHER. THIS MADE ME SPECIAL FROM A RESUME PERSPECTIVE. WHAT I DID NOT FULLY REALIZE AT THE TIME WAS HOW DIFFERENT I HAD BECOME: WHAT I KNEW, HOW I THOUGHT, AND HOW I INTERACTED WITH PEOPLE (ESPECIALLY NON-AMERICANS) HAD CHANGED SIGNIFICANTLY, SHAPED BY THE YEARS I'D SPENT IMMERSING MYSELF IN OTHER CULTURES. I SPOKE ITALIAN FLUENTLY, AND I HAD A WORKING KNOWLEDGE OF FRENCH, SPANISH, AND PORTUGUESE. EQUIPPED WITH MY NEW PERSPECTIVE AND THESE NEW SKILLS, I WAS NOW AT THE INITIAL STAGES OF BEING GLOBAL.

TO COMPARE THEN TO NOW, THESE DAYS ALL TOP EXECUTIVES AT MOST COMPANIES HAVE NOT ONLY WORKED OUTSIDE THEIR HOME COUNTRY, BUT HAVE DONE SO ON MULTIPLE OCCASIONS. THEY ALSO, IN MOST CASES, HAVE RUN SELECT FOREIGN OPERATIONS OF THEIR COMPANIES. WHEN I WAS COMING UP, INTERNATIONAL EXPERIENCE MADE YOU STAND OUT FROM THE REST. TODAY, IT IS A HUGE NEGATIVE DIFFERENTIATOR TO NOT HAVE WORKED OUTSIDE YOUR HOME COUNTRY. NOT ONLY DOES IT MEAN THAT YOU DON'T HAVE THE SKILLS THAT INTERNATIONAL EXPERIENCE CULTIVATES, BUT ALSO THAT YOUR PEERS AND SUPERIORS WILL VIEW YOU AS INEXPERIENCED. THIS IS ESPECIALLY TRUE WHEN YOU

DEAL WITH TOP EXECUTIVES; TO NOT HAVE WORKED OVERSEAS SIGNALS
THAT YOU ARE NOT A PLAYER.

I returned to the U.S. in 1982. From then on, I worked on global companies or global parts of PwC. The number of countries I worked in had expanded to seventy-four by the time I retired. My multiple networks were all global, my close friends were global, and one of the things I am most proud of is that my two children grew up to become global themselves.

What follows are some real examples of what being global meant for me in practice.

Lead Partner on Large, Global Companies

To be the lead partner on very large, global companies, you must be global yourself. Not only must you be global, but because these types of organizations operate everywhere in the world, you must also have a global network. In my two involvements with one particular company that fits this description—first as a first-year partner working for the lead partner and then later as the lead partner myself—I cannot remember ever meeting any senior executive who had not worked overseas. Even back then, many executives were running business units not in their home country (like an American running Japan or a German running Brazil). The best person in the world for the job is not necessarily the best from just that country.

Both times I worked with this company, my responsibilities required me to travel extensively to execute on the services we were providing to them around the world. I knew what the job responsibilities entailed, and they and I expected us to deliver. This is when I started using the phrase "24/7 anywhere in the world." Essentially, to oversimplify, the job was to keep the PwC global network connected to the client's global network for every project and everywhere in the world. This one client alone probably added twenty more countries to my list. Great experience for the right global person.

Global Board Member

In 2003, I was elected to the U.S. and global boards of PwC. The U.S. board was twenty U.S. partners elected by the larger group of U.S. partners to represent them. The global board was also twenty partners, but they had been elected by all the partners from around the world. Usually, between six and eight of the global board are from the U.S. The remaining global board members are from all over the world, as are the staff that assist them. I served four years on both boards. This was in addition to having major client and business unit responsibilities.

To get elected to both boards was a huge honor for me. Being picked by my partners to represent them was indeed a high honor. To be elected to the global board was not only a great honor, but also something that signified my global reach within the PwC global network. It also accelerated and expanded that reach. I was representing our partners around the world, and as a consequence, our board meetings were on different continents on a rotating basis and often in conjunction with global or geographic meetings. I was meeting hundreds and hundreds of partners from all over the world. Add another fifteen countries to the list.

Global Vice Chair

In 2007, I was appointed Global Vice Chairman for Clients and Markets. My responsibilities included market-facing activities in the thirty largest countries, the fourteen strategic industries around the world (e.g., financial services, technology, healthcare), and the 150 largest clients in the world. This job was the most difficult I was given in my career, and truly required 150% of my global experience and my global networks. My teams were from all over the world, and all of our objectives were global. About 60% of my time was spent traveling for this role, and if you excluded meetings in New York (which is a global hub), it would have been nearly 85%. Thank the Almighty that I lived in New York!

Frequently, I would bring teams of partners together to discuss strategy, execution, and progress toward our goals. This ranged anywhere from 50 to 400 partners at a time, meeting in London or New York or some twenty other cities around the world depending on our purpose. New York or London were selected most often, primarily because of my ability to get other senior leaders and major client executives to join us there.

During this time, I often needed to visit a client at a moment's notice to try to help save or in some cases get a client. This work was high-stress, high-impact, and in many cases, high-calorie, if you know what client dinner meetings are like. I also was asked to try to help fix our relationships in certain countries. All these situations required a high degree of effort over a number of years, and in environments that were very different from the U.S.

I often look back on this time of my career. I am very satisfied with those years, I am very proud of what I was able to accomplish, and I am astounded by the number of friends I made and the things I did. I had the opportunity to travel with my wife often and with my kids on occasion (they were in college for most of this time). I also believe that together with my teams we did things that had never been done before, and that may never be done again.

Bottom line: the world is GLOBAL, so you need to be too—especially in business.

Chapter 31

CRITICAL SUCCESS FACTORS IN GLOBAL BUSINESS

Nowadays, all business is global business, from the smallest startups to the Fortune 50. When I started in 1973, it was a differentiator to have non-U.S. experience. Today, it is mandatory. During my career, I visited and worked in seventy-four countries. Of these, I had substantive experience in about forty, meaning that I traveled and worked there many times over my forty-one-year career. There are about eight of these countries where I spent more than a year (cumulatively) and have a very deep knowledge of the country, its people, and its business.

When I think about critical success factors, I include knowledge of the following list of areas: **Culture, Language, Social/Business Protocols, Ethics,** and **Network**.

Culture

Local cultures are different—in some cases *very* different—from country to country. In the U.S., for example, we tend to be very familiar: we hug and even kiss on the cheek people we barely know. In most countries in the world, this is not done, and in many countries, this is even considered offensive. In Western cultures, shaking hands is normal. In most Asian countries, you bow, and the more important the other person, the lower the bow. In India, you clasp your hands and bow your head.

Local cultures can also determine how men and women are treated, and even how they dress and are expected to dress. Many of these cultural differences run counter to how Americans think and act, but navigating them is critical to success in global business.

I remember when Japan was hit by a tsunami, resulting in a breach of one of its nuclear plants. This was clearly a catastrophe of massive proportions. It was far enough away from Tokyo to not be an immediate threat, but that said, there was a lot of discussion in the expatriate community about evacuating to other countries or back to the U.S. Doing so, however, would have been viewed in the Japanese culture as abandoning the country, and thus was considered an affront to the Japanese people. I remember many serious discussions in our firm about what we should do. We relied very heavily on the opinions of our Japanese partners, who were experts on local culture and the related dos and don'ts. Our response was for many of our leaders to stay and assist in the recovery efforts, lending Japan our manpower and other resources.

Some cultural differences can also be positive ones. From 2007 onward, I spent a fair amount of time in Russia. In the first year, I met hundreds of people in our offices in Saint Petersburg and Moscow, at our clients all over Russia, and in government and artistic circles. One cultural difference I was not aware of was that your birthday is considered the most important day of the year. When mine came, I got hundreds of notes and cards and texts and emails. Wow!

In many Latin and European countries, where people tend to be very family-oriented, it is difficult to forge strong friendships if you are from another country. That said, if you are successful in doing so, what you'll find is that you are immediately adopted by the entire family. I remember first meeting my good friend Gianni Iaia in 1981 in Italy. We worked together for about a year, and although it was a very friendly relationship, it really didn't progress the way it would have in the U.S.—or so I thought. One day, Gianni invited me and my wife over for Sunday lunch, where he would treat us to his world-famous lasagna. When we showed up at the appointed time, we were met by Gianni and his extended family. We had a great lunch, and from that point forward, he and his wife have been very close friends. We have become part of their family, and they have become part of ours too.

When I speak about global business and being global, my three years in Italy in the early 80s were transformative. During that time, there were several key individuals who mentored me, showing me the Italian and European ways of life and business, but also much more.

Giuseppe De Carolis (Pepe) was a young partner at PwC Italy at the time, and he essentially adopted me and my wife. He was my "host partner," and he and his wife looked after us. We spoke often, he regularly had us at his house for dinner, and he even invited us on summer holidays. Pepe and his wife had done a tour in Atlanta years before, and I must have benefited from whoever had paid such warm hospitality forward.

Another mentor and friend was (and is) Jagdish Kothari and his wife Mary. They were sort of mother hens to us. By this I mean drinks almost weekly, countless dinners over three years, help navigating all things Italian, and generally helping the "young manager from New York."

I already mentioned Gianni, but another close friend and confidant for almost twenty-five years is Paolo Candini. Both Gianni and Paolo were close associates in those early days in Milan. They both have visited us in the U.S., but Paolo, due to personal circumstances, was able to visit often. Paolo is also a part of my network who has helped me on many occasions. A running joke between us is who makes the better spaghetti carbonara. The answer? He does!

These relationships—which include Angelo Pacillo, Maryann and Lars Flink (Swedish), and others—are long-term trusted relationships that very much changed my life. Whenever we speak, even if after five years, it is as if we have just spoken.

Language

It is obvious that many countries have languages different from English. It is also true that many countries and big cities have many people who speak English as their "first second language." This means many know a number of languages, but English is their second best. In the Scandinavian countries, for example, most people start learning English so young that they are completely fluent in writing, reading, and speaking the language.

When I went to Italy on a three-year secondment, I was committed from the start to learn Italian and to become fluent (and I did). My objective here was simply to learn another language because it would be interesting to do. What I quickly learned was that in Milan, Rome, Turin, and other places where I worked, many people already spoke English. Some Americans concluded you did not have to know Italian. That said, however, there were clear advantages to speaking to an Italian in Italian, even if they spoke fluent English. I learned that an American could quickly win them over if they spoke the native language, even if their Italian was bad.

It was also easier to win certain arguments in Italian. As is true for all languages (including English), some certain words or phrases don't translate to other languages. This was a big learning for me. Over time, I learned how to use these elements of language to my advantage. For example, I occasionally had difficult fee discussions with a client whose English was not that good. We started the debate in Italian, and I switched to English when it got a little contentious. This was probably a little unfair, but he ultimately agreed with my position—I could argue better in English than he could.

Over the course of my career, I met a fairly large number of government officials as part of my various roles in our firm. Most, if not all, spoke several languages in addition to English. I will never forget meeting the Prime Minister of Kazakhstan for the first time. Two of my partners and I were led into a formal room with six chairs—three for us and three for him. Before we met, I'd assumed he would be speaking Kazakh with an interpreter translating the exchange for both parties. After a minute or two, he walks in with two aids, shakes my hand, and—in English—asks how Fordham is doing. I was a little surprised by his English, and by his asking about Fordham, so I asked "Fordham *University*?" He says, "Yes, isn't that where you graduated from, and aren't you still involved?" I say, "Yes, Mr. Prime Minister, and wow you did your homework!" We had a very fruitful half-hour discussion about what our firm was doing in Kazakhstan to help his and the president's initiatives, and how committed we were to his country. This was the beginning of a five-year relationship which, as you can imagine, has resulted in many other stories. From that point forward, I called him "Mr. Prime Minister" in public, but in private, I called him by his first name. Two interesting points: (1) he speaks fluent Kazakh, Russian, English, French, Mandarin Chinese, and maybe others, and (2) he has a Fordham University cap, (which I gave him during one of my trips) which I am told he wears when he plays golf.

Needless to say, a critical success factor in global business is knowing the local language. Many business executives fill this need by drafting local executives to accompany them, usually using them also as interpreters. This is almost mandatory, since there will always be meetings where not everyone in the room speaks English. The impact, however, of one's ability to speak the local language cannot be overstated: it can change the dynamics in the room, and it can strongly influence results.

I remember a proposal in Spain at a famous, Spanish-based multinational company. I attended the proposal with the two most senior partners of our Spanish firm and the Spanish partner assigned to the client. We had a strategy session before our meeting with the client to decide who would do what during the meeting. It had been assumed that we would have an interpreter for me, and we were sure the other firms we were competing against would do the same. I started the meeting by stating that I didn't think I needed an interpreter; I was about 90% fluent in understanding Spanish and about 50% fluent in speaking.

This was a somewhat high-risk strategy, as I was a key member of global PwC leadership and needed to be able to make certain points clearly, as well as at the right time and with the right emphasis. On the other hand, using an interpreter completely changes the pace of a normal meeting, and usually is not a positive. In addition, if the competition needs an interpreter but we don't, that could be considered a big plus by the client.

After some debate, it was agreed—no interpreter. Everyone would speak their native Spanish, and I would speak Spanish or English as I felt appropriate. This was very well-received by the client, and as a matter of fact, they were really pleasantly surprised. I believe they felt respected by my effort. On the whole, the meeting went extremely well and it was clear to all right from the beginning that I knew exactly what was being said—in fact, they raved about my "good" Spanish!

Social/Business Protocols

Social protocols and related business protocols are very important to understand, and even more important to treat as guidance in how one interacts in a given country. If an American acts totally like an American—or even worse, a New Yorker acts totally like a New Yorker—it will generally not be well-received. This is not always true, but most times it is. An exception I found was that my New York approach worked well in Moscow: the Russians responded well to my very direct approach.

Let me give some real-life examples. In Italy, even in a business center like Milan where business executives work extremely hard, it is customary to get up and go out for coffee in the morning around ten-thirty a.m., and again in the afternoon around three p.m. There are "bars" all over Milan—and all over Italy for that matter—that are coffee shops in the morning, panini restaurants/bars at noon, and regular bars from say five p.m. until whenever. It was interesting that many Italians, and even expats for that matter, had "their bar," where they went every day. This was similar to what pubs are in the U.K. and Ireland.

Another example is the different customs of celebrating a business relationship or deal. In the U.S., we typically go out for drinks and maybe have a nice dinner to celebrate. Dinner would typically include good wine.

In Japan, the dinner would be either sushi or steak (very expensive!) and the drink would be sake, followed by Scotch (both very expensive).

In Russia, the dinner would be very international (say French) with good wine and a *lot* of vodka. The amount of vodka would depend, at a minimum, on the number of people at dinner. There would be at least one toast made by each dinner guest. Six guests, six toasts, six shots of vodka. Toasts would be things like "to our deal" or "to our host" or "to our families," etc.

In Korea, the dinner might be Korean barbecue (my favorite) with wine and bomb shots (my least favorite of all time). How many bomb shots? As it was in Russia, the custom was one drink per toast, and one toast (at least) per guest. What is a bomb shot? One-third beer, one-third scotch (usually Johnny Walker Blue—very, very expensive), and one-third soju. When I was offered my first bomb shot, I thought that I could drink beer and I could drink scotch (though I rarely did), so how bad could it be? All I can say is the chemical reaction of all three together is really rough to take.

As you can see, each country has its own custom, which often includes a drink of choice. One thing to remember is that when a celebration is warranted, you must participate. To not participate could be viewed as a personal affront. Also, if you think you made a deal, but there was no celebration, then you probably didn't close your deal.

There was an old saying that "my word is my bond." In many countries, including the U.S., this has been overtaken by "What does the contract or deal sheet say?" In many countries, and particularly those in Asia, conversations might sound like agreements or commitments to do something when in fact they are just discussions; no real commitments have been made until a formal document is completed and signed. Also, many deals get " renegotiated" as you move up the local chain of command. You have to be very careful to understand the nuances of how this works in any country you might be dealing in. If you don't understand it, you will likely conclude that people have lied and thus can't be trusted, when in fact it was just a misunderstanding that can be attributed to cultural differences.

Ethics

Let me say here that ethics is not a defined term. Americans tend to conclude that the U.S.'s way of doing things is the ethical way—a stance that's been reinforced somewhat by things like the Foreign Corrupt Practices Act, legislation that sought and seeks to require companies all over the world to follow U.S. standards. Although I understand this, I always found it odd that eight billion people were expected to follow the ethical guidelines created by 330 million. Also, for religious and other similar reasons, there are dramatically different rules in place in many countries around the world. Whether you agree or not, you must be cognizant of them so that you can make informed decisions. In some cases, that decision will be to not do business in those countries.

Network

Having a global network is a VERY, VERY critical success factor in global business. Having a strong network is so important that I gave it a separate chapter, and I have included it here as being one of my top five.

To me, having a global network is key to success in a global business, but has impacts even beyond this. To me, it is being networked with people all over the world—in my case, more than seventy-four countries. In some cases, there are only two or three connections to a given country in my network (e.g., Malta or Saudi Arabia). In other cases, that number could be twenty-five (e.g., Brazil or the Netherlands), or 100 (e.g., Mexico or China), or many more. My global network includes people I know across the world, and also gives me access to their local networks in their respective countries of operation. In the case of Malta, my two or three contacts know almost everyone in Maltese business or government.

A little story: when I was elected to the Global Board of PricewaterhouseCoopers, I got a note from the senior partner of PwC Malta stating that all Maltese partners had voted for me. At the time, I think there were five Maltese partners out of thousands of partners worldwide. Today, there are almost twelve thousand global partners. By the way, I went to Malta three times, the first of which was as a manager working in Italy to review the PwC practice there.

Also, there are connections I have made with various people and organizations over the years that help to grow my network without me really trying. This is exemplified well by the twelve thousand PwC partners I referenced above. I may not have met them, but the fact that we are all partners of PwC gives me the ability to reach out if necessary. It also works the other way. Over the years, I have been contacted by many of my partners whom I have not met. If they call and need help, I help, and vice versa.

Honorable Mention – Mindset and DNA

To be successful in global business, you need to think global, you need to act global, and above all, you need to *be* global. You need to reference things all over the world, you need to know the best practices (many are from other countries), and you need to reach out to your global network and be known for doing so. Make this part of your mindset, and keep it present in everything you do—even in the little things. Personally, I do little things like if I'm in an Italian, Mexican, German, or Portuguese restaurant, I'll always ask for the check in Italian, Spanish, German, or Portuguese, respectively. If we go to a Russian restaurant, I will always have a shot of vodka. If we are in a Brazilian restaurant, it will be a caipirinha.

As you become more global, you'll find that your global identity and experience will perpetuate itself—you will likely even find that you develop a love for travel and foreign cultures! My daughter and son started traveling with me, but have since become global travelers in their own right. They are both global businesspeople in their early thirties.

Chapter 32

THE INTERDEPENDENCY OF IT ALL

When I decided to write this book, I decided it should only include areas that I thought were critical to making you successful in business and, in many cases, in life. There are many chapters, with hundreds of topics, and maybe thousands of data points or ideas—it's hard to count them all. I included them because I thought they were important, and I hope you found them insightful.

When I think about my fifty or so years in business, I think about the impact that these concepts had on me. I think about how I learned some of them, and occasionally it was ugly! I think about how I used them to achieve success, and in some cases, great success. I reflect on the multiple decisions I made that made me better and better at various aspects of business, albeit not always at the same rate.

It is never just one thing that determines your success when you've had the kind of career I had. In my case, my success is owed to everything in this book, and everyone in my networks and life. The interdependency of it all was critical. This is a fairly complex concept to grasp—it is almost professorial and feels almost theoretical. I never use those two words, and I am never either. In this case, however, I think they have that feeling.

The interdependency of it all needs to be kept top of mind if you are trying to use what's within these pages. A micro example would be the chapter on leadership: the skills and attributes talked about there need to work together to make you a good leader. Just having one or two of those traits will not be enough. If you have them all at a high level, then you might actually have the ability to be a great leader. The concept of having all attributes is applicable to all (or at least most) of the concepts in this book. Many of them are critical for you to have any chance of being a high performer, for example, or of being able to create and sustain a high-performing team.

Being unable to make decisions, as another example, will most definitely impact your career (and life) negatively, and will ensure that you will find it difficult to deal with high-level executives and others.

Some of the topics are foundational. Things like honesty and integrity are must-haves. If you are not honest, everything will be difficult—potentially game over.

Someone who has read this book told me that most people, after reading it, would keep it handy as a reference resource. I don't know if that is true, but personally, I think of it that way and will even use it myself. When I lecture on various topics—such as creating and sustaining high-performance teams, or branding and global branding, or strategy and strategic planning—I will look back to see if I have missed anything. To that point, the chapter on leadership is the basis for my leadership lecture.

I view the areas covered by each chapter as important in and of themselves, but the total content of this book and how the topics impact each other are where I hope the real breakaway value will come. The interdependency of it all is key.

At the beginning of the book, I talked about my early years—about the experiences I had before I began my career. I tried to describe how those years impacted me later in life and business. Some told me not to include those chapters. I didn't take their advice because those experiences were so important to me, and formed the foundation of my life, my career, and my work ethic. Looking back, I believe the interdependency between those experiences and the later years was tremendous. I believe that had I not started out how I had, the rest would have been different. How different, I will never know.

Also, I do not talk much in the book about my wife Gail, and my children, Gabriella and Matt. They have had a huge impact on my life, including my life in business. Conversely, my business life has had a huge impact on them. My wife has been an inextricable part of my life in all capacities since the day we met. She was part of thousands of events, trips, and meetings. Her contributions were intertwined with almost everything, and the results were significantly influenced by her. This is also true for my young adult children. I remember both welcoming guests to my annual Christmas party—my son and his friends even parked their cars! As you know by now, I've traveled to many countries and I act and think globally. So too did my wife and kids. Both my son and daughter have traveled extensively, and I'm sure that the travel bug that bit them came from me. They are both very independent and adventurous, and have even been to some countries that I have not.

When I reflect back, it is clear that who I am and how I operate is a clear result of ALL my experiences. The interdependency of it all is obvious.

LIFE AFTER PwC

Let me start by saying that for most of my life, I have always looked forward to exploring new, challenging, and exciting experiences. This was just as true when I left PwC at the age of sixty-two as it was when I was eighteen. Retirement meant crossing a threshold, and I viewed it less as the end of my career and more as moving on to the next, totally new thing. My view, not to be flip, has always been "been there and done that"—in other words, I never look back. I keep my good friends, my rolodex, and all my great memories, but I'm always looking forward to new challenges and adventures. I am always excited about the road ahead.

Before I left PwC, I gave a lot of thought to what I was going to do with the rest of my life. My planned retirement income stream meant that I would not need a full-time job (thank God), and that I could basically do whatever it was that I wanted to do.

I got tons of advice from many different people, but there seemed to be a sort of "standard model" that many wanted me to follow and that was more or less expected of someone with my experience. The advice I was given by a number of close friends, however, was to do what I was passionate about and not what others thought I should do. I took that advice.

At this point, I also established some ground rules for the way forward. They go something like this:

- I'd work only with people I liked.

- I'd engage only in projects that piqued my interest or sparked my passion.

- I'd focus on endeavors where my contributions would make a tangible impact.

- I'd only pursue opportunities where my efforts were genuinely appreciated.

- It had to be fun; it couldn't feel like work. If it did, it was time for a change.

Broadly, I divided my post-retirement life into two halves: one half would be dedicated to giving back and engaging in meaningful endeavors, and the other half would focus on business-related ventures. I also decided that I would make time for family and travel, seeking new ways to connect with the people I cherished and the places and cultures that had always fascinated me.

Many wanted to know my plans, but most expected an elevator pitch. So, I'd say, "I'll spend half my time giving back and trying to get into Heaven, and the other half making more money in retirement than I ever made working." This would usually be met with raised eyebrows and a "Can you do that?" To which I'd reply, "I don't know, but I'm sure the second part will be easier than the first."

The financial aspect of my post-PwC life involved managing my own accounts and becoming a mini venture capitalist. I strategically invested in technology and healthcare companies, aiming to make a significant return while focusing on projects that could positively impact the world.

Some of these investments have been successful, some have failed, and others may still go either way. As I continue to navigate my post-retirement financial strategy, I remain true to my goals and my values: I invest in companies that I not only believe will be successful, but that will also change the world for the better. Will this result in my "making more money while retired than I ever did while working"? That remains to be seen, but I've still got plenty of time left, and I'm already well on my way.

While the "money part" remains important to me, I have found that I would rather devote more of my time, energy, and resources to supporting worthwhile causes. At the heart of my philanthropic endeavors were several not-for-profits, led by Fordham University and Cardinal Hayes High School—my alma maters, and institutions that I have always felt deeply connected to. Over the years, I've contributed to both as an alumnus, a fundraiser, and a board member. I was asked to join Fordham's Board of Trustees in 2013, and accepting that offer was pivotal in shaping my post-PwC life; my tenure has been equal parts challenging and rewarding. Soon after, I was able to combine my passionate support of both institutions by way of the Fordham-Hayes partnership: a mutually beneficial relationship that offered new opportunities for students and teachers on both sides. This initiative has grown considerably over the years, and I couldn't be prouder of what it has become; providing educational opportunities to young students facing unique challenges has been one of my most gratifying pursuits.

Teaching also became a part of my journey. I took up teaching and lecturing roles at Fordham's Gabelli School of Business, both for undergrads and graduate students. I've enjoyed my time teaching more than I could have expected, and I'm ever impressed by the next generation of business magnates. Their sharp questions and keen minds continue to keep me on my toes, and it has been so rewarding to share what I know and to learn from them in return.

In addition to my work with official groups, I've also been fortunate enough to mentor and support many young learners and athletes on a more personal level. Some of these young adults face challenges that would break your heart, and witnessing their resilience and determination as they succeed in the face of adversity has been nothing short of inspiring.

In hindsight, my path has evolved from the initial plan as my family's needs and my own desires changed. Nonetheless, I remain aligned with my overarching vision. With each passing year, I find myself happier, healthier, and ever more excited for the next venture. The future, as always, brims with possibilities, and the horizon seems more promising than ever. The adventure continues!

CREDITS

 Braden Mayer — Lead Editor

 Dina Kali — Special Advisor and Contributor

 Gabriella Almeida — Assistant Editor

Susan Feeney — Contributing Editor

Matthew Almeida — Contributing Editor

Martha Hirst — Contributing Editor

Olivia Lilley — Media Advisor

Michael Smith — Illustrator

Tim Wilson — Cover Concept Contributor and Don's Caddy/Coach

QUOTES AND REVIEWS

"By the end of the first few chapters, I knew I had to get my kids to read this."

- Daniel Almeida

"In his new book, How to Be the Best (In Business), Don Almeida provides both high-level advice and actionable tactics that will help individuals advance at any stage of their career. His candid storytelling approach to leadership concepts immerses the reader in real-world examples that can be applied to a myriad of industries and situations. What Don labels "Almeida Points" are particularly helpful and informative to anyone who wants to improve their performance."

- Donna Rapaccioli, Dean Amerita, Fordham Gabelli School

"This book offers a treasure trove of wisdom from a man who's seen it all in the business world. Don's dedication to mentoring the next generation shines through every page."

- Mary Bly, New York Times Bestselling Author